DATE DUE

BRODART, CO.   Cat. No. 23-221

COMMANDER AND
BUILDER OF
WESTERN FORTS

COMMANDER AND BUILDER OF WESTERN FORTS

THE LIFE AND TIMES OF
MAJOR GENERAL HENRY C. MERRIAM,
1862–1901

JACK STOKES BALLARD

Texas A&M University Press
College Station

This paper meets the requirements of
ANSI/NISO Z39.48–1992 (Permanence of Paper).
Binding materials have been chosen for durability.

Library of Congress Cataloging-in-Publication Data

Ballard, Jack S.
Commander and builder of western forts : the life and times of Major General Henry C.
Merriam, 1862–1901 / Jack Stokes Ballard. — 1st ed.
p. cm.
Includes bibliographical references and index.
ISBN-13: 978-1-60344-260-2 (cloth : alk. paper)
ISBN-10: 1-60344-260-X (cloth : alk. paper)
ISBN-13: 978-1-60344-633-4 (e-book)
ISBN-10: 1-60344-633-8 (e-book)
1. Merriam, Henry C. (Henry Clay), 1837–1912.   2. United States. Army—
Officers—Biography.   3. Medal of Honor—Biography.   4. United States—
History—Civil War, 1861–1865.   5. Frontier and pioneer life—West (US).
6. Military bases—West (U.S.)—History—19th century.   7. United States.
Army—Military life—History—19th century.   8. West (US)—History—19th
century.   9. West (U.S.)—Biography.   10. United States. Army—African
American troops—History—19th century.   I. Title.
F594.M525B35   2012
978'.02092—dc22
[B]
2011016692

(frontispiece) Maj. Gen. Henry C. Merriam. Courtesy National Archives.

CONTENTS

FOREWORD

Students of American history are often fooled into the impression that between the civil conflict of the 1860s and the murder of William McKinley, it was all just Boss Tweed, Little Big Horn, and Buffalo Bill. Just like the "Great American Desert" between St. Louis and California, once America found its edges, it settled into a humdrum phase of its evolution that just does not make for good television. We are a people who love drama. And in this postwar period, there is not a lot of it that is readily apparent. Once the dust settled and Lee handed over his sword, to a great many Americans, history plays like *Dances with Wolves* without the locals: just a long, remote stint in a forgotten outpost of time. It is a rare student, much less one of history, who can recite the list of US presidents from Andrew Johnson to Benjamin Harrison, and we understand.

To be fair, the second half of the nineteenth century did have drama certainly, but primarily it was of a different kind. It was not so much glory as governance, not so much fighting as uneasy peace. This was when one expanding society, believing in its destiny, searched for its limits and began knitting together a nascent nation. This is the drama of making an American sausage, and a lot of folks just prefer not to watch.

Yet taking the time to explore this portion of our past is well worth the effort. In many ways it brings meaning to that which preceded it. Some of it is indeed compelling, like Custer's Last Stand or that day at Promontory Point, or complex, like Seward's Folly or the silver crash of 1893. Most of it is less so, like expanding and protecting lanes of commerce in the West or establishing forts and dispensing day-to-day justice. These matters are maybe not as eye-catching but are as necessary to the future of our country as air, water, or wheat.

Henry Clay Merriam was a steady force of the developing United States. His vision was always forward, almost always westward. Through the intricacies of the military process and hierarchy, developing and marketing his entrepreneurial ideas, to bumbling about in the strange world of the fourth estate, he remained resolute. He overcame the impediments in his personal life and his professional life that could well have defeated someone made of less-stern stuff. Merriam was, as the author points out, a man of the West, and his eventual prominence was never in doubt.

In the way Americans take a lot for granted in this country, we can thank our predecessors for giving us the luxury. We owe them a debt, be they the combatants or the builders, for their construction of the nation we have today. We salute those who have been noisy in the creation of these United States and those who have stayed the course—and who, through incremental effort, have made just as significant a contribution. Watching them and learning from them may not make good television, but it makes a great read.

W. Bart Berger
Great-grandson of Maj. Gen. Henry Clay Merriam
Chairman, Board of Directors
Colorado Historical Society

PREFACE

A morsel of genuine history is a
thing so rare as to be always valuable.

THOMAS JEFFERSON

Numerous individuals in American history made significant contributions to the progress of the nation but remain practically unknown. This book is about one of them, Maj. Gen. Henry Clay Merriam. General Merriam deserves serious recognition for his role in the evolving American West in the last half of the nineteenth century. During this exciting time of the West, most attention has focused on colorful figures such as Indian chiefs, outlaws, explorers, lawmen, and key settlers. Noted military leaders usually include those who achieved fame in the Indian Wars, those dealing with native depredations and resisters to reservation life. The names of such Indian fighters as George Armstrong Custer, George Crook, and Nelson Miles quickly come to mind. Yet there were many other officers, including Merriam, who also were important players in the West's history and development.

Henry Clay Merriam, born in Maine in 1837, represents the typical easterner becoming a man of the West. Propelled by a patriotic spirit to enlist for the Union cause during the Civil War, he was placed in command of Maine volunteers, beginning a thirty-eight-year military career that led him to an unusual string of assignments stretching from the Rio Grande to the Pacific Northwest. Although born in obscurity, he became one who never questioned his own strength and, with incremental effort, rose to prominence in the US Army, largely due to his time in the western region.

Although involved in some aspects of the Indian Wars, Merriam would never achieve fame in the major western battles. Instead, he was one of a long list of relatively anonymous military men who were builders, men who in one way or another significantly changed the Wild West by establishing military posts, protecting expanding rail lines, and striving to maintain an uneasy peace between settlers and Indians. Merriam and those like him often contended with a far wider range of problems and tasks than just the fight against the Indians. Their contributions to western history have at times been lost or ignored.

Significantly, Merriam's career brings attention to the western builder more than to the western warrior. The narrative of his life, particularly in the West, offers insights into the harsh realities of life for an army officer's family. A truly pioneering experience was the fate of so many wives and children. What emerges in Merriam's story is that his wives truly personified his grit and determination. Merriam experienced an especially tragic family event that typified the powerful and sometimes unexpected natural forces faced in the West.

A study of any military man's life usually offers lessons on leadership. Certainly the career of Merriam provides an interesting and enlightening one. His experience proves even more noteworthy because of his long command of black troops. He earned praise for that leadership and for his great administrative skills honed through his extensive command of forts.

Because Merriam became heavily involved in a wide range of historic western episodes, from conflict with Mexican revolutionaries on the Rio Grande to miner riots in Coeur d'Alene, Idaho, the story of his career provides new information and broader perspectives on some of these events. Wherever possible, Merriam's words and those of fellow participants are allowed to describe what happened. His comments in particular provide a new breath of currency to some old accounts and also follows author Salman Rushdie's advice: "You should never write history until you hear the people speak."[1]

Fortunately, Merriam conscientiously retained many letters and records associated with his long army career. These previously untapped primary sources form the foundation for this story of his life. The heavy use of quotes is intended to permit Merriam's character and personality to emerge and to ground the narrative in credible documentation. This becomes all the more important, because reading through Merriam's papers rarely discloses his thought processes and philosophical musings. One is forced to rely on accumulated evidence, small clues, and the scrutiny of actions and work habits to determine the inner man. In order to better understand environmental influences on Merriam, I visited sites from his birthplace at Houlton, Maine, to the Coeur d'Alene mining district.

While the narrative maintains a steady spotlight on Merriam the man, the historical background has not been ignored. Hopefully the historical context included explains the times as well as the man.

I am indebted to a host of individuals for assistance in writing this biography. Special thanks go to the helpful staffs of the National Archives; the Denver Public Library; the Colorado Historical Society Museum Library; the Colby College Library Special Collections; the Fort Laramie Archives Library; the Cary Library of Houlton, Maine; the University of Tulsa's McFarlin Library Special Collections; and the Friends of Historic Fort Logan. Various sites where Merriam visited have responded generously with materials and advice.

Especially appreciated has been the support of certain individuals, particularly W. Bart Berger in Denver; Baird Todd at Fort Laramie; Catherine Bell, curator of the Aroostook Historical Museum at Houlton, Maine; and most of all the patience and editorial critiques of my wife, Arleda. I am grateful that all have sustained the work and strengthened the product.

Jack Ballard

COMMANDER AND
BUILDER OF
WESTERN FORTS

1

Medal of Honor

*Lieutenant Colonel Henry C. Merriam volunteered to
attack the enemy's works in advance of orders, and,
upon permission given, made a most gallant assault.*

MEDAL OF HONOR CITATION

In the morning of April 9, 1865, Lt. Col. Henry Clay Merriam, commander of the 73rd US Colored Troops (USCT), received disturbing news that the Confederate garrison of Spanish Fort, one of several guarding the approaches to the city of Mobile, Alabama, had escaped the Union siege during the night. "The effect upon us all was very depressing," he soberly reflected, "for the failure to capture that garrison after spending half a month digging them out meant these troops had abandoned a position no longer tenable, only to fall back to stronger fortifications covering Mobile, there to be again besieged, probably under conditions less favorable to us."[1] Merriam's unit was part of a force besieging Fort Blakeley, also a key defensive position for Mobile. The Union troops had spent many an agonizing day advancing on the Confederate defenses.

Fearing that the Fort Blakeley garrison might also find a way to escape, Merriam believed that some decisive action was imperative—perhaps a daring daylight assault. Ominously, he noted an "unusual quiet on the front of the enemy" since about 9:00 a.m.[2] His first consideration went to gaining support from the commanding colonel of the 86th USCT on his right flank. Merriam proposed that the two commanders seek permission from their brigade commander, Brig. Gen. William A. Pile, to capture the enemy's advanced line of works at once (it was then just after noon) instead of customarily waiting for cover of darkness.[3] The 86th Regiment's commander, Lt. Col. George E. Yarrington, disapproved, so Merriam started alone to Pile's headquarters. Before reaching the general, however, Maj. Lewis P. Mudgett of the 86th, a fellow officer from the state of Maine who had overheard Merriam's proposal, asked

if he could join in the appeal. Merriam eagerly welcomed this unexpected but highly appreciated offer, duly noting Mudgett's courage to go around his commander's position. General Pile listened to the two officers and gave permission for Merriam's dangerous and bold assault, ignoring Yarrington's objection.

General Pile may have been more receptive to Merriam's idea of a daylight attack because his Fort Blakeley siege preparations had reached a final stage. In addition, he had good intelligence indicating that the Union troops now numbered over 15,000 while the defending garrison barely exceeded 4,000 men. During the preceding night and throughout the morning of April 9, Pile had directed the First Brigade's skirmish line to move forward and had ordered a new line of rifle pits "one hundred and forty yards" in advance of Yarrington's unit on his right and "one hundred yards in advance of General Andrews's line on his left." Brig. Gen. Christopher C. Andrews was commander of a division of white troops. Pushing the skirmishers forward would work to Merriam's advantage as the battle unfolded.[4]

The decision to launch a daylight attack had to be weighed carefully, however. The Fort Blakeley defenses were formidable. They consisted of well-constructed earthworks and strong redoubts connected by heavy parapets. There were ditches, abatis, wire entanglements, and scattered "torpedoes" (shells bur-

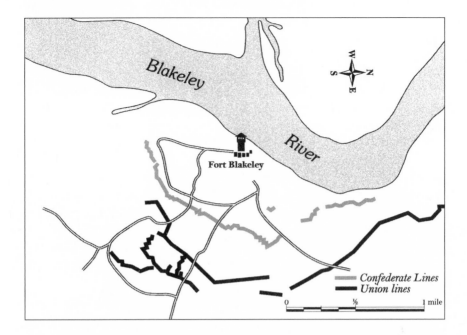

ied as anti-personnel mines). In front of these works were two lines of rifle pits filled with sharpshooters, also screened by abatis and torpedoes. Heavy timber slashings covered the whole front, further impeding troops in formation.[5]

With General Pile's approval in hand, Merriam returned to his regiment and began final preparations for the assault. He now methodically organized and primed his men for the forthcoming charge on the enemy's line. He was so sure that his whole regiment would be needed that he quietly formed it in the advanced parallel trench, "ready for instant call."[6] Although Merriam did not record his thoughts about his black troops at this point, he conveyed confidence that they would act with courage and discipline. After all, in what was to be a Merriam characteristic, he had drilled and drilled his men over many months to instill cohesion and instant response to command. Nevertheless, he must have had some concern since they had not really been battle tested. Furthermore, this would be a charge into the face of withering Confederate fire from well-protected emplacements. What could happen in fierce battle was never certain even with seasoned troops, as Merriam likely knew from his previous Civil War experience.

Merriam designated Company G, commanded by Capt. J. C. Brown, to lead the charge. Capt. Howard Morton, in charge of Company D, was on the left front with orders to "keep a shower of bullets on the enemy's rifle pits on some higher ground." Merriam was aware that these Confederate positions could enfilade his advancing troops unless suppressed with heavy covering fire.

At approximately three o'clock, General Pile, accompanied by Maj. Gen. Peter J. Osterhaus, chief of staff for Maj. Gen. Edward R. S. Canby, arrived at the front to observe the assault. "At near 5 P.M." Merriam received orders to "send forward skirmishers to capture and hold a line of rifle pits which were about three hundred yards distant, filled with [the] enemy's sharpshooters and covered by a strong line [of] abatis." Merriam selected twenty men to engage some troubling enemy sharpshooters in pits on some high ground to his left. As planned, Captain Brown of the 73rd Regiment and elements of the 86th Regiment (part of Major Mudgett's unit) led the way as the troops raced from their parallel trenches and pits to the enemy's fortifications. The capture of the outer line took only a few minutes, despite a "galling fire of musketry and artillery from the three lines of rifle pits and from the main fortifications." But intense artillery and infantry fire on the advancing front, coming from both flanks, threatened to slow or stop the attack. Merriam observed the gathering of enemy reinforcements on his center front and ordered Companies B, I, and A forward in support in rapid succession. Company A's men carried spades, by order of General Pile, to reverse the captured rifle pits. At this point, with his regiment totally involved, Merriam joined the advance. Nearby Major Mudgett fell, shot through the head; Captain Brown had fallen mortally wounded; and Capt. Louis A. Snaer, commanding Company B, collapsed at Merriam's feet with a severe wound. Joined by his only remaining company commander, Merriam took over command of Companies B, G, and I and rushed the enemy's second line of defense. He reported, "The fire from the fort and remaining pits was still unabated, the grape and shell from the heavy guns making havoc over all the ground." In addition, Merriam feared a Confederate counterattack.[7]

Now other Fort Blakeley besieging units became aware of the fury of the First Brigade's assault. Other brigades of Brig. Gen. John T. Hawkins's Colored Division, mostly to the right front, began storming the enemy rifle pits in their sectors and tried to conform their lines with the advancing 73rd and 86th Regiments.

"Having obtained information of the character of the ground beyond the first line of pits," with his "skirmishers having advanced so far as to be able to act effectively upon the gunners of the enemy," and having largely silenced the troublesome artillery fire from the enemy's Redoubt No. 2, Merriam appealed to General Osterhaus for permission to assault the enemy's main works with his whole regiment. According to Merriam's later candid report, Osterhaus refused, saying, "I will go and order the white troops up." Merriam thereupon once again appealed to General Pile, stressing, "We have already fought the battle, unless we get over the main works we will not get the credit." Pile replied: "You are right, Colonel. When you see Andrews's Division start to advance, charge the main works with your regiment and I will follow you with the rest of the brigade."[8]

Merriam gave the signal, and his regiment charged forward with "deafening yells." The regimental skirmishers rejoined the ranks, and the men overcame Redoubt No. 2. Merriam, in his "after-action report," said that he led his men "directly over the remaining lines of pits and then over the main parapet, with small loss and without discharging a musket, planting my regimental flag on the parapet at least two hundred yards in advance of every regiment on this part of the line." He later recalled, "My colored sergeant [Edward Simon] went over the works at my elbow a few steps in front of the line, and was, at my request, promptly commended in department orders for his bravery." In his Civil War diary, Merriam proudly recorded on Sunday, April 9: "My regt first placed its flag on the parapet. It has been a day of laurels . . . was enthusiastically cheered for reaching parapet first and warmly congratulated by Genls. Pile and Hawkins."[9]

With the main defense line breached and other lines crumbling, the Confederates began running in disorder. Merriam and General Pile believed the Rebels were fleeing to the Federals' right in order to escape capture by the First Brigade's black troops. Merriam reported, however, that he captured nine pieces of artillery (including three heavy siege guns and two mortars), several hundred small arms, a large quantity of ammunition. The 234 captured officers and men were placed under guard by the 73rd for the night. Merriam noted as his troops bivouacked following the battle, "Men and officers very much fatigued from the great efforts of the day." There was good reason, as Merriam summarized the action: "Thus we charged over six hundred yards of uneven ground, covered with dense fallen timber, with three regular lines of rifle pits, covered by strong abatis and torpedoes, under a heavy fire from the fort and left flank, and captured a work in itself strong and well manned." Merriam counted his unit's human cost as eighteen men killed and wounded. This small loss he attributed "to the great rapidity with which my movement was executed."[10]

By nightfall, Union forces had captured Fort Blakeley, with its 4,000-man garrison and forty heavy guns.[11] As Merriam would later observe, this assault on and capture of the fort on April 9, 1865, would be overshadowed by the surrender of Robert E. Lee at Appomattox that same day.

The Confederate commander at Mobile, Maj. Gen. Dabney Maury, had little choice but to give up the defense of the city. His remaining beleaguered and dispirited 5,000 men retreated northward to Meridian, Mississippi. The leading part of General Canby's Union forces occupied Mobile and its extensive defensive works on April 12. That same day Merriam noted in his diary: "rode to the fort and examined the works we had captured. The wonder is how we whipped them so quickly."[12]

These April 1865 events, deep in southern Alabama, led to the recommendation that Lt. Col. Henry C. Merriam be awarded the Medal of Honor. The accompanying, ever-so-brief comment read, "Distinguished gallantry at the assault and capture of Fort Blakeley, Ala." These few words hardly reflected the heroic actions of the day. Later, General Pile said of Merriam's regiment and of the colonel's leadership: "The regiment was one of the best in the service, took a conspicuous part in the siege and capture of the Fort—first breaking the enemy's lines and crossing their works—the colonel requesting permission to advance before the order was given. For personal merit, and strict attention to duty, he had not a superior in my command." General Hawkins, Merriam's division commander, stated: "In the assault of Fort Blakeley his regiment bore a conspicuous part, and was the first of all the regiments, white or black, to enter the enemy's works."[13]

Hawkins further praised Merriam, saying: "Colonel Merriam is a gentleman of good moral character, of excellent education, well read in the military profession, and judicious and zealous in all things pertaining to his duties. His regiment was always in good condition, and he had natural talent for a good soldier." Merriam clearly showed his pride in the courageous performance of his black troops when he publicized a report from the captured Confederate commander at Fort Blakeley, who stated, "I had placed the very best troops of my garrison to oppose the colored troops, yet they were the first to break my lines and first on my parapet."[14] Merriam always remained defensive in wanting to ensure his regiment and his black soldiers received the credit for their actions at the Battle of Fort Blakeley.

The Medal of Honor awarded to Merriam at the end of the Civil War added his name to a distinguished and celebrated list of American heroes. It gave him fame as a military commander. It also mightily influenced and shaped his remaining years. He wore the medal proudly. In his subsequent long military career, with its many interesting twists and turns, Merriam would always bask in the medal's prestige, and it gained him favorable considerations in military and even political matters.

2

Civil War Experience

This is a hell of a regiment.

COL. ADELBERT AMES, 20TH MAINE INFANTRY

Henry C. Merriam's Civil War experience began in the summer of 1862. Merriam, age twenty-four and moving into his junior year at Maine's Colby College (formerly Waterville College), had returned to his hometown of Houlton, Maine, in August during a summer college break. In July Pres. Abraham Lincoln had issued a call for 300,000 additional volunteers to fight for restoring the Union. This also meant that there was an increasing likelihood of ending slavery. Although war fever in this far northeastern part of the country had somewhat subsided since the initial excitement of 1861, Lincoln's plea for more volunteers had again rekindled patriotic fervor. This time Henry Clay and younger brother Lewis became volunteers.

The Merriam family had already been touched by the war in 1861, when Henry's older brother Leonard had joined the volunteer ranks. Leonard was a horn player in Houlton's Coronet Band, and in those first months of the Civil War, the group went to war as the 1st Maine Cavalry Band.[1] But Leonard's service ended abruptly on August 26, 1862, for reasons unknown. What effect, if any, Leonard's wartime experience had on his younger brother remains unclear.

Just as Henry and Lewis Merriam volunteered, other young men eagerly responded, and these 1862 volunteers would form a new regiment, the 20th Maine Infantry. Henry was instrumental in encouraging other men in the Houlton area to enlist, and the number proved sufficient to form a company. Quickly marked as a leader, largely because of his college experience, Henry's fellow enlistees elected him company commander. Later he became commissioned as captain of Company H, 20th Maine and thus began a lifetime of military command. Brother Lewis became a sergeant at the time, but he, unlike Henry, would not make a career of the military.

Henry Merriam never indicated what had motivated him to drop his college studies in 1862 and volunteer for war duty. Perhaps he had strong feelings about maintaining the Union. Perhaps he wanted to rid America of the "peculiar institution" of slavery. Perhaps he became caught up in the new outburst of patriotism, however ill defined, as did so many others. Interestingly, he never recorded his true emotions and precise thinking on why he fought in the Civil War.

Several factors may have had some influence on Merriam's volunteer decision. There had been some antislavery activity at Colby College. In 1833 a college literary fraternity had debated the question, "Ought Congress to interfere in the abolition of slavery?" That summer abolitionist William Lloyd Garrison came to speak. As a result, the Anti-Slavery Society of Waterville College was established. Years later, when news came that Fort Sumter had fallen, students quickly formed their own cadre and began to drill along campus walkways. On April 18, 1861, senior Frank Hesseltine stood on the steps of Recitation Hall and yelled, "President Lincoln has called for 75,000 volunteers to save the nation. I am going to be one of them. Who else?"[2] Merriam no doubt was much aware of antislavery sentiment, and he must have felt considerable peer pressure realizing that many of his classmates had already joined the Union ranks.

In an undated text of a speech given after the war, probably to a group in Maine, Merriam offered a collective reasoning of why New Englanders went to war. He began by saying, "Half a century ago our fathers had watched the black cloud of Calhounism and disunion darkening our southern sky, and were filled with sorrow and misgiving." He mentioned Maine-born Elijah P. Lovejoy and his involvement and martyrdom in antislavery activities on the "banks of the Mississippi," first at St. Louis and later at Alton, Illinois. He added, "In our cradles we heard our fathers, with trembling voices, read the stormy debates of Congress" about slavery. All of this conflict, Merriam stated, "was too much even for the sluggish Puritan blood of New England, and we had to confess to a feeling of resentment. . . . Such was the atmosphere which pervaded the home, the school, the colleges and the churches. Such was the atmosphere in which had grown up that men, were destined, in the providence of God, to defend the Constitution of our fathers, and maintain the integrity of the Union."[3] These comments came the closest to explaining his personal decision to volunteer for the army.

Henry C. Merriam, the second child and second son of Lewis and Mary Ann (Foss) Merriam, was born in Houlton, Maine, on November 13, 1837. His father had settled in Houlton from New Salem, Massachusetts, in 1828 and lived on a farm on North Road, two miles north of Houlton, a location at least partially selected to enable his children to attend village schools.[4] Schooling would prove an ever-important consideration as the family grew and eventually consisted of eight boys (although the last, Charles, died at three years) and two girls.

Henry, as he advanced in years, had responsibilities for caring for his younger brothers and sisters, but his main tasks, like those of most of his contemporaries, related to farm chores. Fields had to be cleared, cows had to be milked, chickens and all animals had to be fed and watered, and horses had to be hitched and harnessed. He became an expert horseman as a consequence, and this became a critical part of his later military life. His father had a workshop, and his sons learned many mechanical skills and how to use tools. Typical of life in Maine at that time, men worked cutting trees in the winter, hauling the logs to the rivers and forming them into rafts to float down to the sea. Henry not only cut the prized white pine for ship masts but also worked cutting ordinary lumber, firewood, and fences. He also worked in a sawmill and became adept at all types of woodworking. On one of his military forms, he stated, "As a boy was familiar with lumbering including all lumber manufacturing."[5] Summers would be occupied mostly with farm work, clearing and tilling the land. Whatever the many and diverse tasks, Henry would be imbued with a strong work ethic and with a strong self-initiative.

Despite the family's role in the farming and lumbering economy, the Merriams placed a high priority on education. It would turn out that Henry would be the one most blessed in its pursuit. He attended Houlton Academy, which had been formed and supported by concerned and conscientious community leaders. The academy began in 1847, thus Merriam could have begun his education there when he was ten years old. It became the first high school in Aroostook County, and some students were boarders.[6] From the beginning, the institution was viewed as a preparatory school with emphasis on classical studies, including instruction in Greek and Latin. Eventually, in the 1870s, it would become a feeder ("fitting") school for Colby College and even later would evolve into Houlton's Ricker College.

The challenges Merriam faced as a student at Houlton Academy can be seen in the comments of some of its teachers, who were always in limited supply. For example, school would commence at eight o'clock and continue until dark, with some instruction carried on at a teacher's home in the evenings. One dedicated educator remarked, "I never knew when bed time came as long as a class was ready to recite." The teacher's hard work proved bearable because "nearly all the pupils were anxious to learn, were enthusiastic in the pursuit of knowledge." One Houlton Academy instructor commented retrospectively, "Among the students at Houlton there were an unusual number endowed with more than ordinary talent."[7] Such comments prove enlightening because Henry Merriam evidently was one of these eager, enthusiastic students, and one of those intellectually gifted.

With the Houlton Academy education, it was little wonder that Henry Merriam, upon completion of Houlton's course of study, would matriculate at

Colby College in Waterville. The rigor of his academic preparation is revealed by examining the "Terms of Admission" contained in the Colby College catalog of 1860, the year Merriam entered.

> The requisites for admission to the Freshman Class are testimonials of a good moral character, a thorough acquaintance with English, Latin and Greek Grammar, four books of Caesar's Commentaries, the Catiline of Sallust, the Aeneid of Virgil, Six Orations of Cicero, Latin Prosody, the making of Latin, Jacob's Greek Reader, or its equivalent, Ancient and Modern Geography, Vulgar and Decimal Fractions, Proportions, the Doctrine of Roots and Powers, and Algebra, to Equations of the Second Degree I in Davies Bourdon. It is recommended to students in preparation, to read attentively some convenient manual of Greek and Roman History. Kuhner's Elementary Greek and Latin Grammars, including the Exercises, or Champlin's Greek Grammar and the Latin Grammar of Andrews and Stoddard, are required.[8]

These stringent academic requirements appeared inconsistent with Merriam's family background, economic means, and farm tasks. In addition, the predominately rural farming-timbering economy of extreme northeastern Maine did not suggest a study of Latin and Greek grammar as steps to success. Nevertheless, Merriam's persistence in his studies most certainly signified the high value he placed on a good education and likewise that of his family and the Houlton community.

Merriam's college studies proved most demanding from the very beginning in 1860. His freshman year included geometry and algebra, Latin (grammar and writing), Greek, and exercises in "elocution" and writing Greek. His sophomore year (1861–62) encompassed trigonometry, rhetoric, Latin, Greek, French, and surveying and navigation. The Greek and Latin courses included such readings as *Cleo* of Herodotus, *Iliad* or *Odyssey* of Homer, Livy, Tacitus, Germania, Agricola, and classical history. Lectures on philosophy, Greek and Roman history, chemistry, geology, and "Verbal Criticism and history of the English Language" supplemented the regular presentations. Unfortunately, because a fire destroyed pertinent Colby College records, we do not know Merriam's individual performance. But since he became an elected member of Phi Beta Kappa, one can assume that he studied hard and excelled in his academic marks.[9]

Nowhere did Merriam get into military subjects, with the possible exception of some parts of Greek and Roman history. He did record, however, that it was a custom for the freshman class to listen in the chapel to the experiences of an old French soldier by the name of Charles Martel, who served the college as a janitor. "He also drilled the students on the school of the soldier and company when the war spirit prevailed in 1861," Merriam later recalled.[10]

The Colby College curriculum, and to a lesser degree that of Houlton

Academy, clearly established a very disciplined pursuit of classical knowledge. Merriam mastered reading the difficult material, learned to write succinctly and forcefully (incorporating Greek or Latin in his later speeches and writings), and developed a philosophical thinking process of always finding a solution to any challenge. Of particular importance, Merriam's Houlton Academy and Colby College experience deeply implanted a sense of self-confidence that never left him, a trait that would be crucial to his leadership of men in peace and war.

Less obvious but no less influential, Merriam's education, family, and community experience provided a spiritual dimension to his life. Both Houlton Academy and Colby College were religious schools mainly founded by Baptists. At Colby, morning prayers were held at six o'clock in the chapel followed immediately by recitation.[11] Although Merriam never directly addressed his Christian faith, it apparently was deep seated by the way he practiced it. For example, he and his future wife, Una, held worship services in their quarters at various western forts, with his wife usually playing the piano for hymn singing.

Music contributed still another dimension to Merriam's life. At some point he learned to play the violin. While his older brother, Leonard, played a horn in a community band and then a military band when he volunteered for service in 1861, his younger brother Lewis played the flute. This would seem to indicate that music assumed considerable importance in the Merriam family. Later, during time spent at boring, isolated forts, Henry played his violin, Lewis his flute when visiting, while Henry's wife accompanied them on the piano. This gave some pleasant, recreational diversion from the lonely, mundane days so common in the late-nineteenth-century military West.

Among major questions remaining unanswered is how Henry Merriam financed a college education. No doubt college expenses strained the limited economic situation of the Merriam family, who were not exactly poor but not wealthy either. Did the other members sacrifice and forego expenses so Henry could go to school? Did he earn, through his own hard work and meager savings, enough to pay for tuition and board at Colby College? His silence on this, as in other matters, contributes to a list of unsolved mysteries.

Merriam looked more like the religious, musical, and culturally inclined college graduate rather than a brawny northern woodsman or outdoorsman. According to photographs, he possessed rather refined features with thinning hair and usually a relatively large mustache. His military record indicates that he was five feet, ten inches in height, "complexion dark, hazel eyes, hair brown, occupation clerk." He was slight of build, weighing about 160 pounds. His stature definitely did not establish him as a leader through a commanding physical presence. What did give him an advantage, however, judging from his later years, was his thoughtful, dignified, and calm demeanor. He earned respect by force of character, consistency, and drive. Merriam also possessed a genuine concern for others that would continually prove valuable to his career advancement. Like many good leaders, he would capitalize on his strengths.

apt. Henry Merriam, now commander of Company H, 20th Maine Regiment, had to take his fellow new recruits from the Aroostook region south to the railhead at Bangor, a more than one-hundred-mile trip by stagecoach. Company H joined other new volunteer companies from locations scattered throughout the state to form the regiment. Most of the 20th Maine was formed by men originally "enlisted in the 16th, 17th, 18th and 19th regiments, and afterward found to be unnecessary to complete those organizations."[12] In the Civil War military structure, a regiment, the key battle unit, had approximately 1,000 men, in ten companies of 80 to 100 men per company, commanded by a colonel. Disease and usual army privations could reduce a regiment's strength in short order, and there was no system for states to supply replacements to existing units—new regiments had to be formed.

Captain Merriam's introduction to the regimental organization and its command structure did not prove easy. The colonel commanding was Adelbert Ames, a West Pointer from Maine. Colonel Ames, "not a mild-tempered man" but ambitious, able, and intelligent, had been awarded the Medal of Honor for bravery at the First Battle of Bull Run. With scarcely one look at his new unit, he bellowed, "This is a hell of a regiment."[13]

The lieutenant colonel of the regiment, the second in command, was a much different individual. Joshua L. Chamberlain, age thirty-three, was a distinguished gentleman, a graduate of Bowdoin College, and a member of its faculty at the time of his volunteering. He taught a Sunday-school class and led a church choir but showed, according to one writer, a "most un-Christian aptitude for military affairs."[14] Chamberlain would later achieve fame for his heroic and courageous stand with the 20th Maine at the Battle of Gettysburg, earning him the Medal of Honor. No doubt there would have been interaction between Lieutenant Colonel Chamberlain and Captain Merriam. At the beginning it seems likely, however, that the recent college student Merriam stood in awe of the college faculty member Chamberlain. Military customs reinforced the distance between them by their respective ranks. But many years later, Merriam had established a valuable friendship with Chamberlain and wrote to him seeking his advice and help in military and political matters.

As Ames, Chamberlain, Merriam, and the other officers looked at their volunteer troops, they might have shuddered at the sight of an undisciplined, militarily ignorant, and motley crew. Yet their volunteers represented a cross-section of the state of Maine. "These were flat-bellied, hard muscled fellows from the farms, forests, and coast towns." They knew the "muscular life," whether it was on the farm, in the forest, or on the sea. Additionally, most were from the small towns and rural areas and as a consequence were acquainted with firearms. They were of solid New England stock, with English, Scottish, and Irish origins. Surprisingly well educated, they seemed to readily grasp what the war was about. Merriam, as he launched into the training of his company, which meant drill and more drill, faced many challenges, though he also had some notable advantages, particularly in the character of his men.[15]

By September 7, 1862, the 20th Maine had arrived by rail and steamer at Washington, DC. Merriam left Boston on the steamship *Merrimack*. He had a "little private cabin" in which, he noted, "I recited my first lesson in tactics." He also said the voyage to Washington was when he "first took the field."[16]

The unit's first duty at the nation's capital was the drawing of weapons and ammunition before marching to Fort Craig on Arlington Heights. Colonel Ames, enraged at the way the men straggled in their march, shouted, "If you can't do any better than you have tonight, you better all desert and go home." As the men reached their assigned area, one private wrote in his diary, "Everything looks warlike here . . . flags flying from every hill and for miles the fields are white with tents and troops and army wagons and artillery and cavalry and horses and mules without number."[17]

Five days later, on September 12, the 20th Maine started on the "hot and oppressive" march northwestward to Antietam Creek. Unaccustomed to the heat and humidity, the troops struggled. Experiencing suffocating dust, great drops of sweat, and blistered feet, they traveled some sixteen miles the first day. In the process the regiment "stripped down to light marching order" and finally arrived at their designated area in considerable disarray. The second day they marched twenty-four miles. The 20th Maine, another Maine regiment, and the 118th Pennsylvania Regiment then bivouacked in column of companies. All were now part of the 3rd Brigade (Butterfield's Light Troops) of the 1st Division, commanded by Maj. Gen. George W. Morell, of the V Corps, commanded by Maj. Gen. Fitz-John Porter.[18] As part of Maj. Gen. George B. McClellan's Army of the Potomac, the troops moved into their assigned position in preparation to attack Gen. Robert E. Lee's Confederate army, positioned near Sharpsburg, Maryland, in strong defensive positions west of Antietam Creek.

By September 14 and 15, McClellan's army was still "filing in, hot and dusty from its march." No doubt Captain Merriam and Company H, among those gathered, waited nervously for the battle to begin, which was imminent. The men heard the sounds of artillery and saw their first Confederate prisoners pass to the rear. Pvt. Theodore Gerrish, a member of Merriam's company, wrote the Rebels appeared as "lank, slouchy looking fellows, clad in dusty gray uniforms." Gerrish also commented on his first sight of dead soldiers: "[T]hey lay, as they had fallen, in groups of half a dozen each, and single bodies scattered here and there, all through the scattering oak growth, that crowned the crest of the hill. They were of all ages, and looked grim and ghastly. Old men with silvered hair, strong men in the prime of manhood, beardless boys, whose smooth, youthful, upturned faces looked strangely innocent, although sealed in bloody death."[19]

From a ridge overlooking much of the Antietam Creek battlefield, the 20th Maine men could visually assess the scope and fury of the fighting. The armies arrayed before them impressed these newcomers. As they watched and waited, tension mounted, but they never received orders to move to the battle line. Morell's division and the whole of the V Corps remained in reserve on the east side of Antietam Creek slightly north of Antietam's middle bridge.[20] As the Union assault on Lee's left flank to the north seesawed and stalled and then Union forces to the south almost succeeded in turning the Confederate right only to be thwarted by the timely arrival of Maj. Gen. A. P. Hill's Light Division, what seemed a likely Union victory ended in a bloody stalemate. The 20th Maine men now witnessed their blue-clad comrades falling back.

McClellan would be forever criticized for not throwing the V Corps into the battle at a time when it might have produced a Union triumph. Yet for the very green 20th Maine, being held in reserve proved a godsend. There had been little time to train the men, and limited drilling had only facilitated some efficiency in marching. Colonel Ames, Lieutenant Colonel Chamberlain, and Captain Merriam probably thought they were indeed fortunate that their unprepared troops were not thrown so quickly into the heat of battle.

On September 20, 1862, the 20th Maine experienced its first hostile fire. It and other elements of the V Corps crossed the low Potomac River at Shepherdstown Ford in pursuit of the rear guard of the withdrawing Confederates. While waiting for their turn to ford the river, the men of the 20th Maine became aware of gunfire and ominous whistling in the air above them. They noticed Union cavalrymen and some infantry in retreat back across the river. Furthermore, artillery units, instead of crossing the stream, began setting up firing positions. Even with these disturbing observations, the regiment had not been ordered to halt its crossing.

Indeed, a Confederate counterattack was underway. Lee and Maj. Gen. Stonewall Jackson had learned of the Union advance and on the twentieth Lee ordered A. P. Hill's division "to backtrack and contest the Federal thrust." Hill quickly responded. Forming some 2,000 men, his brigades charged with a yell and seized some bluffs with a clear view of the Potomac and the pursuing Federals.[21]

Receiving the brunt of the Confederate counterattack was the 118th Pennsylvania Regiment. It, like its companion regiment, the 20th Maine, had been in the field barely twenty days. The Pennsylvanians broke under the Confederate charge and, after only thirty minutes of action, had retreated "in an utterly disorganized and demoralized condition."[22]

Under the commanding enemy fire, the 20th Maine was ordered back to the Maryland side of the river, making the recrossing with rife fire all around them. Chamberlain's horse was shot out from under him, and many bleeding men injured by Confederate bullets struggled in this about-face. Despite the adrenalin-laced fear and momentary confusion, the 20th Maine accomplished the withdrawal in reasonable order and took cover in the largely dry Chesapeake and Ohio Canal, which ran parallel to the river. At nightfall the Confederates again withdrew to the south. General Hill, in his report of the action, said, "This was a wholesome lesson to the enemy, and taught them to know that it may be dangerous sometimes to press a retreating army."[23]

The 20th Maine's officers and men, including Merriam and his Company H, had now faced the real psychological stress of imminent death and all the many ways military operations can quickly change and go awry. They had largely survived and had learned valuable lessons of war in the process.

A few days later, on October 1, after their baptism of fire, the 20th Maine men received and recorded a memorable event. President Lincoln came to consult with McClellan, for which occasion a review of the Army of the Potomac was planned, creating an impressive sight. The appearance of the president proved to be a morale booster, and according to Chamberlain, "the men conceived an affection for Lincoln that was 'wonderful in its intensity.'" The men of the 20th Maine long held images of the passing "McClellan—trim, dashing, romantic with his cap cocked at a jaunty angle" and of Lincoln, a figure so tall with his high silk hat, "angular, ungainly on his borrowed mount, with his deep-lined bearded face, his shadowed eyes."[24]

The young, junior officer Henry Merriam remembered these early autumn days of 1862. He had witnessed the bloody Battle of Antietam, experienced Confederate fire when caught in crossing and recrossing of Shepherdstown Ford, and then had been impressed and spiritually uplifted with the appearance of President Lincoln. In an incredibly brief time, he had learned a great deal about war and about leading men in combat. Merriam received more military education from Colonel Ames in the following months. The 20th Maine was assigned relatively calm picket duty near Shepherdstown Ford. During this time, Ames worked to end certain "civilian practices," such as enlisted men gathering around commissioned officers' tents.

Ames began emphasizing fundamental military skills, with the "School of the Soldier" as a guide. Importantly, men needed to be trained in muzzle-loading-rifle procedures to the point where they would perform them automatically without thinking in combat. The "School of the Soldier" required habitual "Load in nine times," with nine consecutive steps for loading. Additionally, it outlined basic facing and marching movements for the trooper. Then followed the "School of the Company" and the "School of the Battalion," with the object of maneuvering units to facilitate advancing on the enemy and massing of firepower. Merriam and the other officers learned that "[t]he ability to go from line of battle into column and from column into line of battle, with a high degree of teamwork in all formations, was a tactical necessity." *Casey's Infantry Tactics* became the basic manual for the regiment's training.[25] All of this instruction and drill proved boring and tiresome, earning Colonel Ames, and perhaps some of the other officers, the slow-burning anger of many men.

Officers like Merriam learned discipline and proper military protocol from Ames as well. For example, a couple of lieutenants left a marching column and took a short cut across a field, for which the colonel had them arrested. When one of the arrested men wrote a personal note to Ames, he promptly was informed that he needed to use proper military form in any communication. All officers also began learning, by necessity, the ardors of caring for their men as cold, disease, and poor sanitation began to create serious problems. Measles, diarrhea, and dysentery quickly became camp nightmares.[26] Morale became a problem. Unfortunately, the rather recent excitement and eager anticipation of the state volunteers gave way to despair and depression.

Winter weather did not help spirits either. As both the Army of the Potomac and the Army of Northern Virginia began a relatively slow march to the southeast, with the Union army on the east side of the Blue Ridge and the Confederates on the west, a heavy snow fell on November 7. As the Federals approached Warrenton, they lay in camp for a week amid the mud and drizzling rain. When the 20th Maine finally reached Stoneman's Switch and encamped for picket duty, four inches of snow fell; in the bitter cold, two of the Maine men froze to death.[27]

Besides the weather, camp talk was abuzz with discussion about army leadership. A change of command had occurred as the army had moved to the vicinity of Fredericksburg. President Lincoln had removed the popular General McClellan. Although the men of the 20th Maine had not been in the Army of the Potomac long enough to develop a deep sense of admiration for McClellan as had other troops, they nevertheless were much aware of the troubling concern of many as McClellan took his leave of the army. There was now wonder about the capabilities of the new commander, Maj. Gen. Ambrose E. Burnside.

The 20th Maine, in camp near the Rappahannock River, soon discovered that Burnside planned to cross the river at Fredericksburg in a drive straight toward Richmond. The crossing would require pontoon bridges, but these had not arrived on schedule. This delay allowed Lee to move his forces to Fredericksburg on the opposite side of the river and then to fortify the heights west of the city. On December 10, Union orders stated, "Get ready to move with three days' rations and 20 extra rounds of ammunition per man." The 20th Maine and the rest of the V Corps marched out on December 11 at daybreak as the army started its forced crossing of the Rappahannock. The men, wearing overcoats because of the December cold, had their knapsack, cartridge boxes, blanket rolls, and other gear loading them. About a mile from the river, the 20th Maine and the V Corps halted and massed on a field near a place called Phillips House. Again, the V Corps appeared to be held in reserve, this time in a field of mud.[28]

The regiment had heard, as the Battle of Fredericksburg unfolded, that efforts to put the pontoon bridges in place had been gravely hampered by Confederate sharpshooters and that Burnside had directed a fierce artillery bombardment of the city to quell sharpshooter fire. Better news followed that a boat crossing had been more successful in squelching the fire. But by then nightfall had come, and the 20th Maine moved a mile to the rear. The men anxiously considered what the next day of battle might be like, particularly with Lee's strong defensive position looming ahead.

Considering Lee's entrenched works on the high ground, Burnside could have considered a different strategy but rather stubbornly pushed ahead with an overall frontal attack. As Civil War historian Bruce Catton has commented, "Lee had both Jackson and Longstreet in position on the opposite shore—75,000 veteran fighters of high morale, ably led, ready for the kind of defensive battle in which they were all but unbeatable."[29] Maj. Gen. William B. Franklin was to lead his two corps downriver to turn Lee's right flank while Maj. Gen. Edwin V. Sumner would send his men out of the city in a frontal attack on the western heights. Maj. Gen. Joseph Hooker, with V Corps troops and the 20th Maine Regiment, would move farther downriver from Fredericksburg to another crossing, but this more southerly force would still act as a reserve.

As the Maine men moved to their position, they became sickened with scenes of the blue-clad troops littering the fields and ominous gaps occurring in the attacking lines. Late in the afternoon, the V Corps was committed to get and hold as much ground as possible around Fredericksburg while sending some brigades to bolster units from the preceding charges. As the 20th Maine crossed a pontoon bridge, Chamberlain remembered that "the air was thick with the flying, bursting shells."[30] The regiment moved into parts of the town and then onto the killing fields beyond. The 20th Maine formed its battle line to move forward, and quickly great holes developed as men went down. Both Ames and Chamberlain were in the thick of the action. As night began to fall, the 20th Maine reached their objective, a small ridge west of town. They took what cover they could find and spent a restless night in this forward position. Unfortunately, a bitter cold swept over the men, quieting the moaning of the wounded and chilling even the hardiest of men.

Merriam, with his company and the other Maine men, wanted the sun of morning for relief from the cold but dreaded the further combat that the dawn would bring. And with the daybreak, the Confederates tried to force the regiment and other Union units from their protective ridge of slightly higher ground. But all day, keeping low and even using the dead as cover, they held their ground. The Federals could not safely retreat, and reinforcements could not easily reach them. With darkness, the 20th Maine received orders to withdraw into battered Fredericksburg. But first the detail of burying their dead had to be cared for, using bayonets or whatever was available to make shallow graves. In town the men tried to get some sleep. Colonel Ames saw fit to walk among the troops, commending their courageous holding action.

They spent the day in the debris of Fredericksburg, after midnight the 20th Maine was ordered to move to the front line again. The move was to be executed with extreme quiet and with entrenching spades. In short time the men realized that they were to be part of a rear guard helping protect the Union army's withdrawal. The Confederates, if aware of this retreat, could sweep down on the rear guard with great fury, possibly overwhelming their defenses. As the Union army withdrew, Colonel Ames and Lieutenant Colonel Chamberlain conceived a plan of retreat while keeping a thin line of battle, guiding their men in rearward leapfrog movements getting the unit successfully back to Fredericksburg. By morning, the regiment managed to recross the river. The battle was over.[31]

General Burnside ordered the Army of the Potomac back across the Rappahannock on the night of December 14–15. A total of 12,500 Union troops had been lost in the assaults. Lee's casualties had been comparatively light, and importantly the Confederate victory resulted in making the "Virginia front . . . stable once again." Also, the Army of the Potomac was out of action for the winter. A Northern newspaperman succinctly wrote about the Battle of Fredericksburg, "It can hardly be in human nature for men to show more valor, or generals to manifest less judgment."[32]

References would be made later about the gallant actions of Captain Merriam during the Battles of Antietam, Shepherdstown, and Fredericksburg. Long after the war, Adelbert Ames wrote: "In August, 1862, [Merriam] entered the service as a captain in 20th Me. Volunteers, of which I was Colonel. From the day on which he reported for duty till his promotion and transfer to another regiment, I found him an able, conscientious, energetic and gallant officer." Joshua L. Chamberlain commented in a similar vein: "He was a captain in my regiment, 20th Maine Volunteers, and his entire service from that time to this, has been of the most meritorious character. With the highest moral qualities, he is a man of active and vigorous mind, of superior education and a laudable ambition in his profession." Brig. Gen. Daniel Butterfield referred to the "efficient, gallant and valuable service rendered" by Merriam "when he was under my command in the Fifth Corps of the Army of the Potomac."[33]

Merriam himself never provided firsthand accounts of his combat experiences, and apparently others did not make reports noting such. Evidently, his behavior, however brave and effective, was lost in the larger perspective of military events in the fall of 1862. Nevertheless, Merriam came through this intense period of military education with courage and success. In only a few months, he had acquired skills in leading men in combat. Fortunately, Colonel Ames and Lieutenant Colonel Chamberlain provided valuable leadership examples and tutorage. As a young, junior officer, Merriam had become a trusted commander.

The trust of Merriam's superiors soon became evident as his name surfaced as a candidate for other commands. Merriam would soon leave the Army of the Potomac and the scenes of the bloody Battles of Antietam and Fredericksburg never to return.

3

Department of the Gulf
Command of Black Troops

Well—the wheels of the watch of ages still revolve! I am not more
convinced of it now than I was a year ago. The year just passed
has not been without its success, like its predecessor. Shall the
new bring still greater good? And ever, ye fates! From force of
circumstances I am obliged to use an old diary. I shall from very
necessity make at least one amend each day of the year—that at the
top of the page. I dare not boast that many days will record any
other amendments, as did when I was assuming to be a man. I shall
now only say, humbly, I will try to do what will satisfy myself.

HENRY CLAY MERRIAM, CIVIL WAR DIARY, NEW YEAR'S DAY, 1865

enry Merriam's conduct during the Battle of Fredericksburg earned him a brevet promotion to lieutenant colonel (some sources say major). Having distinguished himself as "an able, conscientious, energetic, and gallant officer," as "certified by his regimental and brigade commanders," he was then transferred to the Department of the Gulf. Company H gave him an "elegant sword" as a respected parting gesture when he departed the East Coast bound for New Orleans.[1]

There was much more to this transfer to the Department of the Gulf than a simple change from the eastern theater to the trans-Mississippi Deep South. Merriam left a familiar command in the 20th Maine Regiment, with the men he personally knew from the northeastern part of the state, to a startlingly different command situation, leadership of black troops. In addition, he left the East Coast, a geographic section of the country he knew well, for a totally unknown former part of the Confederacy in the steamy South. Truly, all things considered, Merriam was to become a "fish out of water" with this momentous change.

What prompted this transfer remains cloudy. Once again Merriam stood amazingly silent on the subject. Nevertheless, he assumed a role in a series of events unfolding in early 1863. With Lincoln's Emancipation Proclamation, questions arose about the disposition and use of the freed slaves. Political pressure mounted on the president to make some use of the negroes or the colored men, as they were called at that time. Among those urging military utilization of the former slaves was Gen. Daniel Ullman. He, like others, met with Lincoln and urged the president to permit enlistment of the former slaves in the Union Army. After some hesitation, Lincoln agreed to pursue the matter and told Ullman to confer with Secretary of War Edwin Stanton about organizing black volunteer regiments for Louisiana. Vice Pres. Hannibal Hamlin, significantly from Maine, joined in the meeting with Stanton. Afterward Hamlin called upon "his friend and fellow Waterville College [Colby College] trustee, Governor Abner Coburn for help in scouring the Maine regiments for officers willing to lead black troops." Among those nominated was Captain Merriam of the 20th Maine Regiment.[2] With such high-level involvement in Merriam's nomination for a command position in a black regiment, he easily could have concluded that politically he could not reject such an assignment. At the same time, however, as Chamberlain had noted, Merriam was ambitious, and this move could possibly hand him command of a regiment, with a promotion to at least lieutenant colonel or even colonel. Whatever reasoning occupied Merriam's mind at the time in accepting this offer, the decision certainly did not come easy. Considering Merriam's thoughtful character and his education, he no doubt weighed the pros and cons with great deliberation.

Having made his decision, however, to accept working with black troops, Merriam joined Ullmann's expedition to Louisiana in spring 1863 to help organize the first black regiments. His first assignment upon reaching New Orleans could have been a surprise. Merriam was once again a captain and a company commander. On March 11, 1863, he was assigned to the 80th USCT and no doubt faced many new challenges as a white officer in charge of a black company.[3] It is difficult to imagine Merriam's first reaction when facing the black men, mostly ex-slaves, of his new company. He had no previous experience dealing with blacks, for there were virtually none residing in northeastern Maine, where he grew-up and gained his education. His concepts of work and Yankee self-discipline would hardly be matched with the enlisted men he would now command. In so many ways, there would be cultural differences, from food to views about country and duty. Whatever Merriam's thoughts, he barely had time to get adjusted as Maj. Gen. Nathaniel P. Banks, commander of the Department of the Gulf, prepared to launch a campaign from New Orleans northward up the Teche River to Alexandria and Port Hudson, Louisiana. In the Union grand strategy, Banks was supposed to support Ulysses Grant in his thrust on Vicksburg, farther up the Mississippi River, even possibly uniting the two armies, but Banks's push north became distracted by opportunities, at least as he saw them.

General Banks had considerable success in his April 1863 advance northward along the west bank of Louisiana's Teche, a river that runs north to south somewhat parallel to the Mississippi but farther west. His army seized "large quantities of lumber, 500 bales of cotton, many hogsheads of sugar, an inexhaustible supply of salt, and an estimated 20,000 head of cattle, mules, and horses." In addition Banks's column freed many slaves, and Banks, like his predecessor in New Orleans, Maj. Gen. Benjamin Butler, decided to recruit this manpower. He had an example as when Butler accepted the surrender of New Orleans and the 1st Louisiana Native Guard, first organized for Confederate service by Gov. Thomas Moore of Louisiana in May 1862, offered to join the Union forces, and Butler mustered them into Federal service on September 27, 1862. The unit later became known as the 73rd USCT, earning the distinction of being the first black troops mustered into the Union Army. Banks, in his current recruiting effort, was able to form two black regiments of about 500 men each at the captured Louisiana city of Opelousas. One of these new regiments was designated the 3rd Louisiana Native Guards and consisted, as was typical, of ex-slaves commanded by white officers.[4] Merriam now became one of the white company commanders of this 3rd Regiment. With these fresh recruits, slaves so recently freed, his task of developing them into a fighting unit must have been monumental.

Within Banks's army there was considerable doubt about the usefulness of the black regiments. Many believed it inadvisable to put them into combat. What might they do when fired upon and charged by the Confederates? The risks of having them in a battle line would be prohibitive, many thought. General Banks, nevertheless, seemed willing to put them to the test and to decide the issue that way.

The test came during the siege of Port Hudson on the Mississippi River. After reaching and capturing Alexandria (May 6–15), Banks turned east and south, with the reduction of the Confederate fortress at Port Hudson as his goal. By May 25 he had been able to encircle and lay siege to this key Mississippi River bastion. Much to the general's dismay, in two full-scale attacks and an attempted night assault, his army had suffered more than 4,000 casualties. The army was stymied, but Banks doggedly held to his encirclement of the Confederates. His black regiments participated in the siege operations and some of the assaults on Port Hudson. Merriam, commanding Company F, 3rd Louisiana Native Guards, led his ill-trained soldiers in some limited combat action. On May 27, black troops, including the 1st Louisiana Native Guards, earned their first recognition for gallantry, which was later celebrated in a song called "The Charge of the Black Brigade." To the surprise of many, the black Louisiana soldiers had satisfactorily met their first combat test. They had not panicked, had showed courage, and had held their ground. In a way Captain Merriam had passed his test as well. In a remarkably brief time, he had led his black troops into battle with far better than expected results. This was a confidence builder, important for his subsequent command of larger black units. Many years later, a Colorado journal commented on Merriam's Port Hudson action: "In 1863, he was selected as one of the officers to organize colored troops, a service which at that time was more than ordinarily dangerous, and having gone into this branch of the service, led his regiment in the brilliant assault upon the works of Port Hudson, where the bravery of colored men was established beyond question."[5]

The status of blacks in the Union Army had been evolving for some time before Merriam began his leadership of such units. General Butler, the alleged "Beast" of New Orleans, had long urged that freed slaves should be used by the North, if for no other reason than because the South was using them. These men were once viewed as contraband, and as such could be utilized like any other seized material. Butler, during his occupation of New Orleans in 1862, began employing the ex-slaves in labor battalions and then began selecting them as troops for his Corps d'Afrique. Shortly thereafter, a black regiment from Kansas, the 79th USCT , engaged in some skirmishes at Islands Mounds, Missouri, on October 28.[6]

Also, Maj. Gen. David Hunter had boldly begun forming a black regiment that year in South Carolina. His actions included virtual impressments of blacks. By January 1863 Thomas Wentworth Higginson, an antislavery Unitarian minister, helped form the 1st South Carolina Volunteers on Port Royal Island in order to invade Florida. Hunter subsequently had to defend his actions to the Lincoln administration, with Secretary of War Stanton disavowing any involvement or grant of authority, and to face serious questioning and criticism in Congress. Various leaders expressed opinions that Hunter had no authorization to enlist former slaves and then to clothe, equip, and especially arm them. General Hunter's response to charges that he recruited and formed black units began to reflect changing attitudes: "The experiment of arming the blacks, as far as I have made it, has been a complete and even marvelous success. They are sober, docile, attentive, and enthusiastic, displaying great natural capacities for acquiring the duties of a soldier. They are eager beyond all things to take the field and be led into action, and it is the unanimous opinion of the officers who have had charge of them, that in the peculiarities of this climate and country, they will prove invaluable auxiliaries, fully equal to the similar regiments so long and successfully used by the British authorities in the West Indies."[7]

On July 17, 1863, Congress authorized black recruitment, and a War Department order approving the enlistment of blacks and former slaves created a widespread surge of recruits for the Union Army. In Baltimore, for example, Maj. Gen. Robert Schenck received War Department orders to start recruiting blacks. Various Northern states hurried to form black regiments, convinced that this would achieve not only a blow against slavery but also a reduction in manpower levies in their states. As has been noted by many historical commentaries, "the black enlistments were driven by political necessity, not a new found sense of racial sensitivity or political conscience."[8]

Merriam's experience training and leading black soldiers in the 3rd Louisiana Native Guards must have been especially challenging. The recruits had come largely from farms and plantations, most were illiterate, and some spoke only French. Many lacked useable military skills. In addition Merriam and other white officers could not rely on noncommissioned officers to provide key troop-management functions. Instead, they had to perform clerk and quartermaster tasks normally assigned to corporals and sergeants, creating an onerous workload. "Preparation of the accounts, lists, reports, and rolls that made possible the army's day-to-day operations threw the officers of black regiments into fits of despair. The work had to be done, but few enlisted men had the education to do it."[9] A further stressful part of the command in black units was the attitude of fellow officers in white units. There was an element of social ostracizing, with jokes, pointed remarks, and slurs directed at black-regiment commanders. One positive factor in Merriam's favor was the fact that since black recruits often came from one area, they developed a kind of regional esprit de corps, somewhat akin to that of the Maine troops.

Yet most everyone recognized that the success of the black troops depended on their white officers. At first, the black units tended to be detailed to work battalions and guard or garrison duty. In fact, they originally were expected to relieve white troops from the more mundane and distasteful army tasks. As time went by, however, more confidence in black units developed. As General Hunter argued, the recruited blacks proved eager to learn, pleased with their new status of freedom and security the army provided, and were less prone to desert or cause problems. In addition, with good training and discipline, they became effective soldiers. General Butler at one point declared, "I knew that they would fight more desperately than my white troops, in order to prevent capture, because they knew . . . if captured they would be returned to slavery."[10]

After the combat action and long siege at Port Hudson, Merriam became involved in further organizing and training of black regiments in Louisiana. At the same time, he must have watched intently for dispatches and news coming from the East Coast. His former regiment, the 20th Maine, was involved in the furious Battle of Gettysburg. On July 2, 1863, Colonel Chamberlain and the Maine men would earn commendation and glory in the North for their heroic stand at Little Round Top. Merriam must have wondered again about his decision to come to the Department of the Gulf. If he had remained with the 20th Maine, would he have been killed or would he be basking in heroic glory like Chamberlain? What would have been his fate if he had remained in the Army of the Potomac? In retrospect, Merriam surely questioned his career choice in mid-1863. Obviously, here was a case where key decisions seem to be inevitably accompanied with the sobering "what if."

It is evident that Merriam was successful in his training of black troops, for by May 21, 1864, he had attained the rank of lieutenant colonel and was assigned to the 85th USCT Regiment. Only a short time later, on June 3, he became commander of the 73rd USCT, which had also been commended for its performance at Port Hudson.[11] This command represented a two-part milestone. Merriam had become a regimental commander, with the rank of lieutenant

Maj. Gen. Edward R. S. Canby.
Courtesy National Archives.

colonel, and he had taken over the leadership of one of the most-storied black units in the army.

There was a relatively long period of combat inactivity for Merriam and his black regiment, which can be attributed largely to senior command changes in the Department of the Gulf and the region's reduced priority in the North's grand strategy. In 1864, a presidential election year, Lincoln and his army chief, Maj. Gen. Henry Halleck, had decided to do something about General Banks's command of the Department of the Gulf. Banks's campaign up the Teche, followed by his army's thrust up the Red River, had not met with total success nor eastern command approval. But politics (Banks had been Speaker of the House of Representatives) dictated caution in removing him. Lincoln and Halleck's answer was to create the Military Division of West Mississippi, to include Banks's Department of the Gulf, and to assign command to Edward R. S. Canby as a superior rather than a replacement of Banks. General Canby, forty-six and a West Point classmate of Grant, had already shown a desired prudence in his western combat actions and in quelling the New York City draft riots of 1863.[12]

Canby's task in Grant's war close-out strategy was to capture the city of Mobile and then speed into the heart of Alabama with the principal aim of destroying munitions manufacturing at Selma. His immediate concern, however, became the recovery to New Orleans of the scattered survivors of Banks's di-

sastrous Red River Campaign of March–May 1864. Afterward, the army would then be reformed for the campaign against Mobile. Delays ensued when Grant required some of Canby's forces to be sent east as replacements for George Meade's army in Virginia and for William T. Sherman's army in Georgia.[13]

Later in the year, Canby's command received reinforcements from men under Maj. Gen. A. J. Smith; also, a division of cavalry under Brig. Gen. Joseph Knipe was sent down the Mississippi to New Orleans. He now had a force totaling approximately 45,000 men. Grant thought this manpower would be sufficient to begin the long-delayed assault on Mobile with its several strong approach fortifications. Mobile Bay had already been secured by Adm. David Farragut's operations in August, when his fleet successfully passed Fort Gaines and Fort Morgan at the Gulf entrance and then neutralized Confederate defenses in the bay. General Lee and the Confederate commander at Mobile, Maj. Gen. Dabney Maury, had observed the strengthening of Canby and worried that a march on Mobile was imminent. Unfortunately for the Rebels, at this point there was little they could do to bolster Mobile's defenses.[14]

As the planning for the campaign progressed, Merriam had his 73rd USCT in camp at Morganza, about eighty miles up the Mississippi River from Baton Rouge. His diary entries in January 1865 provide insights into his leadership of the regiment and garrison life. Days went by where Merriam noted "nothing beyond the ordinary duties of camp." These "ordinary" activities included problems with mail. On January 13 he complained: "There is still a dearth of mail. We do not understand the cause." There were ordnance requisitions, payrolls, inspections, "property returns, [and] muster rolls" to be administered. But

Merriam was not one to let drill slip if he could help it. On January 27 he noted, "Issued order resuming drills, also instituting a drill for sergeants to be conducted by myself daily." Evenings were often occupied with "officer recitations." After resuming the drills and recitations, Merriam said, "I now feel like myself again." He evidently did not experience serious discipline problems, but some were always present. On January 15 Merriam reported that he had "[i]ssued orders prohibiting gambling." But then three days later, he recorded: "Last night late I was informed of a gambling party in operation near camp, composed of men of my regiment mostly and Adjt and I took revolvers, dressed in disguise, and made descent upon them. By expending a few rounds and alarming the garrison we captured them and a part of their stakes, $20." Even officers got embroiled in discipline problems. For example, Merriam wrote, "Lt. Garrison, having been detailed to go on grand guard, refused to go and went into his quarters in arrest—was afterward allowed to mend his folly."[15]

Always irritating and concerning were the weather and the nearby Mississippi River. Merriam's diary reported on January 15, "The weather is again rainy and unpleasant." Five days later he noted, "The river is again rising very rapidly, and I have taken means to control its approaches to my camp—though it costs the use of a large pump." These efforts were not totally successful, for on the twenty-fourth, he remarked: "Arose late—weather very cold—river and mud very high. Camp half occupied by the river." Somewhat philosophically he later observed, "River threatening—seems to contest my title to the ground on which we are quartered—I believe rightfully—for we are really on the ground belonging to the river outside the levee."[16] The Mississippi remained both a curse and a lifeline as mail and provisions moved up and down the river by the Morganza encampment.

Troop drill, officer recitations, enforcing discipline, and mundane camp activities were occasionally punctuated with surprising excitement. For example, Merriam had to deal with the death of one of his officers on January 8. Diary entries over the next several days told what happened. "While I was engaged writing in evening a soldier came in great haste and informed me that Capt. Guest had been badly wounded while examining outposts. Surgeon Paine hastened with an ambulance. Half an hour later—another message—the captain is dead. I left writing to meet and attend his clay." The next day Merriam added:

I met the ambulance and assisted to bear the body of Capt. G. to his late quarters. It hardly seemed that the wondrous spark had left the body which I bore—it was warm—I half thought I felt pulsation—but no—the femoral artery had been severed in the left thigh high up, and no ligature—he must have died in a few moments. What pity no skillful hand was there to save! It is doubly bitter to lose so good an officer—so brave—so intelligent—so prompt in all his duties in such a way. No one seems to be to blame. I have released with praise the poor fellow who shot the Capt.

Almost as an afterthought, he wrote the next day, "I neglected to state that Capt. G. was shot by one of his own company Private Henry Nita of Company 'H.'" Such an incident required explanation, and Merriam stated: "On investigation it was reported that Capt. G. was shot by Private Henry Nita, Co. 'H,' 73rd U.S.C.T. while on post as sentinel or vedette, that Capt. G. was apparently testing the guard—That no blame can be attached to Henry Nita, and that he manifested a laudable degree of discipline and coolness."[17]

Merriam's superior at Morganza happened to be General Ullmann, the same officer who had played such a large role in his volunteering to work with black regiments. Merriam seemed to have had a cordial relationship with the general, reporting on a number of occasions that he had called on him. For example, on January 12, 1865, Merriam wrote, "Called on General Ullman and explained some official matters concerning ordnance requisitioning." In time, however, the Merriam-Ullmann relationship apparently cooled considerably. A diary entry on the thirtieth sounded an unusual note of criticism: "General Ullman returned from his expedition in the night of Saturday—it is said— so drunk that two men had to hold him on his horse. His staff it appears was worse off as some had to be brought in carriages. Strange stories are about of his exploits, most disgraceful, some of them." Several weeks later Merriam wrote, "General Ullman had one of his usual drunks last night and has relieved Asst. Adjt. Genl. and several others of his staff today."[18] These comments not only tell a story about General Ullmann but also reveal more about Merriam's character. He was, as usual, most circumspect, holding firmly to his religious beliefs, which did not allow drunken or immoral behavior, particularly in full view of his subordinates or his peers.

During early 1865, Merriam plunged into some serious reading. He began a book or volumes by Emmerick Vattel on international law. This reflected his continuing interest in law, suggesting that he at one time might have pursued this as a career. Perhaps he found concentrated reading of law books a bit tiring over a long period, for he later noted that a Chaplain Gardner had given him "Poems by Tennyson in two volumes." On January 13 Merriam's diary reported, "A few pages of Vattel and ordinary duties consumed the day," but then added, "'In Memoriam' by Tennyson was commenced after retiring—am quite well pleased with it." A few days later he stated: "Arose this morning and found Tennyson in bed with me, showing that I had gone to sleep reading 'In Memoriam.' I opened the book and finished the above and commenced to read 'Maud.'"[19] Merriam's reading selections truly mirrored his classical education.

Merriam's diary also reveals a continuing and growing passionate love affair with Lucy Getchell. The two had met when he was a student at Waterville College in Waterville, Maine. Their relationship had blossomed, and therefore it was not surprising that Merriam recorded numerous times when he wrote Lucy. She responded with letters to him, even sending a new pair of slippers; no doubt that is why Merriam personally felt the holdup of mail deliveries in January 1865. On the twenty-second, he wrote, "Felt quite uneasy all day on account of the great delay in our mail—all day I looked—boat after boat arrived and went steaming by but still no mail." The next day he rejoiced. "The long expected mail arrived bringing me a large stack of letters, requiring from 11 a.m. till 3 p.m. in perusal—and no dinner. Nearly all my correspondents were represented—some of them several times—three long letters from Lucy." Lucy must have shared Merriam's interest in music as a diary entry on January 15 reads, "Wrote to Lucy sending ferrotype and small 'greenback' to pay for a guitar as a present."[20]

Despite his love affair with Lucy, to be consummated in marriage after the war, Merriam did not shun looking at and enjoying the companionship of other women. One typical diary observation reads: "In afternoon went to ride with Mrs. H. and had a very pleasant time. She seems to have fallen in love with 'Arab' and wants to ride with me again."[21] In February Merriam was detailed to New Orleans on some official business primarily dealing with ordnance requisitions, but evening allowed some personal diversions. Interestingly, he wrote on February 15: "Called on my creole friends Miss Anna White and Miss Eliza Dubois, accompanied by Luther Anson. We invited them to Varieties where we witnessed again 'Lady Isabel' with as much interest as last eve. I find Anna a very pleasant little companion." Having completed his business in New Orleans, Merriam boarded the "new and elegant steamer 'W. R. Carter'" on the seventeenth for a return upriver to Morganza. The trip proved more pleasant than usual: "Made the acquaintance of a Mrs. Macauley—very pretty and very interesting company during the evening we passed the time at 'Euchre'—slept finely." The next day Merriam added, "The sweet presence of Mrs. Macauley chased away the weariness of the long eve, retired late."[22]

Merriam, a busy letter writer throughout his life, corresponded with family members regularly. On several occasions he indicated that he had written to his mother. Older brother Leonard, back in Maine, seemed to have received special attention. For example, on 8 February the colonel wrote: "Mail arrived. Letters from home. My Bro. Leonard wants some money—suppose I must send it though I must also scold him for so extensively entering into business in these times of uncertainty."[23] Henry Merriam was frugal, and this would not be the only time siblings requested financial help from him. He also, no doubt, honed some business skills through his duties in regimental management, such as continually working requisitions, doing payrolls, and being accountable for property. This would explain some of his reluctant reaction to requests for money.

After returning from his New Orleans trip, Merriam sadly moaned: "orders have come by which regiments of this Post are to make gardens to have fresh vegetables, etc. I suppose this settles us for the summer—unless some accident requires that we go elsewhere." The next day, however, he received a pleasant surprise. "In eve about ten came orders for me to hold my regiment in readiness to embark on b'd transport for Algiers, La. This was very unexpected though I had solicited such when in the city of N. O. Set about packing up, and as I retired was ready for embarking as far as I was personally concerned." Apparently, Merriam had lobbied with the authorities for combat action while in New Orleans, but he must have left with little encouragement on that possibility. Now he reacted with exuberance that at last he and his regiment might have some action. He hurriedly set about packing in minimal time and indicated that he barely slept during the night. One can almost read the joyful tone of his last diary statement for the day: "Salute at midday [February 22] in honor of the Great Father of our Country."[24]

For the next several days, Merriam and his regiment experienced the age-old military exercise of "hurry up and wait": "Spent the whole day in camp packed up and awaiting transportation." Nevertheless, he again showed his excitement by writing letters announcing, "I had succeeded in getting orders to leave Morganzia and do something." On the twenty-fifth the 73rd USCT "commenced to embark" on the steamer *Adriatic* at noon. As the unit moved down the Mississippi, it stopped at Port Hudson, but Merriam reported that "there was so much confusion at the landing that it was impossible to speak to anyone." As they continued beyond Port Hudson, he said that there was great excitement aboard "as we sailed along the river by points where men were acquainted." The *Adriatic* arrived at Algiers at 2:00 p.m. on February 27; Merriam was greeted by Brig. Gen. William A. Pile, who informed him that his regiment would be in his brigade. The next day the 73rd crossed to New Orleans and disembarked.[25]

The regiment marched eastward through the city en route to their camp-site. Merriam was impressed with the reaction the unit received from people on the streets: "Great multitudes were assembled in Canal St. and greeted the regt. (as the old 1st) with much éclat. I have never seen so much excitement on this great thoroughfare." Many in the city evidently knew or were related to the black soldiers. Merriam reported that at their bivouac, "[h]undreds of people have come out from the city to visit friends in the regt."[26]

Merriam and his regiment reached Lakeport on March 1 and boarded the *N. P. Banks,* sailing on a foggy Lake Pontchartrain, running aground and remaining stuck for about two hours, then entering the Mississippi Sound on the afternoon of March 2. Their journey continued eastward until they "touched at Fort Morgan" in Mobile Bay to procure water. From there the ship left the calm waters of the sound and hit the open Gulf, where "it was met by a stiff sea." Many of the men, including Merriam, became seasick.[27]

By March 4 the sea journey ended and land operations began. The troops disembarked and bivouacked on a sandy beach near Pensacola, where Merriam said his men made coffee while he breakfasted with Major Mudgett of the accompanying 86th USCT. (Mudgett was to play an important role later, with Merriam, in the siege of Fort Blakeley.) Merriam then went with his brigade commander, General Pile, to call on their division commander, Brig. Gen. John Hawkins. The 73rd camped on the white sands, which Merriam said "reminds us of winter at home." The black units were now positioned just within the western Florida panhandle and preparing for a drive north-westward toward the city of Mobile and its major defensive positions, Spanish Fort and Fort Blakeley.[28]

Several days were spent in camp preparing the army for the march. Merriam busied himself with getting parts for his Springfield rifles, filling ordnance requisitions, and recommending new officers. As usual, he returned to the drill of his unit, recording that a battalion drill occurred on March 10. He also reported that General Hawkins inspected "and expressed himself well pleased with [the] appearance of the regt." Other officers also reviewed and inspected the 73rd, and according to Merriam, "[g]ave me some compliments as the C. O. of an excellent regt."

Despite their location on the Gulf beach, Merriam and the men found the weather "very cold and disagreeable." He wrote, "Suffered from cold very much last night." The colonel called for more blankets for his men, but he did not indicate that they ever arrived. Rain began on March 14, which continued all day. "[W]eather cold as well as wet," Merriam remarked, "so that it is very uncomfortable." He even had to suspend drill and parades. But the damp, chilly weather did not prevent two other activities that Merriam personally found important wherever he went: riding his horse, Arab, and target practice. He enjoyed riding Arab on the beach, and in his practice firing, he reported, "Had good success." More importantly, the army's pause had allowed Merriam to issue "articles of ordnance to complete [the] equipment of several companies."

Finally, the army resumed the march northwestward from the Gulf on March 19. A column of companies formed at 5:30 a.m. on a route to Pensacola. The city was reached about 5:00 p.m., but the men had encountered considerable hardship along the way, fording two bayous, one of which, Bayou Chica, spread nearly a mile in width and was waist deep. By the end of the next day, March 20, Merriam reported that they had made eight miles in their march in the center of the brigade's column. He noted the many pine trees, the sandy soil, and "then a nice little prairie," where they halted for the night. During the evening, however, a very heavy rain began flooding the Union tents. With daylight, the 73rd had little time to recover since it was detailed to assist the army's supply train, now bogged down in what Merriam claimed was the "worst mud I ever saw. . . . In some places it was impossible for my horse to carry me and mules had to be taken from the wagons and wagons boosted along for half a mile by the men alone." The regiment made only three miles that day.[29]

The next day Merriam received welcome orders to move his unit to the head of the column, leaving the supply train in charge of the 82nd Regiment. This segment of the journey had good roads with overall drier conditions. Merriam said, "we pushed on gaily." Also, the march became more lively with the sound of musketry ahead. Some skirmishing began with the advance guard, and since Merriam's regiment was in the lead, it expected to see action at any time. The column's arrival at Pine Bunen Creek and its high waters necessitated a halt while a bridge could be constructed. Forward movement did not continue until March 25. The road proved good, following somewhat of a ridge with swamps on either side. In the afternoon, cannonading and "brisk musketry" could be heard. A skirmish largely involving the 1st Louisiana Cavalry near Escambia Bridge resulted in the capture of a mortally wounded Confederate commander, eighteen other officers, and 101 enlisted men. Merriam wrote that he "visited the rebel prisoners and had quite a conversation with them."[30]

As the march toward Mobile continued, Merriam saw a "change for the better . . . in the country." The army passed several houses, although the colonel found most country houses in the South "far inferior to those of men in similar circumstances in the North." Noticing farms instead of just wilderness, Merriam sent out details to drive in cattle, resulting in a large supply of beef for the soldiers. This pleased the brigade commander, Merriam happily noted: "General Pile entered into the spirit considerably and was soon riding into the forest with all the enthusiasm of a western hunter."[31]

During the next several days, March 27–29, the advance of the army and Merriam's regiment became very difficult. Merriam complained that his men "marched through horrible swamps for about three miles," the route to Pollard, Alabama, being "circuitous" and of which "almost every foot had to be bridged." At another point he moaned of the "road [being] indescribably bad . . . horse mired several times." He further remarked: "Can now fully realize what is meant by the allusions made in books to the swamps of Florida and southern Alabama. One house was passed early in the afternoon and the remainder of day's march was in a monstrous swamp."

The weather, the swamps, and inadequate supplies began to take a toll on the men. Merriam related, "for the first time during the campaign we had two men sick in the ambulance train." With some pride, he went on to add: "Weather and spirits of the men of my regt. is the theme of conversation among officers. It surpasses anything I ever saw—nine days, hard marching on half rations, and not a man too sick as to fall out of ranks, while the ambulances of other regts. have been full." Merriam favorably compared his regiment in other ways with other units and in particular those of white troops: "Waited till 3 pm for General Andrews' (C. C.) Division to pass, I never saw men so much discouraged and so unreasonably helpless. Their trains wallowing in the mud and the men, instead of assisting them, only cursed and complained, some of them crying—others offering five dollars for a 'hard tack.'" Furthermore, poor foraging resulted in rations being reduced from one-half to one-third. Again Merriam could not help but brag about his soldiers, declaring, "the uniform good spirits of the colored troops under our discouraging circumstances was an additional evidence of the superior efficiency of their officers." He went on to say that despite the roads being blocked by "the unassisted train of the white troops," the 73rd had moved ahead and had "made about twelve miles in not only getting along our own train but also that of the cavalry and leaving the white infantry far behind."[32]

Toward the end of March, troop conditions seemed to improve. Merriam's regiment had made contact with a Union cavalry unit and a railroad. In addition, extensive foraging had brought in fresh meat and some corn, but a "quarter ration of bread" had cleaned out the commissary train. Merriam said,

"I tremble for the health of my men." Yet the colonel personally profited from one foraging expedition: "Major and my servant, Charlie, went and got chickens, sweet potatoes and eggs, so we live high." On April 1 Merriam reported, "Another ration of corn and fresh beef issued to the men and officers."

Hawkins's division again advanced after a one-day bivouac on the Tensas River at Stockton, about twenty miles north of Mobile Bay. The Union cavalry commander sent word of a skirmish ahead, and Merriam's unit came up prepared for action. Nothing developed, however, and the men went into camp to "feel the enemy in the morning." The next day, April 2, cavalry scouts fought a skirmish near the camp. Merriam then got the combat action he had so earnestly desired: "We were called to clear the front and formed a line of battle and advanced rapidly through the woods—charging ravine after ravine—some filled with water as well as infested with [the] enemy. Hotter grew the fight till we came upon strong earthworks and, our skirmishes having driven them all in, we were ordered to halt. Rest of day went in line of battle under fire from the rebel fortifications, both artillery and musketry."[33]

Merriam and the 73rd Regiment had arrived at the outer defense positions of Fort Blakeley. On April 3 he noted, "having entrenched ourselves during the night, we proceeded to prepare for [a] regular siege." Merriam believed that he had chosen his combat line well since enemy artillery, trying his position, had not resulted in regimental casualties but had inflicted losses on both flanking units. Later the 73rd was ordered to move to the rear for a rest break and was relieved on the siege line by the 51st USCT. This allowed Merriam the opportunity to survey the ground where the Confederates had placed torpedoes (land mines). He was impressed by the "carcasses of horses . . . lying in all directions, they having been killed by the torpedoes." The rest time was indeed brief, for the next day the regiment was ordered back to the front to relieve the 86th. Merriam simply complained, "worse ground."[34]

Although the siege of Fort Blakeley had begun, Canby's army sought to keep pressure on the Confederates by closing in on the fortification, moving foot by foot if need be. On April 5, for example, Merriam reported, "Having received orders as soon as I had taken position last night to advance my lines as much as possible, I directed my skirmishers to push in the enemy gradually." By noon he concluded that his regiment could advance about two hundred yards. He was complimented, Merriam said, for "[m]aking so good advancement," particularly since the division on his left had been able to advance only fifty yards. This painstaking forward movement of the besieging lines was not without cost, however. Merriam declared that his line was harassed by enemy fire, "casualties were numerous," and one company commander had been "wounded while withdrawing a working party."[35]

The next three days saw periods of skirmishing and fighting lulls. Merriam mentioned that he could see Mobile with a "glass" from his advanced pits. Federal forces mounted heavy Parrott guns along the river to Merriam's right, positioned to deal with Confederate gunboats. On April 8 a spirited fight erupted between the batteries and the Rebel gunboats. Merriam stated that a "piece of shell struck exactly between his feet" during the artillery exchange: "One inch right or left would have cost me a foot," he said. On another day his regiment, resting in a rear ravine, was ordered to the front "doublequick." He took pride in noting that he spent only ten minutes in getting his troops formed and moving forward, notwithstanding that "it rained hard."[36]

The main assault and fighting at Fort Blakeley occurred on April 9 (see chapter 1). Curiously, Merriam's diary entry for that special day was simple, straightforward, and business like. Without great description or mention of his very important role in the capture of Fort Blakeley, it reads:

> News of Spanish Fort, surrender of, received during the night. I advanced my lines two hundred yards—besting the troops on both right and left by an average of forty yards. Rebs were unusually quiet during morning and I asked to feel them. Granted and it drew on a general assault resulting in the capture of the fort with its entire garrison, 3000 men and its armament. My regt. first placed its flag on the parapet. It has been a day of laurels. Capt. Brown mortally wounded. Capt. Snaer badly wounded. Eighteen men killed and wounded. Maj. Mudgett killed in the charge. Was enthusiastically cheered for reaching parapet first and warmly congratulated by Genls. Pile and Hawkins.[37]

Merriam indicated that his officers and men were much fatigued after the battle and capture of Fort Blakeley. As a consequence, Merriam received orders to allow the men several days to "wash and rest." During this downtime, the colonel noted that the camp was alive with rumors of the capture of General Lee and his army and the occupation of Richmond by Grant. In his diary he wrote, "Considerable rejoicing, but some hesitation—tis too good a thing to be fooled upon—we will believe when we are sure—till then we must doubt." It was not until April 17 that Merriam declared: "News of surrender of Lee confirmed— official correspondence received—salute of 200 guns ordered. Now we look for a speedy peace."[38]

Merriam made his report about the Fort Blakeley battle, and he made a telling remark in his diary: "Made my report of yesterday's battle. During the charge I found a man skulking behind his company which was engaged and I drew my revolver and shot him. Today I find the shot took effect in the neck but is not fatal. He has a mark of which he will be ashamed all his life. He concluded the fire from the rear was most dangerous and went forward lively."[39]

This comment reveals a harsher side of Henry Clay Merriam. When it came to a question of bravery, commitment, and disciplined behavior, he was unequivocal. Duty became paramount, and slacking could not be tolerated. He firmly believed his men, white or black, must learn, mainly by never-ending drill, to respond quickly and completely to the given orders. This applied not only to a charge in face of fire in battle but also to coming to the assistance of a bogged-down supply train. Whatever needed to be done had to be done. At the same time, his diary entries and the recorded events leading to the conclusion of the war also reveal a softer side. Merriam studied the law, read poetry, and wrote copious letters, some of love. He worried about the health, welfare, and discipline of his men. He truly grieved over the loss of an officer, friend, or enlisted man. Merriam even showed interest and some compassion toward his Confederate enemy.

The experience of commanding black troops, as has been indicated, challenged his leadership skills. Merriam's New England background had not prepared him for such a potent interaction of race and Southern slave culture, made all the more difficult by his being thrust into this experience in the Deep South. To his great credit, Merriam adjusted quickly and well. There was a surprising absence of racial comment in Merriam's writings. In most cases one does not know whether he refers to whites or blacks in his entries. Evidence points to a most evenhanded approach in his command of black men. Merriam employed the same leadership techniques whether he led white or black units. His strong belief in tight discipline did not waiver when considering the racial composition of the organization. In this he was successful in the use of drill and discipline to mold fighting units, so he never deviated from this basic premise.

As his command of blacks evolved and continued over many months, Merriam seemed to take pride in the performance of his troops, favorably comparing and contrasting them on occasion with accompanying white units. Also, he recorded times when he felt the need to point out his troops' good actions to senior commanders, even to correcting what he felt were erroneous credits in official reports. Overall, one must conclude that Merriam did not object to command of black soldiers; indeed he may well have welcomed such command.

During the Civil War, often times there was a contrast drawn between the so-called abolitionist officers and the non-abolitionist officers of black troops. Both were greatly influenced by the pervasive social attitudes of the time. The black troops might now be viewed as free men, but their freedom carried racial limits. For example, abolitionist officers tended to hold that recruitment of blacks was not only a means to make them soldiers but also a means to equip them to be good citizens, advancing them from dehumanized slaves to free and contributing members of American society. Non-abolitionist officers, though, might not especially care for the free status of their men, viewing command of black units merely as an avenue of career advancement. Merriam's command, as that of other white officers, blurred such polarized distinctions. Nowhere does Merriam come across as a thoroughgoing abolitionist—he certainly lacked the rhetoric. Yet his care and concern for his soldiers, including instruction and assignment of responsibility to them, demonstrated optimism for their future role. At the same time, Merriam left hints, such as his self-promotion talks with senior officers, that he understood that command of black troops could further his career.

Beyond his attitude toward his command of blacks, Merriam had become part of a larger reshaping of American society. The Union Army eventually had 120 infantry, twelve heavy artillery, one light artillery, and seven cavalry regiments of black troops. These organizations totaled over 186,000 men, with 134,111 coming from the slave states. There were other men informally included in the total aggregate. This black manpower had become a substantial force that not only helped expand Union ranks but also helped bring about social change. Frederick Douglass clearly saw the great importance of enlisting blacks in the Union Army: "Once let the black man get upon his person the brass letters, U.S.; let him get an eagle on his button, and a musket on his shoulder and bullets in his pocket, and there is no power on earth which can deny that he has earned the right to citizenship." In a similar vein, historian Russell Weigley observed, "For black men to march through the slave states wearing the uniform of the U.S. Army and carrying rifles on their shoulders was perhaps the most revolutionary event of a war turned into revolution."[40]

4

Post–Civil War

The Occupation Army

Called at several houses and was received very pleasantly
by the ladies—men having all run away at our approach.
Ladies say they want peace on any terms we choose to
grant them. They are willing to give up slavery but ask
what is to become of the negro? With much emphasis.

HENRY CLAY MERRIAM, CIVIL WAR DIARY, APRIL 27, 1865

With the capture of Fort Blakeley on April 9, 1865, and the simultaneous surrender of General Lee at Appomattox, Civil War fighting came to an end. The South was defeated and demoralized, and Union forces spread throughout the former Confederacy to enforce the beginning of Reconstruction. Merriam had worked diligently for so many months molding his black troops into an effective fighting force. Now he and his regiment would begin an entirely different task of armed occupation. This new mission would not be easy. All armies in postwar times face a decline in motivation, cohesion, and purpose as the focus in preparing for battle is lost, replaced by uncertainty. In addition, the occupation—to pacify, stabilize, and restore the rebellious states to the Union—would occur in an area and environment of civilian hostility. Merriam's leadership ability would be tested in a different way. Fortunately, he provided valuable insights, via his 1865 diary, as to how an army unit, a black one no less, performed in the Union occupation and the beginning of the reconstruction period.

Immediately after the Union occupation of Fort Blakeley, the 73rd Regiment rested. This allowed time for Merriam to read his mail, and as he read his stack of letters, his spirits rose. One in particular, from his brother Lewis, dated from home, told of Lewis's escape from the Confederates. (He had been taken prisoner on May 5, 1864, but had escaped on February 15, 1865, and joined Northern forces at Wilmington, North Carolina, on the twenty-second.) There were also letters from brother Cyrus and, of course, Lucy.[1]

Meanwhile, General Canby's army moved on from Fort Blakeley to seize Mobile. The capture of the city proved easier than expected as the Confederate commander, General Maury, abandoned the Alabama port the morning of April 12. Maury reported the event and commented on his predicament:

My effective force was now reduced to less than 5,000 men, and the supply of ammunition had been nearly exhausted in the siege of the two positions [Spanish Fort and Fort Blakeley] which the enemy had taken from me. Mobile contained nearly forty thousand non-combatants. The city and its population were entirely exposed to fire which would be directed against its defenses. With the means now left me an obstinate or protracted defence would have been impossible, while the consequences of it being stormed by a combined force of Federal and negro troops would have been shocking—my orders were to save my troops, after having made as much time as possible—therefore I decided to evacuate Mobile at once. . . . I completed the evacuation of Mobile on Wednesday morning, having dismantled the works, removed the stores best suited for troops in the field, transferred the commissary stores to the Mayor for use of the people, and marched out with 4,500 infantry and artillery, twenty-seven light cannon, and brought off all the land and water transportation.[2]

The Union Army swept into the city, beginning the occupation. Merriam noted in his diary on April 12, "Mobile occupied this day . . . at 2:30 p.m. without opposition." Several days later he made his first trip to the city, leaving Fort Blakeley on a steamer. In Mobile he met with General Andrews and had "quite a lengthy conversation with him" about the performance of the black troops. Merriam said that Andrews was "much gratified when I told him my regiment had behaved finely on the whole campaign."

Always inquisitive, Merriam toured the occupied city the next day. He observed, "Mobile is a pretty city, though now very dull and shabby in the business portion of the town." He added, "In general appearance it compares well with N. Orleans above Canal St.—visited the fortifications—three lines—all the heavy guns left by rebs, but they are rendered temporarily unserviceable."[3]

Afterward, Merriam quickly returned to Fort Blakeley and to his regiment. On April 20 he was awakened in the night and informed of orders to "embark on transport with least possible delay." He aroused his regiment, and they boarded the transport *Wenville*. Merriam and the 73rd Regiment were to be transported up the Alabama River and become part of the Union forces moving to Selma, Alabama, to seize or to destroy its munitions industry. This was one of the final goals of the whole Mobile campaign and part of Grant's war close-out strategy.

While aboard the steamer, Merriam and all Union troops received a most disturbing report. "In evening came the astonishing news of the assassination of President Lincoln and Secy. Seward!" Despite the initial reaction to want to discount such information, Merriam resignedly said: "The news is official and we cannot doubt it. Every man is furious and exasperated. How can the places of these great men be filled?" The next day he wrote, "News from N. Orleans giving more details of the horrible affairs at Washington—J. Wilkes Booth the murderer of Pres. Lincoln—Secy. Seward still alive."[4]

The movement up the Alabama River was led by the gunboat *Cincinnati*, with two other gunboats behind. The river navigation turned more difficult as the Alabama ran very high, with considerable flooding in the countryside. Merriam remarked that the "stream seems very narrow to one so long associated with the great Mississippi."

Near Black's Bluff, Merriam approached his brigade commander, General Pile, about a proposed march across country to Bridgeport. The distance overland would be about eighteen miles, while the gunboats and transports would need to travel thirty-five miles by water. Pile approved, ordering the colonel and his regiment to lead the way. Merriam obtained a guide and set his men in motion. The road seemed good at first, but soon he reported "pitchy darkness and the roughest road imaginable." Merriam and his horse fell down a steep incline "several yards in the mud on his back," but the colonel merely commented, "I was not injured but had to ride on a very muddy saddle." Fortunately, a plantation provided a suitable camping spot, which allowed Merriam and his men to regroup.[5]

The march to Bridgeport, through Camden, resumed the next morning. During a rest stop, Merriam indicated that he had "visited some ladies—men had all skidadled—and had a very interesting conversation with them." One of the topics discussed must have been the end of the war. Merriam noted, "Scarcely any one will believe that Lee has surrendered."[6] Clearly, he and his black troops marching through represented a new reality for residents of the area.

The black brigade arrived at Bridgeport on April 26. They had successfully foraged in the countryside en route, seizing numerous heads of cattle and 400 bales of Confederate cotton. Many of the animals were slaughtered to provide fresh meat, then the men again embarked on the transports. The next day they landed at Cahaba and marched until dark, bivouacking opposite Selma, Alabama, one of the army's major objectives. On April 28 Merriam crossed the river to inspect the town and found that Union cavalry approaching from the north had already accomplished the destruction of the munitions center. He spent an hour touring the ruins of "C. S. A. Iron Works and Arsenal" and reported, "The destruction by Genl. Wilson's cavalry was most complete and the extent of property destroyed almost beyond conception." Selma "was doubtless very pretty before, but now the ruin is everywhere manifest." In addition, Merriam found the people were not "so pleasant"—understandable perhaps, considering the destruction described.[7]

Merriam's stay in ravaged Selma turned out to be exceedingly short. The day after his touring the city, the 73rd USCT, along with the 47th USCT, received orders to board and escort the transports back to Mobile. General Andrews's division moved to garrison Selma, while General Hawkins's division of colored troops continued on to Montgomery. Although Merriam did not specifically indicate, it appears that his regiment was selected to load seized cotton for shipment downriver. At this time, cotton was urgently needed in the Northern textile mills to keep workers employed. As the flotilla moved downriver, it made stops at several locations specifically to take on cotton bales. The assignment of the 73rd and 47th to this duty, a task that Southern blacks no doubt knew all too well, seemed a return to the early days of detailing black regiments as work battalions.

The troops arrived back at Mobile at 9:00 a.m. on May 2. After disembarking, Merriam searched, with considerable difficulty, for a suitable camp area, finally bivouacking temporarily about four miles from the city's center. Later he rode through the streets and explored Confederate fortifications, still looking for an appropriate campsite for the regiment. He felt there was "no ground very well adapted," with the major trouble being the want of good water. The next day he finally selected a location, near an abandoned redoubt, with suitable water, though he declared the ground was "quite uneven." The officers would be quartered in some nearby houses.[8] This process would assume considerable importance in the future because it provided Merriam further training and experience in selecting suitable places to quarter troops. Years later he would apply such experience many times in surveying and establishing forts in the West.

After establishing his Mobile camp, Merriam followed a pattern he had developed previously. He "called at several adjoining houses in the evening and had lengthy conversations with the people." He always seemed curious about the conditions around him and actively sought to engage the local populace and learn from them. Perhaps this was smart politics—to reduce animosity and conflict in the area around his camp—but at the same time it seemed to be a Merriam characteristic to ascertain what was going on, in a broader civilian context, and to determine what people were thinking. In this case what he found was that the Alabamans were "[a]ll tired of the war, but some still love their Southern Confederacy. They would like independence if it cost nothing."[9] This probably proved unsettling to him, with his strong passion for preserving the Union. Apparently the South, although defeated, would not easily come back into the national fold.

Merriam had opportunities to meet with some of the general officers in Mobile. On one occasion, he heard from Pile that the general had recommended Merriam's appointment as brevet colonel for his conduct at Fort Blakeley and that it had been approved by General Osterhaus and members of Canby's staff. This news delighted Merriam, but it was tempered by the knowledge that the army would be demobilizing soon, and with it would come fewer opportunities for promotion. Despite his success in leading black troops, he must have harbored some doubts about future advancement. A new and different peacetime army was just starting to take shape. Also, Merriam, rather courageously, called on Osterhaus, Canby's chief of staff, to discuss "the recent false representations of the assault and capture of Blakely."[10] The colonel had indicated earlier that he felt the performance of the black regiments had not been faithfully reported. To continue to raise the issue with senior commanders showed his pride in the black units and his determination to have their story told honestly.

During these days in the middle of May, Merriam sought to keep his men both busy and sharp. He scheduled a dress parade, the first since arriving from Selma, and then began frequent battalion drill. One day he remarked, "Not feeling well but had a battalion drill at 8 a.m." Feeling under the weather allowed him to resume his classical reading. This time, he was reading Dante.

On May 19 Merriam had a surprise. After coming back from his conference with General Osterhaus in Mobile, he found his brother Lewis awaiting him. Lewis, as expected, had to provide his older brother with an account of his capture by the Confederates. Merriam then noted in his diary his reaction to his brother's ordeal. "Poor boy! I had not dreamed that he had suffered so much in the hands of the enemy—dastardly villains to torture prisoners so."[11] No explanation was offered as how his brother managed to join Merriam in the Mobile area, after having last written him from Houlton. Lewis apparently was still in the Union Army because a few days later, Merriam said that Lewis had left camp "for Louisiana—to join his regiment now at Bayou Sara."

On May 25 Merriam reported on the catastrophic explosion in Mobile. "Great explosion in the city of Mobile which shook the earth here (7 miles out) and reverberated for many minutes. Rumor says thirty tons of powder exploded in one warehouse, but we believe it was only our engineers blowing up some of the rebel works around the city." Later he acknowledged the terrible truth: "Evening confirms the rumor and says a thousand persons were killed and wounded by the falling missiles. It is horrible if so!" The next day he made this report:

> Morning paper relates the horrifying catastrophe of yesterday. Went to the city and examined the ruins. Whole blocks of the heaviest buildings in the city are literally blown into powder, while the mangled parts of unknown human bodies are being removed from the ruins by the wagon load. Fully half of the city is injured more or less. Some buildings nearly a mile off have their windows entirely broken out, while others nearer have only shattered walls left standing. Two steamers were destroyed in the river and several others much injured. The loss is many millions and lives several hundreds.[12]

The following day, on May 26, the commander of the Confederate Trans-Mississippi Department, Gen. E. Kirby Smith, surrendered to Major General Canby. This was the last major Rebel command to capitulate, prompting Merriam to write: "News in evening of the surrender of 'Kirby' Smith's Trans-Mississippi Army. Salutes fired at Fort Morgan. This is the end of the great Rebellion." That same day, however, Merriam noted that his regiment was to move again. "Four regts. of our division (half of those remaining) are ordered to hold themselves in readiness to embark on transports." It was not until June 11 that the 73rd USCT boarded "an old rotten craft" called *J. M. Brown* and sailed down the bay. The next day the ship crossed the Mississippi Sound, encountering "a strong wind which made our craft creak and bend fearfully." The vessel then moved up Lake Pontchartrain "to an encampment at Greenville, Louisiana." Some days later Merriam received orders to move upriver to Vicksburg. His unit's expected mission up the Mississippi River proved most disappointing: "Visions of railroad repairing seem to dawn darkly in our horizon."[13]

Although ordered to be in readiness for transport to Vicksburg, Merriam and his troops remained a few days in camp awaiting the availability of a river steamer. This allowed him to draw supplies and issue them to his men. He reported that his camp was "filled with wives and friends of the regiment having a general good time." Merriam took notice of the women: "Some of the Creole girls are very beautiful, and, in our unprejudiced New England would be admitted to such society as their education and character entitle them."[14] He probably waxed a bit idealistic on this "unprejudiced" comment, but nevertheless, it did reflect his optimism about the future of African Americans in society.

Also, while awaiting upriver transportation, Merriam returned to his campaign to ensure that his black troops received recognition for their combat performance. He reported that he had written an "article for publication," which had been approved by General Hawkins, "in which the just claims of the colored troops in the capture of Blakely are set forth for the first time." On this occasion Merriam was writing to the newspapers of New Orleans. He sent copies of the article to the *Times* and other publications, hoping to correct what he saw as the omissions and false reports of New Orleans's newspapers. A day later Merriam noted, "Article of yesterday did not appear in the 'Times' and there was no issue of 'Tribune.'" Still later he said: "Article of Sunday appeared in 'Tribune' on 1st page with a happy prefatory remark, editorial, but no mention was made of it in the 'Times'—wrote a spicy note to editor and asked a reason for their neglecting the article. He gave no reasons, but remained quiet as a mule." Merriam became quite frustrated with the absence of his article in the *New Orleans Times*. On June 21 he wrote: "Still no notice of my comments in the 'Times.' Officers of the division of colored troops are becoming very much enraged at the course of the 'Times' and say the editor is afraid to publish it lest he displease some rebel correspondent." He continued his writing efforts, declaring that he "wrote an article additional for publication in other journals of the city explaining the treatment my article had received by the 'Times.'"[15] That same day Merriam and his troops embarked on the *General Quitman* and steamed up the Mississippi. New Orleans editors likely were pleased that the colonel had left their fair city.

Merriam and his command proceeded upriver, stopping at Port Hudson, where he left a body for burial; one of his men had been killed by the "falling of a plank." His brother Lewis was in camp nearby, so the two brothers enjoyed another brief meeting. The next stop was at Natchez, where Merriam had time to mount his horse and enjoy "a gallop . . . through the city." "Tis more of a place than I had supposed," he observed. On June 24 the regiment reached Vicksburg, disembarked immediately, and occupied barracks buildings on Cherry Street. The next day, a Sunday, Merriam called for a dress parade of his regiment down Cherry Street. According to Merriam, this parade "drew out a large crowd of spectators and elicited highly complimentary remarks from high officials." Afterward, he had time to ride over the area where the "armies of the mighty Grant struggled with the rebel host of Pinkerton [*sic*, Pemberton] in 1863." Somewhat sadly he reported that rains and weeds had "been at work on those landmarks that told where heroes fought and nobly died."[16]

Merriam received orders to move his regiment from Vicksburg to Clinton, Mississippi. His unit was to repair a railroad in the Champion Hill area. Merriam began preparation for relocating his troops and the difficult task of securing supplies for rebuilding railroads. He was informed that no mules "fit for service" were available. He tried to get rail transportation as far as Big Black but had to put supplies on the available cars and then march the troops. The early summer weather was very hot and the road dusty, resulting in several days of difficult marching. On June 29 Merriam and the troops arrived at Clinton and went into camp, but since their tents were with the supply trains, "we had to 'lie' out" unsheltered. Other troubles developed. A detail of one hundred enlisted men and two commissioned officers, with ten days' rations, had to be dispatched to Meridian, Mississippi, to secure railroad ties. Company commanders formed details of fifteen enlisted men with ten days' rations and one wagon to work a rail line leading back to Vicksburg. Merriam reported, "Officers all very busy with their papers."[17] Interestingly, the colonel recorded that he had applied for an extended leave of sixty days to go to Maine. He probably did not find railroad repair to his liking and felt it was a good time to be gone.

A very welcome order came on July 1 to discontinue all details until after a July 4 celebration. The next day, however, General Osterhaus issued orders for a review of all troops at the post to occur on Independence Day. A rehearsal needed to be held, so a dress parade took place on July 2. Merriam said the post commandant and his staff "spoke in the highest terms of our parade though we thought it was inexcusably poor." In preparation for the review, Merriam commented that "articles needed" could not be filled at the post, "nor nearer than Jackson." In addition, he had a conflict with the commandant. "Had quite a discussion with him on the point of formation of troops in line for review—he contending that regts. took place according to rank of colonels and giving Genl. Osterhaus as authority also Army and Navy Journal." Merriam no doubt lost any argument as the line formed at 9:00 a.m. July 4 for the big review. He then noted: "Review was excellent." Furthermore, he took pleasure in reporting: "Praise was given my regt. by every one for having done finely. Genl. Osterhaus was heard to speak in the highest terms of our discipline and drill." After the review Merriam reported that the "[c]olored people of the community have made a great preparation" and gave the "colored soldiers a fine dinner." He declared, "They are doing the principle part of the celebrating."[18]

Lewis Merriam sent a telegram requesting that his brother send him a horse so he could come to Clinton to visit. Henry replied with a telegram telling him to come by stage. Lewis complied and arrived on July 5, and the brothers began boarding at the home of a Mrs. Guion, a widow with two daughters and a son. A "Judge Yergen" family also lived at the house, which triggered the following Merriam diary remark: "All are of the real Southern aristocratic order and only consent to board 'Yankee Officers' as a sort of necessity as Greenbacks are only got by some such means. They are not slow to claim their aristocratic standing. They appear to have been wealthy which is the only visible claim they ever had to eminence—and that is very invisible now."[19]

Nearly two weeks later, the 73rd USCT was ordered to move into Clinton to act as a garrison force. Merriam accordingly terminated his stay at Mrs. Guion's place and started boarding at a General McMackin's house; Lewis returned to Port Hudson. Merriam recorded a parting remark about Mrs. Guion and her boarding house: "Settled with Mrs. Guion paying ten dollars per week for very ordinary board—presume something extra was charged for my introduction into the 'first families.'"[20] This was one of the few times that Merriam became sarcastic or very critical of conditions in the South.

Merriam again registered complaints about the Fort Blakeley reports. He called on General Osterhaus and "spoke of the false reports which he permitted to be published concerning the assault at Blakely, Ala." Osterhaus told Merriam that General Canby would do justice to all in his report which was yet to be made. Osterhaus sought to mollify Merriam by compliments. "He spoke very highly of my regt., both at Blakely and in general," wrote the colonel. Later he commented that Osterhaus sent an official note "assuring me of his high regards and asking my wishes in reference to future services."[21]

On July 8 Merriam entered a short note in his diary: "Three years today since I left Waterville College to recruit my company in the 20th Me. I wonder if L. [Lucy] remembers the evening of the day?" This comment, along with the more-strident tone of some diary entries, the sarcastic account of his boarding at Mrs. Guion's, and the aggressive pursuit of correct reporting of the Fort Blakeley campaign, indicates that Merriam was getting fatigued with such long service without leave. It was not until July 24, however, that he would receive word that his leave of absence had been approved, headquarters of the Northern District of Mississippi "directing me to return at once and avail myself of it."[22]

In the days between his noting his three-year service anniversary and the very welcome news of leave approval, Merriam had received orders to collect his detailed men and to move his regiment again, this time to Columbus, Mississippi, as a garrison for that city. The men must have viewed this with mixed feelings. On the one hand, it meant that the arduous work details on restoring the railroads would likely end. Just a few days earlier, Merriam had stated, "no drills are expected as we are furnishing quite a lot of men to assist in repairing the Railroad to Vicksburg."[23] On another day he indicated that orders had arrived for detailing one commissioned officer and fifty men daily for the railroad work. The possible conclusion of the work details must have been welcome news indeed. On the other hand, going to garrison duty meant a return to camp boredom as well as drill and ceremonies.

On July 24 Merriam turned over his command "with some regret" and prepared to return to Jackson. The next day he bade his officers adieu, sold his beloved horse Arab to a lieutenant, and took a train first to Jackson, Mississippi, then on to the Mississippi River, beginning a long and eventful journey upriver to Cairo, Illinois. He then traveled to Chicago, Boston, and finally Waterville, Maine. On August 7 he was met at the Waterville depot by Lucy. Merriam said, "I shall not say how I felt when we met," but he decidedly did not want to "see any body else this evening." Following this romantic meeting, Merriam, with Lucy at his side, spent weeks visiting his father and mother, siblings, and other relatives. This was Lucy's introduction to the family as Henry's fiancée. He noted on August 23, "These are happy days." A mere five days later, however, Merriam received word from Washington that he had been granted a leave extension of only ten days, not the twenty he had anticipated. "This is a great disappointment," he confessed, "as I have made all the arrangements with the supposition that twenty days would be given." Because of the length of the journey back to New Orleans, Merriam knew he would have to leave promptly. On September 1 he sadly commented: "I left my poor Lou in a flood of tears at ten and took the train to rejoin my regiment in New Orleans. Poor Girl!—It seemed as though her poor heart would break." But Merriam deeply felt the parting also. While on his return journey to the South, he wrote: "Took photographs from my trunk and with their dumb company I spent the day—having a deeper sense of loneliness that I have felt for many many months."[24]

Merriam's return to New Orleans was by the steamer *Northern Light* out of New York City. He made reading purchases of "Constitutions—Blackstone— and Atlantic Monthly," but he found the trip unusually boring. In addition, he was seasick again, declaring one night that he "had to sleep on deck my stateroom being too hot and too odorous for my taste." He arrived back in New Orleans on September 15 and found his regiment now posted at Camp Parapet.

The next day Merriam returned to his encamped regiment. "Came out to camp in afternoon and found all glad to see me, though all knew I would be a harder master than they had had for a month." The following morning at 9:00 a.m., he inspected the regiment, finding "quite a number of men absent without leave by the reports—from 12 to 25 each day. Otherwise the condition of the men was fair. Camp is wet—Hospital not well cared for." Additionally, he remarked: "Anniversary of 'Antietam.' 3 years have passed quickly by—three years big with events, and to be ever remembered in American History."[25]

Merriam's future status in the army began to assume greater importance and urgency. In late July he had received a letter from Headquarters, Northern

District of Mississippi in Jackson, Mississippi, stating, "I am directed to say to you, that should you desire to remain in Service after the term of your Regiment expires the General will be glad to have timely information of any views or suggestions you may wish to make on behalf of yourself or the men who remain in Service." Merriam promptly responded, "In reply to your communication this date, I have to say that I desire to remain in service after the expiration of my regiment." He then sought to bolster this request by saying that he had "been four times officially complimented for my behavior and that of my command in battle, Antietam, Shepherdstown Ford, Fredericksburg and Blakely, Ala." As an added observation, he pointed out, "The 86th Regt. at Fort Morgan, Mobile Bay, has no colonel."[26] Merriam began keeping a wary eye out for possible promotion vacancies in the army, a trait he would never lose until his retirement. But some anxious months would pass before his future would become clear.

On September 18 Merriam went to General Canby's headquarters to seek information, any plans, about the "muster out" of his regiment and to learn the possibilities of his being retained in the army. He was referred to Maj. Gen. William T. Sherman, commanding the Eastern District of Louisiana. Sherman said, according to Merriam, that "he wished to so consolidate as to have the new regt. retain the No. '73rd' for its reputation." Merriam viewed this as "a compliment to me" since, he said, "I have commanded the 73rd through all." Other news followed that the 75th and 76th USCT Regiments would be merged into Merriam's 73rd, that Col. S. M. Quincy would be retained, and the consolidated unit would include either Merriam or possibly another lieutenant colonel. This was not what Merriam had desired. "Think it almost certain that I shall be mustered out for the reason that Colonel Quincy is retained," he observed.[27]

Considerable confusion and turmoil developed as the army demobilization progressed. Despite promises to Merriam about retaining his 73rd Regiment, an order was issued consolidating the 73rd with the 96th USCT, under command of Colonel Quincy. The consolidation order directed the mustering out of the 73rd's officers and all men whose terms of service were about to expire. Merriam was now bereft of command. But he was told that anything he wished in reference to recruiting service would be approved by General Canby. Also, it was suggested that he apply to be examined for promotion to colonel, possibly to command the 55th USCT Regiment.

On September 23 Merriam "applied to be examined with a view to promotion." The morning of September 27, he dutifully reported to a board of examiners and later reported how he was greeted: "Col. Merriam, we of the Board consider it our duty only to satisfy ourselves that a candidate is fully competent and meritorious. From our intimate knowledge of you and your reputation we are all agreed in your case and shall give you the best recommendation in our power. We waive further examination." Merriam said he "felt somewhat flattered and replied in grateful thanks for their consideration." At the conclusion there was a "hearty shaking of hands and thus ended my examination."[28]

A couple of days later, Merriam called on Canby's headquarters and received very disappointing news. The general had approved the report of the board of examiners, but he had not recommended Merriam for command of any particular regiment. The 55th USCT had been determined "too small to muster a col. and was not a desirable regt. to command." Further disturbing news came to the fore. Merriam inquired at Canby's headquarters about General Pile's recommendation for his brevet promotion to colonel and discovered that it had been returned to the staff for remarks and was never reforwarded. On October 3 he did learn that his papers for promotion had been approved by Maj. Gen. Philip H. Sheridan and forwarded to the secretary of war.[29]

For most of October and into the first week of November, Merriam remained without a command, a particularly vulnerable position during the army's transition to peacetime status. Almost inevitably, it seemed, he could not survive the army's downsizing, unit consolidations, and preferences given to regular officers (often West Pointers) wanting to remain in the service. Throughout the remainder of October, Merriam waited for some word about his status. He realized that any promotion to colonel likely would not be approved without assignment to lead an organization authorized such a rank. Any command vacancies already had many qualified and long-service officers competing to fill the officer's slots. Despite his earning the Medal of Honor, success in commanding a black regiment, and support from various general officers, Merriam's disadvantages of youth, volunteer-officer background, and lack of seniority overcame any of his advantages. He would be mustered out effective October 24, 1865.

Undoubtedly, leaving army service was a severe disappointment for Merriam. During his three years of Civil War experience, he had grown into a respected and praised commander. He had enjoyed his officer status and found his responsibilities challenging. Based on his leadership successes, he sincerely believed that he had the intelligence, education, character, and skills to advance further through the army's hierarchy. Now his only consolation in such a depressed time was the thought of returning to Lucy, family, Maine, and college.

As this chapter in Merriam's life closed, a retrospective examination of his post–Civil War experience provides interesting and revealing assessments. His diary observations provide enlightening accounts of life in the Union occupation army and conditions in the Deep South states of Alabama, Louisiana, and Mississippi. The black regiments, along with white ones, frequently moved about these states. They constituted a new reality for Southerners, seeing black men in Union uniforms, parading in their cities and marching through the countryside. It would appear that some street parades and garrison assignments were made with the intention of driving home the new reality of freed slaves in a position of prestige, paid service, and authority. One ex-slave delightedly said companies of black and white troops marched past him, all of them "manly and walking proudly."[30]

Merriam noted on occasion how the black populace in the Deep South responded enthusiastically to seeing their race so visibly important. This was further confirmed by the reports of others. One officer, for example, said, "Put a United States uniform on his back and the chattel is a man." An ex-slave declared that his race "was now lifted to the highest gift or elevation: his government protector. Should a foot be lifted to give him a kick, he would reply, 'Don't touch these clothes' and 'Show the eagles on his coat.'"[31] In another way, the parading black soldiers stood out in the ruined South as a symbol of economic security. No doubt some of the joyful black-populace response to the soldiers was due to their steady employment and pay.

Merriam obviously took pride in his black troops and courageously objected to what he believed were efforts to denigrate their performance. He had remonstrated with the newspapers in New Orleans, seeking to correct their reporting about black achievements in combat. He sought conferences with his superiors to complain about the absence of correct combat accounts. These aggressive "rocking the boat" tactics easily could have jeopardized his career. At the same time, however, some questions arise. Strangely, Merriam never addressed the role of his black noncommissioned officers in his regiment. Besides being crucially important to carrying out administrative duties, these sergeants and corporals were often considered "cultural mediators" between the white officers and their black soldiers, so recently released from slavery. The high turnover of white officers made the "mediator" all the more important. Yet Merriam never discusses these key black middle leaders. Also, when he had several opportunities to name the black sergeant who was at his elbow in the charge against the Confederates at Fort Blakeley, he failed to identify him.

What also becomes apparent in Merriam's occupation-army accounts is the shifting responsibilities of the black troops. At Fort Blakeley, the 73rd Regiment had become a true combat unit, demonstrating that blacks would and could fight. In the immediate postwar period, however, the black regiments began to revert to labor battalions. In the eyes of many commanders in the various occupation districts, black manpower obviously came to mind as the need to ship confiscated cotton bales and to rebuild railroads became army priorities. This labor role tended to weaken the image of the black regiments as combat soldiers.

An interesting view of the defeated South also emerges from Merriam's observations. The foraging Union forces, often living off the land, devastated the Southern economy. Losses of livestock and food crops severely hit every area, urban and rural. In fact, under Grant, army policy in regard to foraging had changed drastically. Grant wrote, for example, "I regarded it as humane to both sides to protect the persons of those found at their homes, but to consume everything that could be used to support or supply armies."[32] In addition, the Union Army, as Merriam reported, seized cotton and other means of economic wealth and destroyed industries. That is why Merriam could comment about the need of the Southern widow Guion, in search for a source of any possible greenbacks, to board hated Yankees.

When Merriam reached out to talk to Southerners, he found at first a disbelief of their military defeat and later a deep-seated reluctance to give up their Confederacy. Restoration of the Union would neither be easy nor be a simple matter of victory on the battlefield. Merriam had a sense of history, and he realized that monumental change had come to this part of the country. He also recognized that acceptance of that change and the healing of war wounds would take a long time indeed.

Henry Merriam left New Orleans for his return to Maine on November 8, 1865. He boarded the steamer *Merrimack* for New York. This was the same ship that had transported him from Boston to Washington, DC, in 1862. While still transiting the Gulf, the vessel encountered a storm on November 10, during which a serious leak developed in the hull and extinguished the boiler fires. A sail was hoisted but swiftly destroyed by the winds. Pumps were out of order, so hand bailing commenced. The passengers, including mustered-out members of the 42nd Regiment, had to vigorously use buckets and barrels to keep the ship from sinking as water reached a depth of seven feet in the hold. Merriam wrote, "Our only hope is that the leak may not increase before our strength gives out or succor comes." During the night of November 13, the *Merrimack* managed to reach anchorage off Timbalier Light, Louisiana, and the steamer *Morgan* from Galveston arrived to lend assistance. With "superhuman effort," a rope was attached to draw and beach the *Merrimack* on a sandbar, after which the passengers transferred to the *Morgan*. Merriam reported that the rescued passengers met and published resolutions "severely censuring" the captain and officers of the *Merrimack* and the ship's company for their "neglect in failing to have pumps and other suitable appliances on board."[33]

Merriam penned one last comment in his Civil War diary: "On my 27th birthday, I am delivered from the womb of the Gulf of Mexico."[34]

5

On to the Rio Grande

I regard Colonel Merriam as one of the most efficient commanders in the district.

BVT. MAJ. GEN. GEORGE W. GETTY, FEBRUARY 20, 1869

enry Merriam returned to his home state of Maine in November 1865, probably depressed about his failure to retain his military career in the post–Civil War army but exhilarated with the reunion with Lucy and the Merriam family. He also had definite plans: to reenroll at Waterville College (the school changed its name to Colby sometime after the war), to work toward a law degree, and to marry Lucy. Waterville College welcomed him back as a Civil War hero and facilitated his progress toward a degree. Now older and far more mature, Merriam quickly and easily resumed his college studies. By the end of the spring term in 1866, the college took the extraordinary step of conferring on him a bachelor of arts degree as part of his original class of 1864. Although Merriam had thoughts about further study to become a lawyer, he now had accomplished one of his major objectives, earning a college degree.

Another goal was to marry Lucy Getchell. There were indications that this grand event had been planned for a later time, however, it happened quickly after his return to Waterville from New Orleans. The *Waterville Mail* of January 19, 1866, carried this bit of social news: "Married: In this village, Tuesday morning by Rev. D. Champlin, Brevet Colonel Henry C. Merriam and Miss Lucy Jane Getchell, daughter of Mr. Eleazer C. Getchell, all of Waterville." Lucy in her photographs, hair sharply pulled back from the face and parted in the middle, had a rather severe and somber look with only a bare hint of a smile (somewhat typical for the time). She was, however, likely a quite romantic Lucy. Through letters and Merriam's postwar leave back to Maine, she kept alive Henry's passion. Furthermore, she had some college experience, was active in the Waterville Congregational Church, and apparently had a love for

Lucy Getchell, Merriam's love interest in Waterville, Maine,
and his first wife. Courtesy Berger Family Collection.

music. Particularly important to Merriam, she had a steady, calm demeanor, like a gyroscope maintaining a balance, yet she would not shy away from adventure, exhibiting a somewhat subdued courage, but courage nevertheless. He would see Lucy as a wife who would survive the tribulations associated with an army officer deployed to distant places with relatively primitive conditions. All these factors would have been attractive to Merriam, now a robust twenty-eight-year-old finishing college. Little wonder that the marriage had occurred earlier than expected.

Apparently, despite attaining his two major objectives in short order, a college degree and marrying his Lucy, the thought of a military career had never been far away. One commenter later stated it concisely: "His military instincts, had been deeply stirred."[1] Merriam managed to keep alive his desire and his application for an appointment as an officer in the regular army. He continued to solicit support from his former superiors, stretching from the time with the Maine Volunteers to his service with black regiments in the Deep South. His Medal of Honor here proved to be an asset. Nevertheless, Merriam experienced difficulty in securing a regular-officer commission. In an unusual letter sent to a Boston newspaper, he described the problems he encountered:

> I am an applicant from Maine for an appointment in the Regular Army. I consulted the office of General Grant recently in regard to my prospects, and was told that my military record entitled me to a field appointment, but that two names were already before the President for appointment to the two places designated for Maine applicants, one being forwarded by Gen. Grant and the other by outside parties. I was

then advised to forward direct to the President some papers, which had not been considered. I declined to do this stating my unwillingness to oppose the appointment of the gentlemen mentioned.[2]

Afterward, Merriam learned that one of these applicants would not be appointed, so he made application again. Although the postwar army was still in the throes of demobilizing, consolidating units, and trying to determine its ultimate strength and the officer billets needed, remarkably an appointment was given to Merriam as a major on July 28, 1866. General Orders 12, issued by Headquarters, Jefferson Barracks, Missouri, on February 28, 1867, contained the following comment: "Major Merriam holds an appointment made during the adjournment of Congress as Major in the Army to rank as such from July 28, 1866. He accepted it, passed the examination required by Congress, and for five months has been on duty by of said appointment. . . . [H]e is, therefore, a Major from that date."[3]

But Merriam's first assignment following his appointment with a rank of major may have been a disappointment. He was ordered to recruiting duty, often not the most desirable task to those with battle experience who want to command. Nevertheless, this was now a peacetime army, and one had to seize officer billets wherever they could be found, including recruiting service. Merriam initially had responsibilities for recruiting blacks in the St. Louis area, with his headquarters at Jefferson Barracks.[4]

The recruitment of blacks continued to be an important thrust for the army in the postwar period. Many had been mustered out after the war, but black regiments were in the planning for the peacetime army. Some politicians argued that such units were essential as a means of rewarding blacks for their loyal war service and providing a continuing example of black emancipation. The states of Kentucky, Missouri, and Louisiana supplied the greatest number of recruits for the black regulars. As might be expected, approximately half of the recruits in the late 1860s were veterans of the Civil War. Depressed economic conditions in the post–Civil War years, with high black unemployment and various natural calamities such as a severe drought in Georgia, prompted many blacks to seek army service. Recruiters like Merriam sought to balance the large number of ex-slave enlistments with some from northern states, whose black recruits typically had more skills and more experience.[5]

In addition to recruiting, Merriam experienced courts-martial duty, property surveys, and membership on other military boards. Fortunately, he must have thought, his time in these roles turned out to be relatively brief. By April 29, 1867, he had orders in hand relieving him from recruiting duty and assigning him as major of the 38th Infantry Regiment, one of the army's postwar black units, organized in 1866.[6]

Only a matter of weeks later, Merriam began his westward move from Missouri. On June 14, 1867, he had field orders relieving him from assignment with a battalion of the 38th Infantry, then at Fort Hays, Kansas, and shortly thereafter orders to command Companies D and F of the 38th near Fort Harker, Kansas. Established close to the town of Ellsworth and the Smoky Hill River, Fort Harker was an important supply point and distribution center where the Santa Fe stage route crossed the Smoky Hill. Also nearby was the Kansas and Pacific Railroad. In 1867 the fort had become a strategic base for army operations against hostile Cheyenne, Kiowa, and other Indians. By orders of June 27, Merriam was to proceed with his new command to Fort Union, New Mexico, "without unnecessary delay."[7]

In early August his direction became better defined. His Headquarters, District of New Mexico, orders read: "The Battalion—Companies 'D' and 'F'—of the 38th U.S. Infantry, commanded by Brevet Colonel Henry C. Merriam, Major 38th U.S. Infantry will proceed, at once, via Fort Union, Koslosky's Tijeras Canon, Albuquerque and Fort Craig to Fort Bayard, N.M. to relieve the Battalion of the 125th U.S. Colored Troops, now at that post." Merriam must have delighted in the following paragraph: "Upon arrival of Brevet Colonel Henry C. Merriam, Major 38th U.S. Infantry, at Fort Bayard, the Commanding Officer will transfer to him, the command of the post."[8] Merriam was on his way to again commanding a regiment, and he was to command his first fort. At this point he must have considered his decision to return to the army most propitious.

The hurried southwest movement of Major Merriam and his battalion of the 38th Infantry Regiment to New Mexico Territory was prompted by Indian conflicts (both real and potential), friction between the black troops at Fort Bayard with the local citizenry, and trouble among miners in nearby Silver City, New Mexico. These were the exact precursor challenges Merriam would later face during his years in the Southwest and the Far West. He seemed always to have major responsibilities for preventing and resolving Indian problems and dealing with western mining troubles.

Merriam marched his 38th Infantry battalion on the hot, thousand-mile summer journey from Kansas to Fort Bayard, in southern New Mexico Territory. Lucy accompanied him, which provided not only a new joy but also a new responsibility.

Merriam's expedition started amid an Indian war on the Central Plains. The expansion of the railroads and the growing number of pioneer wagons and freight caravans on the Smoky Hill road and the Santa Fe Trail, through the Indian buffalo range, angered the Cheyennes, the Kiowas, and other tribes. An attempt by Maj. Gen. Winfield S. Hancock to intimidate the Indians by a show of force moreover had tipped the scales in favor of Indian war chiefs. As a result, Indian raiding parties plunged the Central Plains into widespread hostilities in the summer of 1867. Custer and his cavalry had a season-long pursuit of the warring bands. Merriam and his troops moved through Kiowa country, and he had to contend with the more war-minded Kiowa chief Satanta. An able and cunning leader given to oratory and boasting, Satanta had bluntly told the soldiers that he wanted them out of his land.[9] He represented a continuing threat that could never be ignored. This was the beginning of Merriam's long and challenging experience with Native Americans.

During the summer of 1867, the 38th Infantry Regiment suffered an outbreak of cholera, but by August the incidence of the disease had declined. Interestingly, Merriam did not record problems with cholera on his long march, but undoubtedly he had worries about the possible effects on his troops and delays in his journey.[10] Sanitation and disease would forever be a concern for Merriam's commands.

Along the way, he also had the usual taxing problems of securing food and water for both men and beasts. There were great expanses of prairie, and farther west pinon pine and cedar-encrusted hills and canyons, that had to be crossed. Merriam was confronting a new environment, decidedly different from either the East Coast or the southern states. The arid nature of the southwestern country would put a premium on securing good water.

As the column approached the Arkansas River in July, Merriam dealt with two unexpected events. First, he had some "tourists," or self-proclaimed "excursionists," attach themselves to his army train. Then he believed that he encountered Kiowa chief Satanta as his column came within fourteen miles of the Cimarron Crossing on the Santa Fe Trail. Merriam reported that, upon a 10:00 a.m. meeting with the Santa Fe stage, he "was informed that a large body of Indians had been following and apparently preparing to attack the stage since early in the morning; some approaching so near as to exchange shots with the escort." He indicated that he observed groups of Indians riding to some nearby hills and believed that they were examining his movements. The column halted, and Merriam assembled a party of fifteen mounted men along with a portion of the mounted escort from the 1st Cavalry. A few members of the excursionist party also joined, including an assistant secretary of the Treasury Department. Merriam intended that this mounted party would "reconnoiter with a view to determine the strength of the Indians."[11]

The reconnaissance group soon came upon about fifteen Indian warriors with thirty ponies, some being used as pack animals. The Indians fled rapidly to the south, and Merriam's men pursued them "vigorously for four or five miles" until they came within rifle range and began exchanging shots. According to Merriam, "the Indians answered without diminishing their speed." He ordered a continued charge against the warriors, pressing closely on them for about two miles. "The best mounted of the Indians made a stand," Merriam reported, "and a sharp little fight was had at less than two hundred yards, till the remainder of my party came up, when they again rushed off."[12]

I now received notice from one of my flankers that a large body of Indians was passing around my left. In consideration of this, and of the fact that many of our horses were exhausted, I resolved to return, which we did, leaning toward the flank where the other party had been seen.

I reached the road considerably westward of the column at 2 P.M., having been out nearly four hours, without seeing any more Indians, which indicates that the other party was making off in another direction, and not passing to my rear as reported.[13]

Merriam stated that the skirmish had resulted in a slight left arm injury to an accompanying citizen. He could not discern any evidence of Indian casualties, though he thought it possible slight wounds could have been inflicted. Merriam quickly gained an appreciation of the military prowess of his Plains Indian adversaries: "These Indians were all armed with breech loading carbines, revolvers, and bows all of which they used according to circumstances during the skirmish. Their chief was mounted on a pony peculiarly spotted, and which was recognized by wagonmaster Thomas of my train as a favorite pony of Satanta, Chief of the Kiowas. The manner in which they covered their retreat would have done credit to disciplined troops, while their skill in the management of their horses, entirely without the use of their arms, was wonderful."[14]

Subsequent to this engagement with the Kiowas, on July 19, 1867, at Fort Lyon, Colorado, the "excursionists" wrote a letter to Merriam commending his leadership:

The undersigned, a party of Excursionists, having traveled from Fort Harker across the Plains of Kansas in company with and under the escort of your command, desire to express their warm appreciation not only of the protection but also of the many kindnesses and courtesies for which they have become indebted to you upon the journey. We have witnessed your faithfulness and ability as a Commanding Officer upon a march sometimes perplexing and troublesome, and are also able to bear testimony to your personal fearlessness and bravery. . . . Be pleased to accept, Sir, for yourself your estimable wife . . . our gratitude.[15]

The letter was signed by individuals listed as from St. Louis, New York, and New Hampshire. While the eastern excursionists provided an additional burden for the arduous march, they still offered conversational and intellectual stimulation for Merriam, Lucy, and the other officers.

Merriam's column mostly followed the old Santa Fe Trail to Fort Union in northern New Mexico, then continued on to Santa Fe. Fort Union offered supplies and ample forage for the horses, but movement south along the Rio Grande, from Santa Fe through Albuquerque and Fort Craig, posed a more-desertlike terrain, with the concurrent problems of obtaining good water for the men and feed for the horses. Leaving the Rio Grande Valley and reaching Fort Bayard in the Silver City mining district entailed penetrating some mountains to attain the higher elevation of the mining towns. The roads were little more than

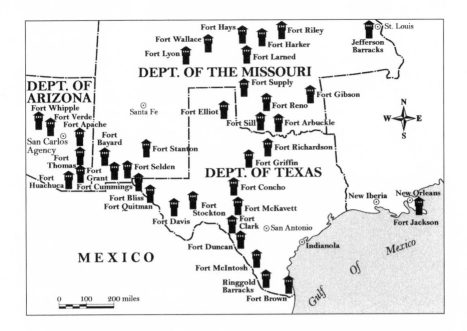

trails and most difficult to negotiate. But once reaching Fort Bayard, Merriam, Lucy, and his troops found a more-pleasant environment of cooler temperatures and some forests, all created by the surrounding southwestern mountains. This was certainly a welcome contrast to the intense heat of the Rio Grande Valley. The climate change must have been particularly welcome to Lucy, who was now pregnant with the couple's first child. Later she would give birth to a daughter, who they lovingly referred to as "Mamie."

Besides encountering a new western environment, Merriam now faced a far different adversary, the Southwest Indians. He arrived at Fort Bayard in August 1867 amid ongoing warfare with the Apaches. He had confronted the Plains Indians, particularly the Kiowas, earlier, but the Apaches presented a truly formidable military problem. At Fort Bayard, he and his regiment were positioned in traditional Apache territory, an area laced with mountains, canyons, and deserts, which hostile bands knew well and could easily exploit to hide and to strike with guerrilla-type warfare. Indeed, the Indians, with their fast ponies, could attack and then fade away, constituting some of the best cavalry that had ever existed. Merriam's New England background and his southern military experience hardly prepared him for what he now faced. He quickly had to learn Indian ways and their methods of warfare.

What Merriam found at Fort Bayard was basically that Apaches were considered "hostile" if they were not living directly under fort control. Thus, a troubling division in treating the Apaches came about. Some Apaches proved to be invaluable as scouts, while others were the enemy. Upon encountering the white invaders, many Apaches saw only a few options: fight, go to captivity with farming and ranching on a reservation, or work for the US military. Since hunting and warfare constituted their long-held cultural definition of manliness, for many Apaches resorting to war was often the preferred option.[16] Thus, the military commander, like Merriam, had to fight the "hostiles."

But Merriam had lessons to learn in the utilization of the Indians as scouts, "auxiliaries," or "friendlies." These Apaches were absolutely necessary to provide intelligence, reconnaissance, and search techniques in battling marauding bands. This meant that Merriam had to understand the Apache as best he could and earn their trust.

It should be noted that Merriam now had a new racial complex under his command, one that could be frustrating and volatile. An intersection of three cultures was occurring, that of white officers (like Merriam), black troops (largely emancipated slaves), and Native Americans. An added element was that Merriam had Indian laborers and servants, termed "colonized labor" by one historian, on post.[17] These Indians required a different kind of attention. Further complicating his dealings with the Apaches was their divisions into Mescalero, Chiricahua, Mimbres, Western Apaches, and sometimes even subdivisions into extended families. Subtle differences often had to be considered in the approach to one Apache clan or another.

Merriam's attitude toward Indians was never clearly articulated or defined, much like his feelings about blacks. It very likely evolved over the years as he dealt with them. For the most part, however, Merriam seems to have held a balanced view of their nature and an evenhanded approach to their actions. In one way he did see Indians as vicious and as savages. In a letter much later in time sent back to Colby College, he referred to the Apaches of New Mexico and Arizona as "probably the most savage and bloodthirsty of all other tribes." In another way, and in the very same letter, Merriam went on to dispassionately write, with considerable understanding, that the Apaches had cause to go to war:

> Their history before our Civil War is not familiar to me. In 1862, the territory was occupied by California volunteers under Genl. J. H. Carleton. A branch of the tribe was located in the upper Gila in New Mexico under an able chief Mangus Coloradas. He was invited to visit a vol. command in camp at Warm Springs south of the present Fort Bayard, New Mexico for a talk with the commanding officer. He was seized and made a prisoner, and while under guard was murdered by the troops, who claimed that he was shot while attempting to escape. The result was that all of the Apache tribes made the bitterest war against white men in the two territories for a quarter of a century, under various leaders among them Cochise, Victorio, Young Mangus Coloradas, and Geronimo. . . . In an interview in 1900 these chiefs confirmed to me the murder of Mangus Coloradas through treachery of the California troops was the cause of their prolonged and bitter war.[18]

Fort Bayard was officially established on August 21, 1866, with the permanent posting of Federal troops. Located approximately ten miles southeast of the mining communities of Silver City and Pinos Altos, near the foothills of the Santa Rita and Mimbres Mountains and several springs, the post commanded Mimbres Apache (sometimes called Warm Springs Apache) trails and dispersed area mining operations. Some of the 125th US Colored Infantry soldiers under command of 1st Lt. James M. Kerr had originally selected the site as an encampment in 1863, but transient troops had been used to try to keep in check the Mimbres Apaches, led by Chiefs Victorio and Geronimo. Merriam assumed command of Fort Bayard only a year after its official beginning, with the charge of getting it fully organized and firmly established. His primary mission remained, however, to protect the prospectors and miners from the hostile Apache bands.

During Merriam's relatively short time at Fort Bayard (1867–69), he mainly faced Mimbres Apache chiefs Loco and Victorio, who had risen to leadership after the death of Mangas Coloradas. Loco, an elder chief, inclined more toward peace with whites, but Victorio remained distrustful and essentially at war with the white invaders of his land. A very courageous and wily leader, Victorio had ably learned warfare from Mangas Coloradas. He was a formidable military opponent, skillfully conducting raids across the vast stretches of desert and barren peaks stretching southward into Mexico from the mountains and headwaters of the Gila River. Noted western historian Robert Utley believed Victorio, in his skilled tactics and "greater mastery of guerrilla warfare," was one of the best Indian war chiefs.[19]

Since Merriam had a principal responsibility for protection of the mining communities, his infantry rarely engaged in chasing the Apache warriors, a task generally left to cavalry units. The exception occurred in June 1869, when Merriam commanded an expedition against the Apaches that led him into western New Mexico's Mogollon Mountains and the capture of an Apache village. Meanwhile, his maintenance of relative peace in the Fort Bayard–Pinos Altos–Silver City area resulted in a petition by the citizens of New Mexico's Grant County to Headquarters, District of New Mexico in Santa Fe, dated January 30, 1869, requesting that "Brevet Colonel H. C. Merriam, Major of the 38th Infantry, may be retained as commander of Fort Bayard, New Mexico." On February 20, 1869, district commander Bvt. Maj. Gen. George W. Getty forwarded the citizen's petition to department headquarters, stating, "it is not my intention to relieve Bvt. Col. Merriam from the command of Fort Bayard, nor to make a recommendation to that effect. I regard Colonel Merriam as one of the most efficient commanders in the district."[20]

Nevertheless, barely six months later Merriam received orders transferring him to Texas to become commander of Fort Bliss at El Paso. By Special Order 178, Headquarters Fifth Military District, Austin, Texas, dated July 30, 1869, "Brevet Colonel Henry C. Merriam, Major 24th U.S. Infantry is assigned to the command of Fort Bliss, Texas, to which place he will immediately repair." This assignment was concurrent with the transfer of the Headquarters, 38th Infantry, from Fort Bayard to Fort Bliss. The question of Merriam's continued command of Fort Bayard may have arisen due to a serious incident that occurred during the 1868 Christmas holiday. On December 24 a riot "occurred near that post, between soldiers of the 3rd U.S. Cavalry and 38th U.S. Inf." The melee resulted in the death of two enlisted men of the 3rd Cavalry and three enlisted men of the 38th Infantry. Headquarters, District of New Mexico sent a general officer in January 1869 to Fort Bayard to investigate the incident.[21] This was the most serious breach of discipline that ever occurred under Merriam's command. While it may have influenced his change of assignment to Texas, it apparently did not derail his appointment to command of units and forts, and obviously the soldier riot had not weakened his reputation with the local citizenry.

Another factor in Merriam's orders to go to Texas was the further consolidation of the army's black regiments. In the evolving post–Civil War army, there was great debate as to the disposition of the black troops and their total percentage in the peacetime army. General Sherman at one point stated, "The experiment of converting them into soldiers has been honorably & in good faith tried in the army of the U.S., and has been partially successful, but the army is not and should not be construed as a charitable institution." The debate resulted in a determination that the black units would be limited in number. On July 28, 1866, the Thirty-Ninth Congress passed an army reorganization act that provided for six black regiments—two cavalry (the 9th and 10th Regiments) and four infantry (the 38th, 39th, 40th, and 41st Regiments)—in a total army of sixty regiments. By 1869, through further legislation, the black troops would constitute "slightly less than 10 percent of the army's entire strength." An outcome of the legislation was a War Department order for consolidation of the 38th and 41st Regiments, forming the 24th Infantry, and the merger of the 39th and 40th Regiments to create the new 25th Infantry. In addition, the War Department called for a reduction of 140 enlisted men in each of the black regiments.[22] Reduced congressional appropriations dictated further consolidations and reductions.

On March 15, 1869, Merriam was assigned to the newly created 24th Regiment, keeping companies of his old 38th Regiment with him in the new unit. Shortly thereafter, at the beginning of September, he received orders relieving him from duty at Fort Bayard and directing him to proceed to Fort Bliss to assume command of that old fort. A military post at El Paso had been established originally in 1849, but from that time it had occupied six different locations. Early in the Civil War, Fort Bliss had been seized by the Confederates, who largely destroyed it when they abandoned the fort in the summer of 1862. Rebuilding of the post was completed in 1866, but the Rio Grande forced yet another move, with Fort Bliss beginning anew in 1869. Thus, Merriam, as in the case of Fort Bayard, transferred into a settling-in period, a fluid situation, of Fort Bliss in its newest location.[23] Merriam was not destined to be there very

long, however, for he and his troops would be ordered to move east and south from El Paso.

While Merriam and companies of the 24th Infantry were still at Fort Bliss, other black units had moved to Texas via ships from Louisiana. In 1867, companies of the 9th Cavalry and 41st Infantry had deployed into the lower Rio Grande and west of the Pecos River. Col. Ranald S. Mackenzie of the 41st Infantry would become the new commander of the 24th Regiment and therefore would have authority over Merriam and his elements of the 24th.[24]

The consolidation of the 38th and 41st Infantry to form the 24th brought together two longtime leaders of black troops, Colonel Mackenzie and Brevet Colonel Merriam, who probably held similar attitudes toward their black soldiers. Mackenzie expressed the opinion at one time that his experience had been "that the best class of negroes make very good soldiers while the poor worse than useless." He went on to say that peacetime soldiering attracted the "poorest classes of whites in the country," while the "United States can probably receive the services of the best" among blacks. On another occasion, however, Mackenzie had noted about his black troops: "The men run up bills with several [stores] and are unable to pay or do not and if allowed to go unpunished for their dishonesty the slave habit of stealing is made more difficult to break up." Despite that negative judgment, both Merriam and Mackenzie were fully ready to defend their black soldiers against any mistreatment. Whatever the views about their effectiveness, at this time in West Texas and along the Rio Grande boundary, black troops would have to play a major role in establishing peace. Brig. Gen. Edward O. C. Ord, commander of the Department of Texas,

Merriam's first wife, Lucy Getchell, and daughter Mamie.
Courtesy Berger Family Collection.

had earlier stressed to the War Department the need to reinforce his units on the lower Rio Grande to improve policing and security.[25] He would have to rely on the black regiments to supply an important part of that augmented force.

Merriam's journey south from Fort Bayard to the Rio Grande at El Paso and then farther east would bring him into a new troubled area. West Texas still suffered Indian raids. Ranchers were killed and abducted, cattle seized, horses run off, and property destroyed. Both sides of the Rio Grande had experienced this conflict and turmoil. War parties, particularly those of the Comanches, had caused deaths and property loss on the north side and also into Mexico. In addition, on the south side of the river, bandits and revolutionary Mexican groups created violence and unsettled conditions, severely affecting American traders there. Merriam and his elements of the 24th Regiment black troops were to be deployed into this Texas region to restore and to maintain peace and to protect American interests.

In April 1870 Merriam and some of his troops left Fort Bliss and traveled eastward, following roads and trails connecting a string of southwestern Texas forts. His destination was Fort McKavett, where he could meet the commander of the 24th Infantry Regiment, Colonel Mackenzie. Lucy and daughter Mamie accompanied him. This was not particularly unusual—after all, Lucy had joined him on the long trek from Kansas to New Mexico.

The hardships faced by family members accompanying their army husbands in the western United States in retrospect seemed overwhelming. Besides the real threat of death by nature's elements, disease, accidents, or hostile Indians, they had to survive long, tedious, and hazardous marches from one post to another. Either riding on horseback, traveling by ambulance (spring wagons with four mules), or taking a stagecoach, they had to endure the bumps and jostling of these western conveyances on the primitive trails and roads. Sometimes they could stay in garrison quarters or an occasional ranch house, but oftentimes when on the move, their fate was shelter in army tents. Always there were unsanitary conditions, frightening pests (including rattlesnakes and scorpions), extreme heat or cold, rain, wind, and dust. The wives, like their husbands, experienced true frontier living. Some could not stand such conditions and returned to the East, but a surprising number endured and treated their frontier existence as a "great adventure."

Capt. R. G. Carter, who served with Colonel Mackenzie and the 4th Cavalry at this time, reported on his experience bringing his "bride" to Fort Concho, Texas. He noted the harsh times that would be encountered, but when a decision had to be made whether to join him or not, his "bride" thought accompanying him would be "so lovely, romantic, charming, delightful!" She did not want to stay in that "lonely old city of San Antonio among so many strangers." After all, Captain Carter said, "hadn't we just been married?"[26]

Perhaps Lucy had similar thoughts. Certainly, she did not safely stay behind but chose to go with Merriam on his journey in West Texas. Unfortunately, this time having his wife and daughter along resulted in a most tragic event, one that would shatter Merriam's life and his young family.

It all began quietly enough. On the night of April 24, 1870, Merriam's army column camped at the headwaters of the Rio Concho in West Texas (near the site of the present-day San Angelo). In a report after the tragedy, Merriam graphically described what happened:

We arrived at the head of the Concho at noon on Sunday, the 24th, after a very tedious ride of twenty-five hours from the Pecos, and went into camp on the ground usually used by travelers—a pleasant camp—on the same ridge, but a little lower below the mail station and that of the detachment of troops, Lieutenant Cortelyou pointing out my camp. Early in the evening, I had been out, and returned about eight, finding my darlings in bed, Mamie asleep. Mrs. M. said Mamie had said her little prayer followed by her usual "goodnight mama, goodnight papa," and then added "Mama, I want to go find papa," and dropped off to sleep. I retired soon but before going to sleep I heard the storm approaching, and got up and dressed, had my tent put in the most secure condition and then awaited the shock. It soon came in the form of heavy torrents of rain mingled with hail. Soon the hail became heavier, and increased to the size of hen's eggs. The sound was terrific beyond description. Mrs. M. now arose and dressed, and took in her arms little Mamie who had awoke in turn. During all the remainder of the storm—near an hour—Mrs. M. sat watching me with wild searching eyes, to know if I was alarmed. Little Mamie too would peep out from her hiding place at intervals and timidly say "Papa," then I would stoop and kiss her burning face and say "darling, don't be afraid." Such was the scene in our tent while the elements were preparing the terrible flood which was to follow.

People who live in the Southwest know how quickly monstrous thunderstorms can develop, particularly in spring and summer, cascading torrents of rain and hail as Merriam related. They also know that dry washes can become thunderous rivers, creating dangerous flash floods. The 24th Regiment's chaplain, John N. Schultz, recalled: "[T]here ensued a flood of unprecedented volume and force. The waters rose 25 feet in 15 minutes."[27] Merriam's report continued in graphic detail:

As soon as I could safely venture out of our tent I did so, and found the water fast rising in the creek—which at dark lay twenty feet perpendicularly below us. It was already very near the level of our tent. I immediately called out my escort and placed Mrs. M. and Mamie in the ambulance, and we started toward higher ground with it. When we had almost reached safety the current became too strong and we were swept from our feet. Then, to give a ray of false hope in the same means of escape, the troops who had just escaped from their quarters came riding to our rescue. I tried to get men to ride to the end of the pole so that I could lay hold of his horse and so bear up the pole against the current and continue our course. Several tried to do so, but either through fear or panic of their horse, would sweep away from me before I could get hold of them. I then tried to get a horse myself for the same purpose, but couldn't so far control a man to get his horse. Several, perhaps ten, precious seconds were lost in this fruitless work. Meantime the water rose in successive waves like an ocean tide. I soon abandoned hope of saving them in the ambulance and made a struggle to get them out, but before I could scarcely touch the ambulance, I was swept by and far down the seething stream. With great difficulty I swam ashore, and ran back to make another struggle, when I was met with the crushing announcement that the ambulance had rolled over and gone tumbling down the current behind me!

I was almost unconscious the rest of the night! I should judge this was about eleven o'clock.

Besides Lucy and Mamie, two soldiers and "one male and one female servant" were drowned in the flood.[28]

With the dawn, a search began for the bodies.

At daylight I alone commenced search for the ruins. I was soon joined by several, and found the wreck of the ambulance about a mile below the camp, but no bodies in it. The top was all broken and scattered over the country. This was a very heavy disappointment, for I had strangely hoped it might be strong enough to keep the precious cargo. One after another the lost soldiers and servants were found, from one-half to one mile down stream. At about 9 A.M. we found, and I took from the water with my own hands, my darling wife's body! Cold—Cold and dead! I took it into a tent and put it in as good condition as I could, there being no female living within fifty miles. Her face, when first found, bore expression of fright and terror, but when I had washed and combed the hair, and carefully and tenderly wrapped the form in a clean blanket, her expression changed to one of sweet, smiling slumber, as if conscious of the presence of affectionate care.

All day we made fruitless search for the little darling's body. I resolved to wait until Tuesday morning, and make one more search. I did so, but still without success. I then offered a reward for its recovery and hastened to bring the remains already recovered to this post [Fort Concho] for temporary interment. My agony at turning my back upon the spot which held my sweet Mamie's body I cannot express.

Chaplain Schultz had been with Merriam and his family since the organization of the 38th Infantry in 1866 and now provided comfort to Henry in his grief. He conducted the funeral service for Lucy at Fort Concho, later reporting that the fort's commander and the "officers and ladies of this post have acted nobly toward our desolate brother, while several officers from Fort McKavett were providentially present to sympathize and aid." In the chaplain's letter to the *Waterville Mail*, he further eulogized Lucy: "I must bear witness to the intelligence, refinement, social goodness and Christian excellence of Mrs. Merriam. She stood in the front rank of Christian ladies in the army. Her influence was a pure and quiet light. Waterville may well be proud of sending such an inestimable Christian young lady to bless and grace the army in cities and camps, on marches and in garrisons, from the Mississippi to the Rocky Mountains."[29]

The funeral and burial of Lucy Merriam at Fort Concho had barely been completed when word came of the discovery of Mamie's body. "During Wednesday the precious body of my darling Mamie was found four miles below the camp, and arrived here before daylight on the following morning. We placed her dust with 'Mama' on Thursday." Merriam closed his detailed report on his great personal tragedy with a remarkable and sorrowful lament:

Thus they are both gone! The gentle vine and tenderest bud which clung so sweetly about my life, softening every care, and sweetening every pleasure, ruthlessly torn away without a moment's notice, and so cruelly that my very soul shudders at the picture. Mrs. M. was a firm Christian, and member of the Congregational Church at Waterville, Maine, and was not afraid to die. The soldiers who were near say they heard her say calmly, as the ambulance turned over in the seething flood, "My darling husband, goodbye." Those were her last words.[30]

As a soldier, Merriam knew the tragic consequences of war. There would be casualties, and they would be grievous. He had experienced this. But the unexpected, the peacetime loss of loved ones, had hurt deeply and produced an overwhelming grief. Merriam's personal world suddenly had been destroyed.

Fortunately, the camaraderie of army personnel, often little understood by civilians, immensely helped his recovery. Merriam's military family closed around him with support and comfort. Officers, high and low, flooded him with condolences. Symbolic was the role of the regiment chaplain. Not only was he there to stand by Merriam as a friend in his sorrow, but he also represented the Christian faith that was so significant an influence in Henry's and Lucy's lives. Although he had lost his wife and daughter, he still had the army.

Merriam took a relatively brief leave to grieve and to recover. Then he returned to soldiering.

6

A New Wife and
Troubles on the Rio Grande

Presented to Col. H. C. Merriam, U.S.A., By
American Merchants of Nuevo Laredo 1876

INSCRIPTION ON SWORD PRESENTED TO
MERRIAM AT NUEVO LAREDO, MEXICO

After Merriam's great tragedy at the Concho River and the burial of his wife and daughter at Fort Concho, he took leave and then returned to Fort Bliss. His original objective of contacting Colonel Mackenzie and the 24th Infantry's headquarters at Fort McKavett had come for naught. At that time, in the spring of 1870, as Merriam's column approached McKavett, Mackenzie had been on detached service and then on an extended leave. Furthermore, when Mackenzie did return to Fort McKavett on October 1, 1870, he was ordered to Washington and shortly thereafter was relieved as commander of the 24th Infantry and given command of the 4th Cavalry.[1] Meanwhile, Merriam retained his companies of the 24th and resumed command of Fort Bliss.

Merriam's command at Fort Bliss, from September 1869 to May 1871, remained largely uneventful. His tenure ended when he was ordered to proceed many miles to the east to Fort McKavett. His orders indicated that there was still a major redeployment of black regiments taking place. "Upon the arrival at Fort Bliss of Companies H, 9th Cavalry and B, 25th Infantry, Major H. C. Merriam, 24th Infantry, will repair to Fort McKavett, and report to his regimental commander for duty." Since the 24th Infantry had headquarters at Fort McKavett, Merriam in effect was consolidating with other elements of his regiment. Other than command of a 24th Infantry battalion, Merriam's duties during his time at Fort McKavett remain unclear. A year earlier, under Mackenzie's command, the 24th had a number of skirmishes with Indians and had participated in a number of scouting parties. By the spring of 1871, when Merriam arrived, the regiment apparently acted as more of a reserve and support force for a planned offensive that would begin against the Kiowas and Comanches. A grand strategy had developed to once and for all stop the Indian raids in West Texas. Four army columns striking from Kansas, New Mexico, Fort Sill in Indian Territory, and from Mackenzie's troops from Fort Concho were to push the Indians into a compressed area of the high plains and then finally crush them.[2] Merriam apparently had little part in these operations.

Fort McKavett, Merriam's new destination, was an old fort, first established in 1852. It sat on a high bluff near the source of the San Saba River, some fifty miles southeast from San Angelo and Fort Concho. It functioned as part of a fort system to battle the high-plains Indians. During the Civil War, it had been occupied by the Confederates and afterward fell into virtually complete disrepair. Colonel Mackenzie began the rebuilding using his black troops of the 41st Infantry when he occupied it on April 1, 1868.[3] Thus, when Merriam arrived in 1871, he did not have to reestablish the post as he had in some of his other assignments.

Merriam's time at Fort McKavett was very short. He arrived in May 1871 and on January 15, 1872, he went on leave, an extended one, until March 23 but never returned. While on leave, he was ordered to go to Fort Duncan, Texas, by Department of Texas orders issued on March 9, 1872. The directive simply stating, "Major H. C. Merriam, 24th Inf., is relieved from duty at Fort McKavett, and will proceed without delay to Fort Duncan."[4] Another old fort, having been established in 1849, Fort Duncan was on the Rio Grande River at Eagle Pass hundreds of miles almost due south from Fort McKavett. As a consequence, Merriam had to face more long-distance travel. He now had returned to the Rio Grande, a region that during the next several years would prove most significant in his life and his career.

Upon arrival, Merriam took command of Fort Duncan. Orders in May 1872 also listed him as a member of a courts-martial there. His tenure at Fort Duncan was most brief, for by November he had further orders to move down the Rio Grande to Ringgold Barracks, where he would "assume command." Ringgold Barracks was one of a string of posts established along the river and the Mexican border after the Mexican War. It occupied a spot at David's Landing at the head of navigation of the Rio Grande. But his stay there proved to be even more brief. By an order on January 3, 1873, he was told: "On arrival of Colonel Hatch, 9th Cavalry, at Ringgold Barracks, proceed to Fort McIntosh, Texas, and take command of that post."[5]

Troubles with cattle thieves, Indian bands, and Mexican revolutionaries had continued to plague the lower Rio Grande, necessitating Merriam's succession of moves. In March 1873, cattle rustlers were reported to be active in the vicinity of Brownsville. These security problems led to still a further reassignment: "In compliance with verbal instructions from the General Commanding the Department relative to the protection of this frontier, Major H. C. Merriam, 24th

Infantry will proceed at once to examine the country adjacent to the left bank of the Rio Grande from Ringgold Barracks to Fort Brown, Texas for the purpose of determining the most important points to station companies of cavalry with the view of so occupying the country that mounted men may operate effectively for the protection of this frontier against the incursion of stock marauders."[6]

These orders underscore Merriam's rising reputation in Texas and the high level of trust that his superiors now held in his ability to select appropriate positions from which to conduct military operations. It constituted considerable responsibility for a relatively junior officer, moreover one who commanded infantry and whose command experience was largely with black troops. Such confidence was a recognition of Merriam's attention to detail and his astute observation skills. He had moved about in southwestern Texas, and in his travels he assessed the geography and terrain and applied military common sense to the location of camps and fortified posts. Furthermore, he developed a reputation for a strong hand in the organization and command of military units, a problem along the Rio Grande, where personnel were scattered and often left to manage as best they could in their assigned areas through their own devices.

Ironically, despite Merriam's extensive experience as a post commander, he remained seriously concerned about the strategy and tactics of dealing with a very mobile enemy, whether they were cattle rustlers or Indians. On April 22, 1872, while he commanded Fort Duncan, he sent a letter to the headquarters of the Department of Texas outlining his military plan for mobile detachments to confront the roving Comanche bands. US Army mobile units would be preferable and more effective to manning fixed posts, he argued. Merriam stressed that the mobile units would need to move secretly and employ Indian methods of ambushes. This startling proposal must have surprised headquarters. Perhaps it was too great a departure from the currently employed system, for he failed to change the basic strategy in the region but continued to command forts.[7]

Merriam's new charge apparently countermanded his being detailed to command Fort McIntosh. During the period March 1873 to June 1873, he commanded troops patrolling the lower Rio Grande and at the same time selected deployment points so the army could stop cattle rustling. In May he had an additional assigned task as "Special Inspector to inspect certain unserviceable horses belonging to Co. C, 9th Cavalry with a view to their disposition for the best interests of the service."[8] Apparently, his horse knowledge also was appreciated.

On June 12, 1873, a telegram from Headquarters, Department of Texas to Col. Abner Doubleday at Fort Brown stated, "[b]efore leaving Fort Brown, transfer command of the post to Maj. Merriam, 24th Inf." Orders issued that same day directed that Merriam was "assigned temporarily to the command of Fort Brown, Texas." Two days later he also was assigned to participate in a Fort Brown general courts-martial. Fort Brown, near the mouth of the Rio Grande and across the river from Mexico's Matamoros, held one of the most strategic positions on the entire river. It had been established by Col. Zachary Taylor in 1846 just prior to the beginning of the Mexican War. Merriam's command of the fort, even if temporary, represented a major advance in responsibility and prestige. Even more telling in regard to the importance of the assignment was a handwritten order from Headquarters, Department of Texas to the commanding officer of Fort Brown, dated October 9, 1873, declaring, "the duty of guarding the line of the Rio Grande from its mouth to Santa Marie is hereafter entrusted to you."[9]

Merriam's detail to Fort Brown became significant for another, personal reason. Shortly after his arrival at the post, a fellow officer in the 24th Regiment invited Merriam to accompany him on a social call across the river in Matamoros. At this time Merriam was introduced to twenty-five-year-old Catherine Una Macpherson MacNeil. Una, the name she preferred and used, had come to Matamoros in May 1872 to visit her favorite uncle, Jasper Lynch, who had business affairs in that part of Mexico and was currently based in Matamoros. Born on September 29, 1848, in Kingston, Jamaica, the daughter of attorney John Macpherson MacNeil, who served Jamaican sugar plantation owners, Una had grown to womanhood experiencing many of the social and economic privileges associated with the plantation class, including slave servants. Her father arranged for a nanny from England to ensure that Una and her two sisters and brother received proper educations. Music assumed an important place in the family; Una's father dearly loved the old Scottish hymns and tunes, and Una learned to play the piano to accompany his singing. Both her mother and father were devout in their Protestant faith, and the family established close relationships with various Jamaican ministers. Her mother died when Una was ten, soon after which her father's law practice floundered and he died suddenly. So by the time of Una's arrival in Matamoros, much of her previous privileged life had changed. The visit with her uncle, originally intended to be temporary, turned into a more-permanent affair. Within Uncle Jasper's merchant class, she quickly became involved in the social activities of Matamoros, Brownsville, and Fort Brown.[10]

There seems little doubt that Merriam saw in Una some of the same qualities that he had loved in Lucy. She was young, attractive, intelligent, educated, skilled in conversation and the social graces, steady in temperament, and inquisitive. He could not help but note the music and Christian background, and again feeling most comfortable with these aspects. The one thing that perhaps differed was that Una had an aura of sophistication that Lucy of Maine had not possessed. Once more, Merriam saw a potential wife who would be a wonderful complement to an army officer. Una felt attracted to Merriam, a handsome man of integrity and a dashing officer seemingly moving upward. In short order Henry Merriam and Una MacNeil were engaged in late 1873. It was not until June 1874, however, that they married at Fort Brown.

Una in 1868 or 1869. Courtesy Berger Family Collection.

Una explained why the wedding was held at Fort Brown: "There were many reasons for making a wedding easier on the American side. Colonel Merriam had many friends in the regiment, to which he belonged for some time; they quite insisted we should be married at the Fort as it was really the best and pleasantest way, so we were married there by the army chaplain, many friends from Matamoro   s, as well as Brownsville being present."[11]

Merriam had approval for an extended leave for a honeymoon, so immediately after the wedding ceremony, the newlyweds departed on a very long trip to New York, the British Isles, and the European continent. Una provided some description of their trip:

> That afternoon we went down to Brazos in the small launch, several friends going with us, and that evening left on the steamer for New Orleans, in route for New York and England. Arriving at New York we stayed at the Brevoort House. . . . After about a week in New York we sailed for England. . . . We were in London for some time and spent some days with Uncle Robert and his family. . . . Then we went to the Continent; France, Switzerland, a trip up the Rhine, etc. . . . Returning we went to Scotland. . . . We sailed from Glasgow to New York, Colonel Merriam making a short trip to see his mother in Maine, while I remained with the Girods for the few days he was away.[12]

On the way back from New York to Texas, Henry and Una stopped at Mobile. Una wrote that Henry was most anxious to visit the Fort Blakeley

Photographs of Merriam and Una made in London on their
honeymoon in 1874. Courtesy Berger Family Collection.

battlefield, where he had won his Medal of Honor, and an interesting adventure
ensued:

> It was a great undertaking as there was no regular map we could fol-
> low. We cruised around all one day in a small boat, (rowed by a negro)
> among the bayous in that region, with corn pone for lunch. Finally
> coming to a point that seemed to give some promise, we landed. In-
> quiring at a clean, small, thatched cottage occupied by negroes, we
> found we were on the right road, not far from the battlefield. It was
> late afternoon and no other resting place in sight so we were thankful
> to accept the hospitality of the family for the night. Leaving Rufus
> [Merriam's brother] to look out for our "traps" we started off on foot
> through tangles of bushes and brambles, often having to cover our
> faces with our hands to avoid being scratched, as we scrambled on.
> However we were rewarded by finding the exact country; trenches,
> earthworks, etc., all overgrown and rough. It was a great pleasure
> to Colonel Merriam. The evening and a lovely sunset, we felt it a suc-
> cessful and enjoyable trip. Arriving at our thatched cottage we dined
> delightfully on fried chicken, sweet potatoes and corn pone; then all
> retired to the only available guest chamber, all so tired that the accom-
> modation was not criticized; and it did not take us long to forget our
> tired feet! We slept well, leaving the next morning for Mobile; from
> whence we continued to New Orleans where we spent several days
> waiting for the steamer for Brazos.[13]

Henry and Una's long honeymoon trip allowed the couple to make acquaintance with many friends and relatives. It also gave them an introduction
to the European world, which would be important to Merriam when he later

sought to market his innovative military backpack. Perhaps the trip was most revealing as to the character of Una. She seemed at ease visiting with friends and relatives from New York to London and especially in her father's homeland of Scotland. She proved to be an immense help to her husband in moving into new social circles. It was the tour of the Blakeley battlefield, however, that demonstrated her willingness, even eagerness, to take on unexpected circumstances associated with her army-officer husband's interests. It constituted a beginning of many frontierlike experiences for Una.

After arriving back at Fort Brown in December 1874, Merriam returned to many of his usual duties as a commander in the 24th Infantry Regiment. He apparently had earned a reputation for good service on courts-martial boards as he had details to a series of such trials at Fort Brown. Also, the newly married couple settled into post quarters and its lifestyle. Una took note of her new living conditions:

> Our quarters at Fort Brown were comfortable, tho' small and lacking many conveniences; double houses to accommodate two families, each family house with two rooms downstairs and a hall running beside the rooms, and stairs ascending to two small, half-story rooms. A front porch and at the back a sort of shed, or extension, leading from the main building, this contained our dining room, kitchen and small room for a servant. There were many of these small houses for officers, between each double house a plot of grass; in front more grass and brick walks, and a few rather insignificant trees, all taken very good care of. At one end of this "run" of houses, a larger building; used for officers, the soldier barracks at the other end. Back of the buildings a lagoon, large enough to have a boat on. There was an island in the lagoon on which, I think was the cemetery. We had very delightful neighbors in our building, Mr. & Mrs. Wygant, who became our dear friends, and many happy times we had on our porch and driving in our double surrey.[14]

On August 2, 1875, Henry and Una welcomed their first child, a daughter named Caroline Augusta. In her memoirs Una said that her infant daughter was "the most wonderful creature I had ever seen so far, and my days were busy, assisted by a young and very faithful Mexican girl, as nurse. She was devoted to the baby, kind and faithful." Merriam's marriage and now the birth of a daughter prompted him to request a change of station from the Rio Grande. In January 1876 he even wrote to James G. Blaine, a politically powerful congressman from Maine, asking for his assistance in securing a move to a more-healthy climate. He was not alone in requesting such transfers, for many officers complained of being "condemned" to service on the border and along the Rio Grande. But at this time there was more military activity in this region than most anywhere else in the country.

While still at Fort Brown, Merriam became absorbed in a personal enter-prise, the development of a new military knapsack. He believed the army-issued knapsack was heavy, cumbersome, and did not distribute its weight well while worn on a soldier's back. Una assisted in making models of the knapsack by cut-ting, sewing, and putting together the original backpack. Merriam enlisted men to try it on marches. On February 14, 1876, he wrote to the US Army's adjutant general proposing that the army should look into the use of his design. He en-closed photographs of his model and included commendation reports from offi-cers and enlisted men who had tried the pack. This was the mere beginning of a very long effort by Merriam to convince the army to adopt his new knapsack.[15]

Merriam's hopes for leaving the Rio Grande were abruptly dashed when he received orders on February 22, 1876, directing his move upriver. The instruc-tions read, "Major Henry C. Merriam, 24th Infantry, is hereby relieved from further duty at Fort Brown and will proceed without delay to Fort McIntosh, Texas, assuming upon arrival command of the post."[16] After his "temporary" command of Fort Brown, Merriam likely saw command of Fort McIntosh as a welcome change back to being officially in charge of a fort. This time, however, he had to consider the effect of uprooting his wife and infant daughter.

The assignment to Fort McIntosh represented part of an increased effort to curb violence and lawlessness on the lower Rio Grande. General Ord, com-mander of the Department of Texas, had complained to the War Department in June 1875 that reinforcements were needed to improve policing on the border. Later, Ord's annual report, dated September 26, 1876, and addressed to his su-periors at the Military Division of the Missouri, headquartered in Chicago, de-scribed the situation that he faced, which in his mind justified the actions that he had taken thus far and planned to take in the immediate future:

> In regard to expeditions after hostile Indians, all the Indians who come into, or temporarily occupy, this state, are, and have been for years, hostile; they never come around the settlements except to rob or mur-der, and the peculiarly wild, rugged and inhospitable character of the immense and almost unknown portion of Texas, extending from the 100th meridian, in a line due west, to El Paso del Norte, a distance of four hundred miles, and from the Red River, south to the Rio Bravo, a distance along the meridian of four hundred and sixty miles, make it, next to impossible, with the limited force at my command to do more than guard a few important settlements along or near the Rio Grande, protect the stage routes, and occasionally pursue a raiding band af-ter it has struck its blow and is in full run for a hitherto safe retreat among the recesses of the mountains in Northeastern Mexico.
>
> Many of these Indians have in years past, been driven by the troops and Texans from this state to the uninhabited mountains of Mexico, whence they have carried on their depredations with impunity and great profit, selling their plunder to the nearest Mexican towns

or villages, and returning to Texas for more booty as soon as the proceeds of previous raids were spent.[17]

Ord had been besieged with requests for protection of the border area. He had difficulty providing the requested help, and he believed there was only one answer:

> Some of the settlements along the Rio Grande have been almost abandoned by the stock ranchers because of the want of safety to life and property, and I have had summer camps established at two such places for the protection of the settlers. The stock interest exposed to these raids is very large and is entitled to consideration, and I here repeat what I stated in a former report that there is only one way of checking the raiders or of recovering the stolen property and that is to pursue them to their retreats in Mexico, where they can be punished and the stock sometimes recovered, they always have the start of troops sent to overtake them while in United States territory, and they always have the plundered horses to ride—changing as fast as needed—so that they nearly always reach the river in safety and taunt us from the other side as they ride leisurely along, driving the stolen American stock and sometimes displaying the scalp of our people.[18]

The general had also informed department headquarters that the 9th Cavalry, a black regiment, was incapable of performing patrol duty along the border. The Senate Military Affairs Committee soon after began investigating events and troubles on the Rio Grande and the Mexican border. Ord had indicated that black regiments serving there might be contributing to tension in the area. In the course of the committee hearings, Civil War hero General Sherman told the senators that all four black regiments were located in the Rio Grande region because they were better suited to its hot climate. While that opinion was common for the time, a more-practical reason for keeping them there was the cost of moving regiments from one department to another. Regardless of the reasons, the black troops, and particularly their white officers, were becoming restless and more vocal in wanting to leave the Rio Grande.[19] Merriam was one such officer.

Fort McIntosh, over 200 miles upriver from Brownsville at the town of Laredo, had been established on March 3, 1849, several months after the Mexican War. Originally known as Camp Crawford, it was renamed Fort McIntosh in 1850. Like other posts on the river and the border, it was meant to block and control Indian movement along the border and to protect American interests from Mexican intrusion. After the fort was reoccupied by Union troops during the Civil War, it had to be rebuilt. During the period 1868–77, it went through a series of upgrades and changes. Companies of the 9th Cavalry and 24th Infantry arrived in the spring of 1873. Since barracks had not been completed, cavalry units had to make do with quarters in a storehouse, while the infantry occupied the hospital; patients were displaced into the town of Laredo. By 1876, the cavalry companies had left and the infantry had moved into the storehouse.[20]

Merriam's orders to go to Fort McIntosh occurred as part of yet another reorganization of the military in the lower Rio Grande region. On April 7, 1876, Headquarters, Department of Texas in San Antonio issued an order stating, "a district to be known as the District of the Rio Grande, with Headquarters at Fort Brown, and embracing the posts of Brown, Ringgold and McIntosh, with their dependencies, is hereby established and Colonel J. H. Potter, 24th Infantry, is assigned to the command thereof."[21]

Merriam, his wife, and their daughter, Caroline, left Fort Brown on March 24, 1876. Una recounted the hardships of the journey, the "first of many wanderings" as she termed it:

> The journey from Ft. Brown to Laredo took several days. We traveled in ambulances—a wagon with two seats facing each other to accommodate four or six persons; a driver's seat outside; drawn by four horses or, generally, mules. The wagon had a flat top, or roof, and curtains that could be fastened down in case of storm. Our worldly goods and tents for the journey, packed in wagons with canvass tops, called "Prairie Schooners," went with us, and a detachment of soldiers as guard for, at that time, "The Border" was unsafe for traveling, the region being infested by dangerous characters from both the Mexican and Texan side of the river; many fleeing from justice and trying to gather in all they could in their flight. We traveled all day, making an early start and stopping in the afternoon; these stops were chosen with reference to finding water and a little grazing for the animals. When we went into camp tents were put up, a guard surrounding the camp, and animals tethered near by; supper prepared by the Army Cook, provided for the trip. Soon after we went to bed in our tent the guard walking around giving, at least, a sense of protection! In places said to be infested by rattlesnakes, a rope was put around the tent and fastened down to keep the snakes out! This was my first experience of Army travel! But we got through alright, the most disagreeable feature being a "Norther" the fierce and cutting wind almost upsetting our wagon and filling everything with sand and dust, tho' the curtains were fastened down as tightly as possible. The baby, on her pillow, was held close to one or the other of us, to save her as much as possible from wind and dust.[22]

The Merriams stopped at Ringgold Barracks, about midway between Brownsville and Laredo, and rested for a few days before proceeding on to Fort McIntosh. Una called the second part of their journey "more trying than the first and full of dangers." Six days after leaving Fort Brown, the family arrived at Laredo and Fort McIntosh. Una quickly concluded that Laredo "fully deserved the fearful epithets hurled at it by desperate Army people who found themselves stationed there." In 1870 the population of Laredo was only 2,046.[23] Fort McIntosh quarters proved equally depressing and challenging: "Tarantulas, centipedes and an occasional rattlesnake, as well as snakes of less fatal varieties, were found in, and out, of the house." Una went on to provide wonderful insights as to what life was like at this primitive army post:

Laredo, in those days, was a most forlorn, unattractive place. Sandy soil going down to the Rio Grande which moved by the garrison, sluggish and dirty. No growth except the low chaparral scrubby and brown from constant dirt and heat. The Garrison consisted of a few desolate looking houses with nothing round to give a look of cheer. The Commanding Officer's house was a rather long, one story adobe building, originally built for a hospital, later divided into two buildings, one used as a hospital, the other quarters for the Commanding Officer. The porch at front and, at one far end, steps which opened into our dwelling, the same arrangement at the end which formed the Hospital entrance, Our portion consisted of a living-room, a good-sized bed room and one other small room. A narrow hall led to a dining room and out to a kitchen. Behind the dining room, separate from the house, was a small building originally used as a morgue; fortunately discontinued for this purpose before our advent. This place Col. Merriam transformed into a tank for catching any rain that fell (not often) a good change as our sole supply of water was the Rio Grande. A Mexican, with a large barrel attached to him by a strong rope or chain, waded out into the water, disturbing mud and dirt, the barrel was filled and dragged back to our house where the water was turned out into a rather cleaner barrel and various measures used to settle the mud and render the water less objectionable. Our supplies all came in cans and, as there was no ice, we had to devise various methods for keeping the butter—always served with a spoon—for heat was intense. We had no fresh vegetables, occasionally potatoes transported from the "States" at a very high price and, very occasionally, a few ears of corn—not "Country Gentleman!" No fruit except, now and then, a few figs—not a tree or blossom of any kind. Much cactus, some bearing fruit that could be eaten but not very palatable. . . . Those were days of hearty breakfasts, the beef was always fresh-killed and had to be hung up and used the next day. Often the steak for breakfast would have to be discarded as the cook would announce that a centipede had crawled over it! How she knew I never asked her as we did find the creatures in the house and Col. Merriam was painfully stung by one.[24]

Merriam arrived at Fort McIntosh during a time of violent revolutionary activity across the Rio Grande in Mexico. There had been little peace in that country before 1876, and Gen. Porfirio Diaz was trying to seize the reins of government that year. In an interview given to a Mexican newspaper in 1905, Merriam claimed to have "met General Diaz several times during the winter and spring of 1876, at Brownsville, Texas." He added, "we met socially several times and I remember him to have been a fine fellow."[25] Diaz would bring more stability to Mexico eventually, but in the beginning, lawlessness reigned on the border.

Inevitably, American merchants trying to do business on the Rio Grande became embroiled in the turmoil. Mexican revolutionaries, outright bandits, and even federal troops saw Americans as targets of opportunity to be incarcerated or threatened with arrest unless they paid a tax or ransom. This was one way they could obtain money and supplies for their particular cause.

In characteristic fashion, always curious and closely following events, Merriam did not shy away from becoming involved in the armed conflict going on between Mexican factions across the river from Fort McIntosh. At one time he personally crossed the border to see the results of one skirmish. He found the commander, a Colonel del Valle, of one group badly wounded, with one arm shattered and a doctor preparing to amputate it. Merriam believed the arm could be saved and received permission to move the officer to the Fort McIntosh hospital. The arm was saved, and del Valle became a Merriam house guest for several weeks. He departed American soil a most grateful man.[26]

US policy fluctuated with respect to the troubles in Mexico, especially in the border region. In early April the situation near Laredo and Fort McIntosh became far more serious and volatile. On April 9, 1876, Merriam sent a telegram to department headquarters in San Antonio:

Diamond—an American merchant of New Laredo was imprisoned and his life threatened last night by the federal commander of that Plaza . . . for hesitating to contribute his property and refusing to pay a fine of one hundred dollars levied by the said military commander. At the insistence of our Commercial Agent I have today called upon the Mexican commander and demanded the release of Diamond and revocation of fines. Demand completed with but threats against his future safety. I shall therefore hold all the forces at my disposal in readiness to aid our Commercial Agent in protecting American citizens. I ask definite instructions and more troops immediately. The regular force on the other side is about thirty.[27]

Merriam's bold action must have triggered some alarm since the next day the department telegrammed him: "You will remain strictly neutral in regard to all matters transpiring in Mexico and not post any force on that side of the river unless ordered."[28]

That same day, April 10, Merriam dispatched a series of telegrams to the department and district headquarters reporting on Mexican actions across the river. "New Laredo attacked at daybreak this morning [April 10]—after fighting two hours revolutionists were repulsed. Many shots came to this side wounding one man and two women. Fight seems now over but as yet no communication can be had as boats are all held on the other side." A following telegram stated "Mexicans have fired many shots across river I believe intentionally. One citizen mortally wounded. . . . I have put a twelve pounder in position near U.S. Custom House and notified Mexican commander that I would resist any further intentional shots. All is quiet now." Clearly an international incident was at hand, and Merriam, despite his decisive actions, wanted further guidance. Still another telegram to department headquarters asked, "Shall I continue to defend our side against deliberate attack or not?" Apparently Merriam did not receive instructions on what he should do, and at 5:35 p.m. he acted on his own, later informing his superiors that he had returned Mexican fire by retaliating with "the first two shells over their position."[29]

The next day at 7:00 a.m., Merriam filed more telegraphic reports:

At sunset last night the guard placed at the ferry by the U.S. Marshal to protect improper crossing was fired on by Mexican federal troops and driven away. Lt. Gaston again replied by firing two shells into their position. Revolutionists renewed their attack at about midnight and have been fighting ever since with occasional lulls. No more deliberate firing to this side and no more damage done. Revolutionists hold about half the town and both sides are fortifying. Have just had an interview with a Mexican federal officer who admits the firing on the Marshal's guard, but claims that the Marshal's guard also fired, which is being investigated.

Merely three hours later, at 10:15 a.m., Merriam informed headquarters, "New Laredo just captured by revolutionists." This evidently caused some of the Mexican federal troops to flee across to the American side. Merriam now had a further problem. "I have fourteen of the federal troops as prisoners with a portion of their arms. Some are wounded. One was drowned crossing." Some of the Mexican federal troops escaped downriver. Merriam posed a new question: "What shall I do with the prisoners? All quiet now."[30]

At 12:30 p.m. on April 11, Merriam conveyed some disturbing intelligence to his district commander: "I learn from prisoners that General Quiraga with three hundred federal troops was hourly expected from Lampsas. If this is true we may have more excitement soon." He wanted reinforcements for the small Fort McIntosh garrison, but if denied, he proposed an alternative: "If I cannot have more troops, I would like authority to arm a large posse for the U.S. Marshal." The next day saw a further update on the situation: "Have released Mexican prisoners retaining their arms. Have just had an interview with our Commercial Agent at New Laredo. Rumors of approach of federal troops under Quiraga not confirmed. Revolutionists have committed no excesses in New Laredo thus far, they have sent out several foraging parties beyond town today."[31]

Several days later Merriam received pertinent instructions that evidently had emanated from Washington: "You will prevent any revolutionary movements from our side and also military expeditions in aid of the revolutionists and all violations of neutrality to arrest, disarm, and intern any troops who may cross from Mexico."[32] This message seemed to confirm the US position of neutrality and perhaps offer a cautionary note for Merriam's responses to the Mexican problems.

That restatement of a policy of neutrality had barely had time to be digested when further developments plunged New Laredo into renewed crisis and thrust Merriam once again into its midst. Merriam telegraphed Fort Brown at 11:15 a.m. on April 16: "Revolutionists levied a prestamo on merchants of New Laredo including five Americans and threaten to break open their stores and sell goods to double account assessed, unless paid by 8 o'clock am tomorrow. Commercial Agent has appealed to me but I have no authority." This new incident of intimidation of Americans produced a different headquarters reaction: "In reply to telegram stating five American citizens in New Laredo had through the Commercial Agent asked protection against revolutionary officers on account of refusing to pay prestamo from being sold out, the Secretary of War directs that you will grant the protection asked by its American citizens in New Laredo against such lawless outrages as the government is unable to prevent—but consider caution—thinks notification of intention to protect will perhaps prove sufficient."[33] Merriam now had the authority to protect American interests that he had sought, though not without an added caution.

The New Laredo confrontation eased unexpectedly on April 19 as revolutionary elements left the city to pursue a federal force under Col. Pablo Quintano. Quintano had been the previous commander at New Laredo and had engaged in the confrontation with US forces across the Rio Grande. Merriam indicated to his superiors that he now had information that fighting was underway twelve miles downriver. He also noted a new development, that the revolutionists had chased Quintano to the American side, remarking, "If I had a few mounted men I might capture him I think." That would not happen, but Merriam had momentarily succeeded in protecting US merchants in New Laredo. Merriam reported to his headquarters on April 20, "Result of report about the prestamo upon American citizens is that I have orders from the Secretary of War to protect them against enforcement of it and it has not been enforced."[34]

From the end of April to August 1876, although the military and political situation at New Laredo (Nuevo Laredo) remained unsettled, an uneasy lull prevailed between the Mexicans and the Americans. During this more-quiet interlude, Merriam received some good news in July that he had been promoted to lieutenant colonel. Furthermore, his request for transfer from Texas and the Rio Grande had been approved. He would be relieved from his duties with the 24th Infantry and assigned to the 2nd Infantry at McPherson Barracks at

Atlanta in the Department of the South.[35] Merriam's and Una's joy was short lived, however, as the Laredo troubles again flared to a new crisis.

In August 1876 Merriam received a letter from J. J. Haynes, the US commercial agent in New Laredo, about additional forced collections from American merchants in the Mexican city. Haynes included handwritten accounts from US citizens and merchants being assessed. Problems came to a head at the beginning of September. Agent Haynes had incurred the anger of Mexican authorities, and he was arrested with preparations made to move him into Mexico's interior, away from possible military protection. With the aid of his friends, he appealed to Merriam on September 3, 1876, requesting the army's intervention and protection. Merriam immediately endorsed the request, sending it on to Fort Brown: "United States Commercial Agent appeals to me for troops to protect himself and Americans in New Laredo enclosing copy of petitions made by merchants to him; represents town entirely without authority, civil or military, of either contending party, and that a band of twenty or more armed men under Cecilio Benavides, a notorious robber and murderer, has just entered town to the terror of the people. Shall I take action now or await acts of robbery?" Merriam obviously believed he would need to take some action, but the question was when. In an uncommonly fast response, he was told, "Take such action as you deem necessary for the protection of U.S. Commercial Agent and American citizens." Simultaneously, word came from General Ord in San Antonio: "If there is no alternative, and American citizens are in danger, do not wait till robberies begin but act at once. In case you cross to protect such, remain only long enough to enable American citizens to remain with you and secure their property by bringing it to this side. You must be the judge of the time necessary to do this; we cannot garrison New Laredo."[36]

With this backing, Merriam led American troops across the Rio Grande, freeing Haynes and seizing control of New Laredo. The next day, September 4, Merriam informed headquarters at Fort Brown and San Antonio: "Took necessary steps to secure order in New Laredo last night. . . . I think all will be quiet for a little time."[37] Later Merriam sent a follow-up report to Fort Brown on all the hurried activity: "Valdez abandoned New Laredo yesterday and the civil authorities at once came to our side for safety as Benavides band was still in the vicinity. Being unable to induce the chief Alcalde to return and try to keep order, I put Lt. Donovan and forty-two men in possession last night. I have assured Alcalde that when he returns and organizes a small armed police, I will withdraw the United States Troops. He has now gone across to make the effort." In reply to this information, Fort Brown sent a welcome confirmation to Merriam's action. "Your telegram of this date received. Action approved."[38]

Actually, a precedent had been set back in 1873 with a somewhat different border crossing. On May 18 of that year, some men of the 4th Cavalry had attacked three Kickapoo and Lipan villages near Remolino, far into the Mexican state of Coahuila.[39] But this incursion into Mexico had been largely forgotten with the new crisis at New Laredo.

On September 8 Agent Haynes sent a telegram to General Ord:

United States troops have been guarding my office and stores of American merchants for two days. Colonel Merriam says that he is not authorized to continue occupation and wishes to withdraw the troops which would be simply abandoning us to the power of the bandit Cecilio Benavides, who is the terror of both parties here. Civil authorities are afraid to stay at night. Benavides was in the suburbs of the town last night with about fifty men and was only prevented from sacking the stores and murdering American merchants here by presence of the U.S. soldiers. He stopped every one who entered or left town, inquired for Mr. Constance and myself, said he would hang us both as soon as he could catch us. He has planned the murder and robbery of Messrs. F. Levy, M. Diamond, T. Walsh, J. Villegas, and Raldrode & son. This is reliable. Mexican citizens here indignant at occupation. Many threats but no action so far. It would ruin American merchants to cross their goods and persons to Laredo, Tex.[40]

The next day Merriam filed another report. "I reduced . . . force to twenty. At about 9 p.m. I received word . . . that Benavides party had grown to above fifty (50) men and that attack was likely to be made. . . . I am determined to hold New Laredo until some show of good order is made unless otherwise ordered."[41] Merriam's superiors began to have second thoughts about the US troops in the Mexican city. A factor in this reconsideration was angry reactions in Mexico. On September 7 a letter from a B. Garcia, New Laredo, in Spanish and with an English translation, was sent to Merriam and other American officials:

Complying with my duty and in the name of the city and of the national integrity, I protest solemnly against the offense committed by the forces under your command in breaking treaties existing between both Republics. Not only by placing yourselves on our soil and occupying this city with armed forces, but by stationing yourselves here since 10 o'clock a.m., without your having been called by this authority.

But what is more unreasonable is that you should come to assist some of our bad neighbors resident here, for only through their artful tales could you have committed the transgressions you are guilty of in occupying our country with armed forces taking undue advantage of the deplorable conditions which now exists therein.

There has not been one single act that could be considered a motive for such an ostentatious defiance of the law, to the disgrace and dignity of Mexico. Meanwhile I make report of these acts, I have given orders to all chiefs of armed Mexicans to lay aside their questions of internal political strife and unite in defending the integrity of their

soil and I will not be responsible for the consequences of your trans-
gression if you persist in maintaining an armed force in this plaza.[42]

The threat of a broader international incident brought forth new instructions from Merriam's superiors. On September 8 he was told: "[T]he
United States cannot be expected to perform police duty in Mexican territory. . . . [T]he American citizens must withdraw their property or assume the
risk." That same day General Ord at San Antonio wrote to Commercial Agent
Haynes in New Laredo, through Merriam, as follows: "Dispatch received. I am
perfectly aware of the dangers of doing business at New Laredo, and the sus-
pension of all authority, but U.S. troops cannot remain in foreign territory for
protection of special interests. Col. Merriam is hereby instructed to give American merchants four days including tomorrow to get out of the country with their
valuables; at the end of that time to withdraw the troops. This is the best I can
do for you."[43] Merriam now appeared to be caught in the middle, between his
desire and his actions to support Agent Haynes and American citizens in New
Laredo and a renewed US government and military concern about American
troops remaining across the border and the serious international implications.
Merriam had acted decisively and on several occasions with considerable tact.
At first, he had the backing of his superiors and firmly believed that he was protecting American interests. In his mind what he had done was fully justified. His
support obviously began to weaken as questions arose regarding the presence of
US military forces within Mexico.

Abiding by the deadline set in Ord's letter, Merriam reported to San Antonio on September 12, "Local authorities with federal Alcalde completed organization yesterday but my troops remained in possession by their request until
this morning when they withdrew and I received thanks from Mexican authorities for my action."[44] It is noteworthy that Merriam intended to leave a func-
tioning Mexican authority in place as the troops withdrew. He was not content to simply pull out American forces regardless of the consequences in New
Laredo.

The immediate problem with the bandit Benavides eased, and an uneasy
quiet prevailed, with American merchants wondering what would happen next.
They did not have long to wait. On September 20 Merriam telegrammed San
Antonio: "Revolutionary collector at New Laredo orders American merchants
to make a new entry and pay duplicate duties on all goods imported through
Federal customhouse since August 23. If not complied with by 3 o'clock treble
rates to be charged, besides fines. This is a new form of robbery and if carried
out will injure one house to amount of several thousand dollars. They have refused to comply and I expect another appeal for protection." Apparently this
message did not strike a chord of urgency nor a sense of military responsibility
with Ord, and the next day Merriam received a telegram in reply that brusquely
stated, "The Department Commander does not intend to interfere with the
Collector of Customs at Laredo."[45]

General Ord did not see the New Laredo customs collecting as Merriam had viewed it. "This is simply not a new mode of robbery," he declared. Instead, the general commented, "the business of collecting revenue in goods, money, or anything, is one that is taken up by any leader in the country who can gather a few armed followers with whom to divide the plunder."[46]

Fortunately, Merriam was not called to the rescue again. Mustering his considerable diplomatic skill, he worked with Mexican leaders to restore law and order in New Laredo. It was remarkable that he was largely successful, considering the turmoil on the border. Also, aided by Mexico's Porfirio Diaz gaining greater control in Mexico, the American merchants in the city could count on relatively peaceful and orderly commerce again. As a gesture of their sincere gratitude, the merchants presented to Merriam a beautiful, inscribed sword.[47] This was the second presentation sword that Merriam had received, but this one represented a diplomatic victory brought about by his decisive and timely use of military force.

Laredo-area merchants later petitioned US senators in support of Merriam's promotion, asserting, "Colonel Merriam possesses in a high degree those qualities of energy, discretion, valor and judgment which distinguish the true soldier." They recapped and praised his actions in New Laredo. "These acts were done for the immediate protection of the lives, liberty, and property of American citizens in a foreign country," they stressed.[48]

In a similar vein of commendation, Ord wrote to General Sherman, commander of the US Army:

General: During the Revolutionary struggles of 1876 on the Rio Grande frontier, and when on account of the delicate and important questions likely to arise with the people and authorities of the vicinity of across the river, it became necessary to select an officer of discretion and energy to command the small garrison at the town of Laredo, I selected Major, now Lieutenant Colonel H. C. Merriam, 2nd Infantry, relieving the then commander.

By reference to my subsequent annual report, you will see that serious and threatening difficulties did arise at the town of New Laredo on the Mexican side of the river, and that Major Merriam acted with energy and judgment, proving that I had not mistaken his fitness—for he proved equal to every emergency.[49]

Now that the New Laredo crisis had successfully ended, Merriam could turn his attention to his transfer to Georgia. Special orders of September 22, 1876, stated, "Lieutenant Colonel H. C. Merriam, 2nd Infantry, will, upon the arrival of Captain F. M. Crandal, 24th Infantry, at Fort McIntosh, Texas, comply with SO 137," the initial order detailing him to McPherson Barracks at Atlanta. It was not until October 10, however, that Merriam gave up command of Fort McIntosh and left the Rio Grande.

Army wagon transportation, Summer 1886. Courtesy National Archives.

No doubt Una was overjoyed at leaving Fort McIntosh. During most of her time there, she was the only white woman at the fort. "The troops were colored but faithful and good to us," she wrote. She had experienced not only the hardships of life on the post but also had learned what it was like to be in the line of fire. "During any fighting across the river we were instructed to lie on the floor with the babies in order to be out of the path of bullets which might come through the windows." She also noted, not surprisingly, "The heat was intense during our stay at Laredo."[50]

Henry Merriam, Una, and daughter Caroline (now called Carry), left Fort McIntosh by wagon bound for San Antonio. Una remarked, "We had no sorrow at leaving Laredo and packed up in short order, discarding many useful articles in order to make the weight of our household effects come within the Government allowances." At San Antonio they paused to rest from the arduous wagon journey. Una rejoiced in being able to purchase "a presentable hat to continue the journey with." They had to travel thirty miles beyond San Antonio before they could catch a train that would carry them on to Atlanta.[51]

Thus, in the latter part of 1876, Merriam's long, difficult, and varied experience in Texas and along the Rio Grande came to an end. A review of Merriam's time there points to several significant conclusions. First, this chapter in his life had showcased his talent in selecting strategic locations for military garrisons and building up existing forts. Most telling was the order directing him to establish locations for deploying army units in the lower Rio Grande region. Merriam gained a reputation for his astute choice of points to better control a wild and lawless area. This was all the more remarkable considering he was an infantry and not a cavalry officer. Also, he served as commander of several important forts, particularly up and down the Rio Grande from Fort Bliss to Fort Brown, despite being a relatively junior officer. His growing experience as a post commander, including all the multitude of details ranging from health and sanitation to logistical matters, became a highlight in his expanding military resume. This background would prove important in his forthcoming career assignments in the Far West.

Second, Merriam greatly strengthened his command and leadership credentials, exhibiting sound judgment and decisive action when he believed circumstances warranted. While on the border, with its chaotic conditions, he actively gathered intelligence and firsthand information on conditions in Mexico. The number of revolutionary leaders and Mexican federal officials that he had to deal with was extraordinary. There also was always the question of who was in control. In the New Laredo crisis, Merriam demonstrated unusual and successful diplomatic skills despite being personally fired with a strong sense of American nationalism. On occasion he sought to befriend and use Mexican leaders. At times he evidently saw opportunities to play off one Mexican faction against the other; the Garcia protest letter was an attempt to foil this strategy and unite Mexicans against the Americans. As a person with a passion for discipline, Merriam continually worked to bring law and order to New Laredo as an answer to protecting US interests there. Also, like any smart military man, he was careful to keep his superiors informed and earnestly sought their backing but was not hesitant to act when he felt the situation required a timely response. Overall, Merriam showed measured restraint and diplomatic skill both with his own military and governmental authorities and with Mexican leaders. At the same time, he was always cognizant of the value of timely application of military force in diplomatic situations.

Third, Merriam's departure from Texas terminated his command of black troops and his long tenure with the 24th Infantry. It is important to note that in a number of events, the regiment must have been ready for a fight. Maintaining combat readiness while stationed at distant posts was not easy and at times ignored. Troops were often caught up in mundane activities of garrison life and lost the discipline of arms. Merriam apparently had no hesitancy in sending his men into a possible hostile situation. He remained ready to use force or the threat of force on either side of the border even though he could muster only a small number of men. He seemed totally confident in his black troops. Going back to the last years of the Civil War and to his last days at Fort McIntosh, he had commanded black troops for twelve years. Remarkably, he had registered little comment in all those years about the attributes or character of his men. Apparently he did not see black-troop problems or successes as very different from those of white soldiers and thus worthy of special notice. This constituted a surprisingly unprejudiced view for the time and a commendable broad vision of the future of black soldiers. This Merriam characteristic, along with others, made him eminently successful in his leadership of black men.

Fourth, Merriam had found a wife in Una who was a perfect complement to his military career. She added grace and easy rapport with all types of people, energetically maintaining the social side to their oftentimes harsh military life. In addition, she supported his enterprises, like his innovative knapsack, and willingly joined him in his worst frontier assignments. Una and the beginning of a new family continually sustained Merriam's high spirits and happiness and promoted his set course as a career military officer.

Now that Merriam was leaving this part of the United States, he no doubt felt that he had done his best—perhaps penance—in serving in an unwanted, often hated, assignment on the hot and rather isolated Rio Grande. Also, he probably felt proud of his long leadership of the little-understood and often-shunned black troops.

During this transition from one command to another, news arrived about the "Custer Massacre" on the Little Big Horn. Merriam knew George Custer, apparently not well, and he, like all army men, was shocked and angry at the loss. He was dismayed that such a thing could have happened, much like his reaction to Lincoln's assassination. Little did he know at the time, however, that this event would influence his future, and relatively soon.

7

To the Pacific Northwest

Sites selected and plans prepared for new post
Coeur d'Alene by Lt. Col. Merriam are approved.

COMMANDER, DEPARTMENT OF THE COLUMBIA, TO
COL. FRANK WHEATON, MARCH 27, 1878

After another long, cross-country journey from San Antonio to Atlanta, mostly by train, the Merriams arrived at McPherson Barracks near the end of October 1876. This move represented a major transition not only in geography but also in scope of size and civilization. They had left small Fort McIntosh and the equally frontier, diminutive town of Laredo and came to "a large garrison, many troops, a Regimental Band, etc." and a bustling city. The Merriams were overjoyed with the change, no doubt strongly feeling it was long overdue. Una exclaimed, "We were delighted, and especially by the warm welcome given us by the officers and their wives," referring to her husband's new regiment, the 2nd Infantry Regiment. The Merriams, while awaiting assignment to some quarters, were invited to stay with the unmarried regimental adjutant, who also had his mother and sister living with him. Una remarked, "I felt weary of travel, gladly accepting the Dempsey's invitation to be their guest."[1]

Apparently Colonel Merriam, unlike his wife, did not feel quite so wearied by the travel from Texas. Shortly after settling his wife and daughter with the regimental adjutant at McPherson Barracks, he went to see the US Centenary Exhibition in Philadelphia. Although he never stated why he wanted to see the exhibition, it was one more indication of Merriam's innate curiosity in a broad range of subjects. Perhaps also he saw some advantage in viewing some of the latest inventions and deriving ideas as to how to advance his own innovative army knapsack. Certainly, a visit to Philadelphia could open contacts with possible East Coast manufacturers for his knapsack. His timing of the visit, despite leaving Una on her own to get settled at a new post, likely came with the thought that it was best to be done before he received very specific, time-consuming assignments with his new unit—and after all, the centennial year was drawing to a close.

· Upon Colonel Merriam's return to Atlanta, he and Una began moving in to new quarters. "Our household furnishings were next to nothing," His wife recalled, "so we made many expeditions into the City, the attractive shops being most enticing." The Merriams' new place soon "presented quite a homelike atmosphere with many new things, and our old treasures to lend dignity." Una, however, described the quarters as "[a]n ugly old house but comfortable, large rooms; living room, dining room, two bed rooms and a wide 'barren' hall running through the house with a door at the back, opening onto a covered passageway, joining the kitchen to the main house, for the kitchen and servant's quarters were separate from the main building; fire places in all rooms."[2]

An especially treasured new acquisition for the Merriam quarters was a "hired piano," which Una declared enabled her to feel "very much at home." The piano not only provided immense personal enjoyment but also enlarged her social circle. "There were many charming women among the officer wives, some good musicians, one in particular, wife of the chief doctor, Elbrey by name, from Virginia, was lovely and played beautifully. We became great friends." She added, "Tho' a gifted musician she was not above playing with me and we had a delightful time playing duets, etc." The Merriams entered into a new social whirl, with dinners, dances, and staged theatricals, something they had not experienced for a long time since their days in Brownsville.[3]

Una also reported that "the markets of Atlanta were well supplied with most tempting food of all kinds." She admitted, however, "I was never a good cook, but I knew how things should be done, and made an effort." Materially aiding her in "returning kindnesses shown" was the availability of cooks, which the Merriams hired at ten dollars a month, a combined nurse and housemaid hired at six dollars a month, and a boy retained for what she called a jack-of-all-trades but a master-of-none. Even with this help, not all things turned out according to plan. She recalled one incident at Christmas in Atlanta: "I tried to carry out a Xmas dinner as we had it at home. A delicious plum pudding was concocted and I gave strict instructions how it should appear, a branch of holly on it and flaming brandy round. Imagine my surprise when it appeared with the Headdress of Holly but no burning brandy! I said nothing and the pudding was much enjoyed; afterwards, I learned that servants had felt the flame was to keep it hot and see it safely from the kitchen, then before entering the dining room, carefully extinguished the flame."[4]

The Merriams truly enjoyed the winter of 1876–77 in Atlanta. In the spring Una noted that "Atlanta was such a pretty city" and "the peach trees a joy." She was aware, nevertheless, that the "soreness between the North and South had not yet worn away." During these pleasant months, Henry and Una arranged to have daughter Carry christened. They affiliated with an Episcopal church in town, and although Carry, now over a year old, "objected to the prescribed method of becoming a Christian," the "ceremony was duly performed." Una expressed great happiness "that my little daughter was a member of my own church."[5] She felt most pleased with again making associations (plum pudding and the Episcopal church) with her Scottish-Jamaican roots.

Not all things proved pleasant, however. In February the Merriams experienced a fire in their kitchen area that "destroyed everything in it and the passageway to the main building." The fire alarm had sounded at two in the morning, and Una and Carry had to flee to other quarters, far down officer's row, during a very cold morning while soldiers "took everything the Merriams's [sic] possessed out on the parade ground under guard for the remainder of the night." The next day the family examined the "mangled remains" of their possessions. It took some time to get them into another house and to get their "pretty new things in some sort of shape again."[6]

More personally serious for Lieutenant Colonel Merriam was the reaction to his persistence in pursuing a relatively longstanding courts-martial case going back to January 1876 at Fort Brown, Texas. He had become involved in charges and specifications against Capt. John M. Claus of the 24th Infantry as a result of being detailed as "special inspector" at Fort Brown on January 11, 1876. One charge against Claus was for "conduct unbecoming an officer and gentleman," revolving around a matter of a deserter named Sergeant Long. The case also embroiled Col. Joseph Potter, commander of the 24th, who had been charged with "drunkenness on duty in violation of an Article of War."[7] Merriam doggedly believed that justice was not being served with respect to Captain Claus and continued to press for what he personally thought was right. This pursuit for resolution put him in conflict with Colonel Potter. Despite being counseled to drop the case, Merriam had appealed, through channels, to be furnished copies of certain papers related to the charge and specifications against Claus. The application for papers went all the way to the desk of the general of the army in Washington. Merriam had become concerned that his actions had caused army headquarters to believe that he had preferred charges unnecessarily, and he was right to be worried.[8] He received at McPherson Barracks a third endorsement, dated November 15, 1876, to a stinging letter from the army's commander. The letter to Merriam read as follows:

I have the honor to inform you that Lt. Col. Merriam's application was laid before the General of the Army and the following are his views and instructions on the subject.

Major, now Lieut. Colonel, Merriam has pushed this case too far. The duty of a good officer is simply to call to the attention of his superiors any wrong or irregularity, leaving to him to judge whether the good of the service calls for action.

If the Department Commander decides this case, all should submit promptly and gracefully.

No further steps must be taken in the case of Captain Claus, but Lieutenant Colonel Merriam should be informed that his duty as commanding officer must be to prevent strife, not cause it.[9]

This was not the kind of recognition that Merriam wanted nor needed as he began his duties with the 2nd Infantry at McPherson Barracks. This written slap on the wrist, coming from the army's highest officer, could have been devastating to his career. It was to Merriam's credit that he survived this chastisement, although some future events hinted at some lingering concern in Washington about his persistence and aggressiveness in some matters.

This incident further reveals aspects of Henry Merriam's character. His supreme self-confidence led him from time to time into some cases of stubbornness, a willingness to contest when he believed justice was concerned. He tended to see, in his mind, matters of fairness largely in terms of black and white, eschewing the more subtle shades of gray. He felt obligated to charge on to make things right. At the same time, some of his commanders, most of them fortunately, saw Merriam's aggressiveness and tenacity as positive attributes. In their overriding view, Merriam would and could get the job done, whatever time required.

During the spring at McPherson Barracks, troubles developed with area moonshiners, or "Illicit Distillers," as Una called them. Troops were sent out to arrest them, and a McPherson lieutenant was killed in a skirmish. The young officer was married with several children, and Una recorded how this greatly distressed the army community. "A Lieutenant's pay was small and little chance for one with children to put away anything for a Rainy Day." She noted that everyone was anxious to help. "Among other little activities to raise funds was a very good play given by the officers and ladies, so successful that, by request, it was repeated; and in this way they were able to contribute a fair sum to help with the present needs of the widow and children."[10]

During Merriam's time at McPherson Barracks, he also kept busy with many assignments to courts-martial boards, some of them time-consuming general courts-martial. Some cases involved travel to other posts, such as Chattanooga in January 1877 and Newport Barracks, Newport, Kentucky, in February of that year. He also received a significant detail to inspect money accounts of officers at Chattanooga and Newport Barracks in March 1877.[11] There was no evidence that Merriam was much involved in day-to-day command of troops.

In June 1877 Colonel Merriam applied for a leave. His goal was to take Una and Carry to Houlton, Maine, to meet his parents, brothers and sisters, and boyhood friends. Also, he had in mind a stop at Waterville to introduce Una to his college town. They closed their McPherson quarters, expecting to return in August. They had been gone two weeks when Merriam received a telegram ordering him to return to Atlanta. The message from Col. Frank Wheaton read: "Second Infantry has been ordered on active service in Idaho. General Hancock directs you proceed to join it without delay." Merriam responded by telegram to Colonel Wheaton, asking a question to which he likely already knew the answer, "Do families go?" The very next day, July 8, the colonel replied, "Start Friday families do not go your horse left here."[12]

When Merriam arrived back at McPherson Barracks, he found their belongings had already been packed by the army and stored awaiting a time for a future home. Una would not see their possessions for a year, and some "treasures" from their Atlanta home were never seen again—lost or discarded by the packers while the Merriams were away.[13]

A decision was made for Una to remain with Merriam's mother and sister in Houlton while he moved west with his regiment, with all the troubling uncertainties of her joining him later. An important factor in this decision was her late-term pregnancy. In addition, shortly after Merriam's abrupt departure, daughter Carry came down with scarlet fever. Una in turn contracted the disease and endured "a very uncomfortable time." On October 10 Una gave birth to a son, Henry Macpherson, born in his father's hometown of Houlton.[14] Thus, in a relatively brief time, Una had experienced a series of shaking events without the help of her husband.

Una's greatest trial, however, was the winter in Maine. Her childhood in Jamaica, along with the time in Texas and Atlanta, had not prepared her for the cold she now endured. "The winter was a very dreary one for me in spite of much kindness from Col. Merriam's family. I had never before experienced such cold and preparation for meeting the winter, almost alarming. Double windows, 'banking' the house all around with boughs, etc.; stoves in every room, for we had no furnace, and stoves had to be well supplied with wood. Water freezing hard at night in the rooms. We had, or I had occasional sleigh rides on the river which ran by town; but it was too cold to be a pleasure."[15]

Perhaps fortunately, Una was kept busy caring for her children, for there was not much other activity. Worthy of note, she felt, was the Christmas of 1877, "[a]nd a lovely Christmas tree which gave us all much pleasure, the elders in preparing it and the children enjoying gifts and tree."[16] They would remain in Maine until May 1878. She would always remember her winter in upper Maine.

Colonel Merriam and members of the 2nd Infantry moved from McPherson Barracks to Fort Lapwai, in northern Idaho Territory, via rail. This long-distance train travel for troops represented a significant change from the long marches Merriam had experienced from Kansas to Fort Bayard in New Mexico back in 1867. It was now possible to transport and concentrate army units in the vast expanses of the West by an emerging rail system. In the latter part of the nineteenth century, this would lead to the closing of some of the many scattered western forts. General Sherman fervently believed that railroads would help resolve the Indian problem in a number of ways, and he actively sought to use the army to support railroad construction. While the lines aided the troop movements and the influx of settlers, they greatly angered Indian tribes as tracks increasingly knifed through their lands.

Brig. Gen. Oliver Otis Howard. Courtesy National Archives.

The 2nd Infantry's deployment west resulted from the ongoing Indian Wars. Since the end of the Civil War, sporadic conflicts and set battles, highlighted by the much-publicized Custer disaster in 1876, had occurred in many areas of the West. These had taken place despite President Grant's Indian peace policy. The encroachment of miners and settlers on Indian lands had continually sparked conflict and open warfare. The army's role oscillated from protecting the building of railroads, to trying to keep peace by interposing themselves between the natives and settlers, to trying to confine the Indians to designated reservations, to actual combat.

In 1877 the Pacific Northwest saw the development of a war in Idaho with the Nez Perce. Chief Joseph, sometimes admiringly called the "Red Napoleon," and his tribal factions, angered by what they considered betrayal regarding their lands, had resisted efforts to assign the Nez Perce to a smaller reservation. They embarked on an amazing flight and fighting retreat to try to escape from Idaho to Montana or Canada. Brig. Gen. Oliver Otis Howard, the one-armed, praying abolitionist commander of the Department of the Columbia, had begun a difficult campaign in pursuit of the fleeing Indians. Chief Joseph skillfully retreated and deftly led his tribe over the Bitterroot Mountains into Montana. The Nez Perce War did not end until Maj. Gen. Nelson A. Miles finally cornered and defeated Chief Joseph and the Nez Perce at Bear's Paw Mountains in October 1877. The army's campaign against Chief Joseph had been intensely followed by eastern newspapers, so this conflict was well known throughout the country. The press coverage engendered greater sympathy for the Indians.[17]

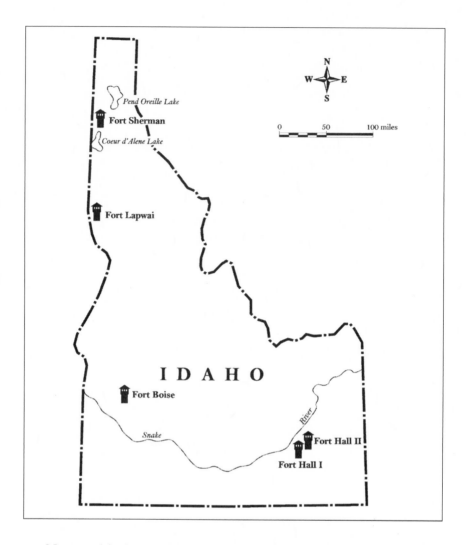

Not surprisingly, Merriam and the 2nd Infantry were deployed to northern Idaho amid the Nez Perce War, arriving at Fort Lapwai in July 1877. It remained unclear whether General Howard intended to use the troops specifically to join in the campaign against Chief Joseph or whether they were meant
to provide a force to deal with other restless tribes. Tribal neighbors of the Nez
Perce, notably the Bannocks, Paiutes, and Sheepeaters, were threatening to turn
to warfare in their longstanding grievances with settlers. More to the north and
west, "charges and countercharges of duress, deceit, and plotted treachery in
connection with treaties" had stirred tribes east of the Cascades. Gold strikes in
the Colville (Washington Territory) and Coeur d'Alene country also threatened
conflict with those tribes.[18]

Fort Lapwai had been established in 1862 to guard the then-friendly Nez
Perce during the Snake Indian War and later to guard the Oregon Trail. Like
some other posts in the post–Civil War period, it had been evacuated several

times and then reoccupied, with the latest habitation occurring in November 1867. The fort was located on the left bank of the Lapwai River, a Clearwater tributary, and was principally positioned there to separate and to keep peace between the Indians and the on-pressing miners and settlers. Lapwai was actually within the Nez Perce reservation, and the old Spaulding Mission originally was nearby.[19]

The 2nd Infantry, based at Fort Lapwai, soon received clarification of their mission a relatively short time after their arrival. General Howard decided to send some companies northward as a show of force for other tribes expressing discontent. As a consequence, Colonel Wheaton moved troops into the Spokane area to militarily impress discontented Indians in that region of northeastern Washington and northern Idaho Territories. In one of his first actions, Wheaton arranged a meeting with tribal leaders on August 10, 1877, not only to listen to their complaints but also to convey the army's intention to maintain peace, by force if necessary. One result of this council was the creation of a new military district, with Wheaton in charge.[20]

Meanwhile, in the months leading into 1878, troubles came to a head with the Bannock, a tribe to the southwest of Fort Lapwai. In August 1877 some Bannocks from the Fort Hall reservation killed two settlers, for which one chief was executed. The next spring, as the tribe gathered on the Camas Prairie to collect Camas roots, their anger at whites grazing stock on their prairie led to an attack, and the so-called Bannock War ensued.[21]

Apparently Merriam was only indirectly involved in the fighting of the northwest Indian conflicts. One of his first assignments after arriving in Idaho was to replace Brig. Gen. Alfred Sully as commander of the supply depot at Fort Lapwai and the Lewiston area.[22] Fort Lapwai was a key communications center at which councils with Indian leaders had been held, including one between General Howard and Chief Joseph. Special orders also indicated that Merriam once again had been detailed to some courts-martial. These various responsibilities were meant to capitalize on his administrative skills.

On February 8 and 9, 1878, Merriam received orders from Colonel Wheaton, commander of the District of the Clearwater, to move to northern Idaho Territory to explore sites for a new post. His instructions specified that he would "proceed to Coeur d'Alene Lake via Camp Spokane Falls for the purpose of carrying out the instructions of the District Commander contained in a letter of Feb. 8, 1878, from these Headqtrs." Accompanying Merriam was Lt. C. W. Rowell, who would have the responsibility "to make a topographical sketch of the country between Ft. Lapwai and Coeur d'Alene Lake." This expedition became necessary for several reasons. Indian tribes in the region, such as the Coeur d'Alenes and Spokanes, were threatening war, and the Northern Pacific Railroad needed protection for its survey and construction crews working westward toward the Pacific. Merriam, utilizing his knowledge of commanding and reestablishing forts in Texas, selected a site on the northern shore of Lake Coeur d'Alene. Although one could imagine that he was attracted to this location because of its natural beauty, more pragmatic considerations held sway. Trails had long been used both north and south of the lake. The northern shore, from where the Spokane River emerged, provided important access points and good water for troops and animals. Nearby there was excellent timber for fuel and construction and a grazing area for livestock. On March 27, 1878, a letter from the commander of the Department of the Columbia to Colonel Wheaton stated, "Sites selected and plans prepared for new post Coeur d'Alene by Lt. Col. Merriam are approved."[23]

It was at Coeur d'Alene that Merriam employed skills he had learned in the northern Maine timber industry. Land had to be cleared, roads established, sawmill equipment purchased, a sawmill built, trees cut and sawed for construction, and soldier teams organized and supervised to raise the buildings. The fort was planned for six companies, so it would be significant in size. Another consideration for Merriam was the money allocated for the work. Later General Howard would note, "The appropriation was small, and therefore great economy was demanded." A fort emerged after much planning, hard work, and consideration of a multitude of details, such as a system for water and disposal of sewage. The building of Fort Coeur d'Alene drew Howard's praise: "For administrative ability, diligence and success in that work, and in fact for all his work under my command, I have heretofore highly commended Colonel Merriam."[24] At the same time, while engaged in building, 2nd Infantry troops had to remain vigilant to deal with Indian troubles and provide protection for the railroad.

The new post was first called Camp Coeur d'Alene and in 1879 officially became Fort Coeur d'Alene. Much later, in 1887, it would be named Fort Sherman. Merriam became its commander and remained there until September 1879.

While at Fort Coeur d'Alene, Merriam's continued effort to sell his knapsack to the army received a serious setback. Before he left Atlanta in 1877, the colonel had received a letter from the army's chief of ordnance, stating: "In reply to your inquiry of the 23rd, I have to state that no action can be taken on account of want of money. During the next fiscal year, should Congress make a sufficient appropriation, I will be glad to consider your case, and assist you all I can. Now, I can do nothing." Merriam persisted, and despite the army's budget problems, he asked for consideration of the knapsack in 1878 and again in 1879. A letter reached him in the field in February 1879, which informed him: "The Board on Army Equipment have had under consideration your knapsack supporter, but no model accompanied the papers to it. Will you be kind enough to forward to the Board at your earliest convenience a pattern of your invention."[25] Merriam wrote to the adjutant general of the army from Fort Coeur d'Alene on May 9, 1879, commenting:

[M]y combination Pack and Supporter for foot troops did not reach Washington in season for trial by the Board, I have the honor to request that a special board, composed of officers of skill and experience, may be appointed to make a thorough competitive trial of my equipment against all other known methods or devices for the same purpose and to report upon its merits.

The equipment is the result of more than five years of study and experiment, and the unanimous reports in its favor by nearly thirty companies of troops, and large number of line and medical officers, copies which I have forwarded to Chief of Ordnance from time to time seem to warrant my belief that no other known device for carrying a soldier's necessaries in campaign can bear competition with it, hence I feel justified in making this application.[26]

Merriam's plea for a special board was soundly rejected. On June 14, 1879, the Adjutant General's Office responded: "Your 'combination pack and supporter for foot troops' did not arrive in time to receive the action of the Board . . . and requesting the appointment of a Special Board to examine and report upon the merits of your invention, I have respectfully to inform you that the General of the Army—before whom the process was laid—does not approve the appointment of a Board for the purpose indicated."[27] While Merriam was again momentarily frustrated in his attempt to get the army to adopt his backpack, he would not give up.

During the construction of the fort, Indian conflicts had diminished and a decision was made to allow 2nd Infantry officers' wives to rejoin them. No doubt Henry and Una were excited with the thought of reunion. Thus, near the end of May, Una and their children left Houlton, Maine, on what she called "almost a perilous journey." Most interestingly, they stopped for a few days in Waterville, where they met the parents of Henry's first wife, Lucy. Una reported that the Getchells were most anxious to see her children because of the loss of their own daughter and granddaughter in the terrible Texas flood. She said the "Getchells were most kind" and that she and the children "spent a couple of days most happily with them." Then mother and children traveled on to New York City, where they joined two other army wives whose husbands were in Merriam's regiment.[28]

The three wives and seven children, three of whom were less than a year old, headed west by train, stopping at Chicago and Omaha. After pausing for several days in Omaha, Una said, "our journey really began, when we started for San Francisco."[29]

Una recalled that since this journey occurred before the advent of dining cars, trains would stop at "eating stations," where passengers "could get a fairly good meal—eaten in a hurry," though their "chief reliance was on a good sized lunch basket fitted with the most necessary things to sustain life." The three army families arranged so that one mother would leave the train at an eating station, have food herself, and bring back supplies while the other mothers watched the children since they were "all too small for us to cope with at a lunch counter."[30]

Una fondly remembered one incident in Utah when they had an extensive delay while the train underwent some repairs. "Our provisions were at a low ebb; we always kept a good supply of condensed milk for the babies but we older members had to make out as best we could." While debating their chances for getting a good meal, the train porter handed them a card that read "General John Gibbon, 7th U.S. Infantry." To their delight the general provided the answer to their needs. The women knew of Gibbon's reputation, and Una called him "one of the finest of our officers." He had heard about officer families on the train, and he invited them to go with him, carrying young Henry in his arms, to replenish their baskets. Ironically, years later Merriam would replace Gibbon as commander of the 7th Infantry.[31]

Una and the family groups finally arrived at San Francisco, waiting a few days in the city to regroup before continuing their journey. Una found the "winds of San Francisco very cold," and warmer things had to be purchased for the children. The next leg of their journey was up the West Coast to Portland, Oregon, a trip "not very pleasant, small boat, rough water and a sea sick crowd, even the babies." Spirits peaked, though, when husbands met their wives and children at Portland. Una greatly rejoiced because, she said, "we gladly turned over our cares to them."[32]

From Portland, the Merriams took a steamer up the Columbia River to The Dalles. That voyage was easy compared with the more-difficult upriver travel and the ultimate return to army wagons for the final overland leg to Fort Coeur d'Alene. No doubt this return to the frontier travel experience came much to her dismay.

Life in the Pacific Northwest frontier required some unusual measures. A cow and a crate of chickens accompanied the families to the fort. At one point a wagon carting Una's new Webber piano tipped over and rolled down a slope, with driver and mules. All were recovered, and the journey resumed. Also, she always remembered with a shudder shooting some rapids on the Columbia River in an Indian dugout canoe.[33]

Una and the children remained at Fort Coeur d'Alene until September 1879. She never forgot the beauty of the area. Lieutenant Colonel Merriam received new orders to go north and west from Coeur d'Alene to the Okanogan/Columbia River region of Washington Territory. But first he took his family back to the Pacific Coast to Department of the Columbia headquarters at Vancouver Barracks, across the river at Portland. This was another hard journey, through some wild country, and Una again was pregnant. A short time after safely arriving at Vancouver Barracks, on December 16, 1879, son Cyrus Lincoln was born.[34]

After getting Una settled at Vancouver Barracks, Merriam began his new assignment. He was to explore areas east of the Cascade Mountains for one or more new military posts and to make recommendations as to locations. This mission stemmed from a promise of the president to establish a new military

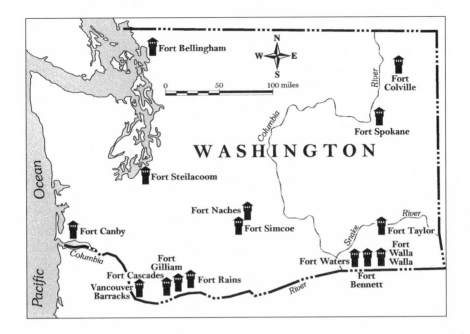

post to be positioned somewhere between white settlements and Chief Moses's reservation. Also, the military leadership in the Pacific Northwest wanted to seize this opportunity to locate forts, as a precautionary measure, near Indian tribes that were still restless and threatening warfare.

This new assignment to explore fort sites on the east side of the Cascades and west of Spokane greatly angered Merriam. In a remarkable but rare fit of temper, he used almost fighting words to express his frustrations to higher headquarters:

> Inviting attention of the Division Commander to Paragraph 9 of SO 94 of Department of the Columbia, copy enclosed, I feel compelled to remonstrate against the injustice and unusual hardship it imposes on me, which I think are manifest as follows to wit.
>
> Having served on the extreme frontier ever since the war, I came to the 2nd Infantry in November 1876 shortly before its transfer to this department. Since then, I have incurred the privations and labor of locating and building one post under many disadvantages and with a limited appropriation, I am just now for the first time provided with shelter and a degree of comfort for myself and family; and to be deprived of all this now, without apparent military reason, or to gratify more personal choice of one who has not shared such privations, and to be sent again into the wilderness, without even the privilege of taking with one the troops whom I have instructed in this duty, often with

my own hands, appears to me an unusual hardship—one to destroy my faith in the justice of military administration and in a partial violation of duty upon which we depend, and without which esprit de corps is impossible.

I am unwilling to believe the Division Commander has intentionally authorized this wrong to be done me, and I appeal to his sense of justice for relief from the requirement of the order.[35]

This letter of bold protest likely was triggered by the relocation of his family to Vancouver Barracks and the subsequent separation again after their brief months together at Coeur d'Alene. It also represented some building resentment with repeated moves and multiple exploratory expeditions. Although the letter reflects Merriam's study of law, it still has a very sharp edge. Once again, Merriam threw army caution aside when he believed justice was involved. It remains unclear what reaction this letter generated at headquarters, but his appeal went nowhere.

Only a short time after submitting this letter, Merriam returned to the field, checking out possible sites for a new post. He did offer an explanation for this turn of events: "Having become familiar with northern Idaho and Washington during the location and construction of Fort Coeur d'Alene in 1878–79, I was ordered by Genl. Howard to locate and build another new post on or near the southern boundary of the Indian Reservation beyond the Columbia, then recently augmented westward to Lake Chelan for Chief Moses and his people." After conducting explorations, Merriam wrote to Howard, saying, "convinced that the object contemplated could be met economically and effectively attained by combining the troops with those at Fort Colville in a large post at the mouth of the Spokane River." Despite his recommendation for a fort at the Spokane River, the colonel was surprised to get instructions limiting his "selection to the region lying westward of a point on the Columbia River about six miles above the mouth of the Okanogan, a region of many difficulties—timberless, and almost waterless south of the Columbia."[36]

On August 27, 1879, while in the field, Merriam received a telegram from General Howard via "Indian courier" informing him that "troops are not sent into the field simply to establish a new post, but to fulfill promise of Government to whites and Indians. They must be got under some shelter before cold weather. If there is no timber south of the Columbia and it is impracticable to float down, we shall be forced to go to the west side of the Columbia. Select site quickly and report."[37] Merriam was thus under pressure to make a fast and judicious decision. He and Lt. Thomas Williams Symons, an army engineer, met in September 1879 at the juncture of Foster's Creek and the Columbia. They journeyed down the river, examining both banks and exploring potential sites.[38] Merriam had to work within specified limits, and this greatly complicated a site selection. On September 10 he filed a report via a handwritten letter, which conveyed the problems he encountered and his thinking process:

In compliance with instructions given me by the Department Commander I have examined various points on the south side of the Columbia, within limits specified, and found that on which I have located my temporary camp to fulfill more of the requirements as a site for a military post than any other. The great objection to all points on this side of the Columbia is the difficulty of obtaining lumber and fuel. None can be had except by the very difficult and expensive process of rafting down the Columbia from the timber region beyond Spokane. How expensive this would be may be seen by the rates of wood contracts at Fort Lapwai, where the distance and difficulties of the process are much less. I estimate the cost of lumber alone for a four company post on this part of the Columbia at thirty thousand dollars, to say nothing of the great annual outlay for fuel supply after the post is constructed.[39]

Despite Merriam's misgivings, he dutifully complied with his instructions. In early September he told his headquarters: "Site south Columbia four miles above Okanogan fulfills most requirements. Camp established winter shelter commenced." Yet he could not help but repeat the problems with the site. "Both land supply routes circuitous and difficult will be impracticable for transportation from December to July. Distance Walla Walla exceeds two hundred miles."[40]

While work at Camp Okanogan, as it was labeled, progressed, Merriam and Lieutenant Symons explored other areas, realizing that sooner or later a different location had to be chosen. Moving down the Columbia, they camped at the outlet of Lake Chelan, which they considered to be a far better site for a military post than the one at Camp Okanogan. Symons recorded: "Lake Chelan is a wonderfully beautiful sheet of water, about 60 miles long and from 1 to 5 miles wide. It seems to be and is in fact a dammed-up mountain canon of the most rugged and pronounced description. The water is of diamond like clearness and yet in places no sight can penetrate to the bottom of its liquid depths."[41]

Merriam added his reasons for favorable consideration of this site. "On visiting Lake Chelan I found that, at twenty miles above the outlet, good timber, which appears elsewhere north of the Columbia only on the summits of the mountains and in canons equally unaccessible, comes down to the very shore of the lake where it can be easily cut and made into rafts upon the quiet water to be towed down the lake. There was no longer any question in my mind as to the economy of locating the post on Lake Chelan, and I selected a site on the north side of the outlet just below the lake." Merriam further outlined advantages of his Lake Chelan selection: "The plateau is abundant in size for all purposes including gardens, and the extensive slopes adjoining afford sufficient grazing for thousands of horses. The water of the lake is excellent, its transparency rivaling the famous Lake Tahoe, and the outlet affords sufficient fall for working hydraulic mains, by which an abundant and excellent water supply can be procured at very little expense. There is also good clay on the site for bricks and excellent sand on the lake shore for building purposes. I did not discover limestone, though it may be found." Of critical importance in locating a new fort was its accessibility to transportation routes. The Lake Chelan choice, "about one mile from the Columbia River," was ideal in Merriam's view: "This opens communication with the Columbia River, which should be made the highway for supplies and operations in both directions without delay, both for economy and the efficiency of the garrison whenever it may be stationed." He envisioned an army steamer that would move the necessary supplies on the river.[42]

Despite all of Merriam's reasons for selecting the Lake Chelan site, presented in his September report, he nevertheless felt obligated to make a comparison with Fort Coeur d'Alene. "The site I have chosen at Lake Chelan, though having so many advantages over all others in its vicinity, is yet far below Coeur d'Alene in advantages for economical building, and even with the proposed steam-launch for towing rafts down the lake, and the sawmill & attachments necessary for manufacturing lumber, it will require more than twenty thousand dollars to advance the construction of the post as far as Coeur d'Alene now is."[43]

Merriam concluded his long report by informing headquarters, as he had in telegrams, that he proposed to remain in camp south of the Columbia at Okanogan during the winter of 1879–80: "measures are already in hand for providing temporary shelter." He would then move to the Chelan site "as early in spring as work can begin." In the meantime, with characteristic determination and self-initiative, he planned to keep busy by detailing a detachment, "supplied with tools, etc., to open and work a wagon road from Chelan to Priests Rapids or White Bluffs."[44]

Most maps of the area under consideration for a new military post were inadequate, so it was appropriate that an army topographical engineer, Lieutenant Symons, should accompany Merriam to assess the terrain and draw maps. Symons had graduated at the head of his class at West Point in 1874, thus he was very young and relatively inexperienced, yet he performed his task well, earning Merriam's praise. Merriam wrote in his site report: "For a map of the country examined in making the selection for a site for this post I refer to the one being prepared with great care by Lieut. T. W. Symons, Engineer Corps of Army, who has accompanied me, and rendered me valuable assistance." At one point in their explorations, Merriam and Symons traveled twenty-four miles up Lake Chelan in a dugout canoe.[45]

Headquarters, Department of the Columbia special orders on July 24, 1879, had directed that a new four-company infantry post would be established "on, or near, the east bank of the Columbia River." These same orders assigned Companies D, E, I, and K, 2nd Infantry to the new post, and the troops were to go into camp and await further orders. In the same directive Merriam was designated as commander of the new post.[46] Thus Merriam had a significant force when he went into camp during the 1879–80 winter. Just as the colonel had foreseen, however, the camp site near Foster's Creek proved expensive largely because of the absence of good timber. A newspaper report said that wood was obtained at a "cost of $20 per cord, and grain at eight cents per pound."[47] This made Merriam most anxious to relocate to the Lake Chelan site in the spring.

During the 1879–80 winter encampment, a Merriam family crisis developed at the Vancouver Barracks. Son Henry, then two years old, came down with diphtheria, a serious and dreaded disease for the time. In January 1880 the colonel returned to Vancouver Barracks on detached duty because of his son's illness. In short order daughter Carry contracted the disease, followed by two maids being afflicted. Vancouver doctors had almost given up hope for son Henry, but Una and the colonel took turns caring for him at his bedside night and day, and he began to recover. It was then that Una and Colonel Merriam also became ill with the disease. The family's situation soon became desperate because of the difficulty of securing nursing help, many being fearful of contracting the disease. The Roman Catholic Sisters of Charity in the town of Vancouver came to their rescue and remained with the family until health was restored. The baby son, Cyrus, came down with measles during this nightmarish period for the family. The Merriams forever remembered this family trial and how grateful they always felt for the services of the Catholic Sisters.[48]

In May 1880 Colonel Merriam, recovered from his bout with diphtheria, returned to winter camp on the Columbia. Despite the hardships that could be expected in the forthcoming construction of Camp Chelan, he brought along Una and the children with him. Thus they were very much amid camp movement and new construction.[49]

With the spring of 1880, Merriam moved his 2nd Infantry companies to the selected location at Lake Chelan. A camp was quickly established at the juncture of the Chelan River and the lake, and close by was "a beautiful bunch-grass covered plateau on the south bank, stretching about a mile to the rocky and timbered hills." After setting up a sawmill, the troops began building. Merriam, as he had in other assignments, wanted to know and to understand the topography of the Lake Chelan area. At one time in the summer of 1880, he navigated the entire lake in a canoe. Lieutenant Symons noted one of the colonel's observations: "Merriam afterward went further up the lake, and says that the timber becomes better and better as the lake is ascended, and cedar is foudn [sic] about the head of it, which region he describes as being wonderfully grand. At the extreme upper end he found solid vertical walls of rock and on these, several hundred feet above the water's edge, were a large number of hieroglyphics written in a horizontal line, evidently by people in boats when the waters were at this higher level."[50]

Lieutenant Colonel Merriam always had doubts about the Camp Chelan site as a fort. He supported the Chelan location only because of the site parameters given to him by headquarters. A primary disadvantage of the site was the cost associated with construction and maintenance, particularly fuel. On more than one occasion, Merriam had warned that significant budget allocations would have to be made for construction costs. In one instance he asked for an appropriation of $10,000 to construct a road, but Congress failed to act on this expenditure. The expenses associated with the camp and questions about its protection role with respect to Indian movements were disturbing. As Merriam became more familiar with the region's topography, he came back to his original first choice of a fort where the Spokane River meets the Columbia.

The decision about locating a new fort, however, became political. One proposal, which Merriam favored, would combine Camp Chelan with Fort Colville to the north and then build a new, larger post at the Spokane River site, with eventual closure of Fort Colville. Debate about a new fort location reached the army's highest level. In a letter to Merriam marked "personal," General Howard wrote, "General Sherman holds to Colville with tenacity & hopes to enlarge it. . . . [M]ust be used as a post for several years at least." Even senators got involved. In another personal-type note to Merriam from his headquarters was the comment, "Senator [John] Logan [of Illinois] working for Colville and he seems not to be discouraged." At the same time, the two generals closest to the situation, Oliver Howard and Nelson Miles, supported Merriam's recommendation of the Spokane site. This confidential communication continued: "I wish I could tell you anything definite about the Post business, but I cannot. Gen. Miles I am sure is in favor of Spokane and is laboring to have it (the big Post) built there. He has ordered them to make all preparations to build the bridge which is to be located there as soon as possible next spring. . . . [N]obody knows exactly what will be done although I believe that Gen. Miles will have his own way. As far as I am concerned, if there was any possibility of doing it, I should like to see all three Posts concentrated at Spokane Falls, but I fear that it could not be done."[51]

Meanwhile, as a result of further exploration, Merriam again evaluated the Spokane River site and filed more reports in its support:

> I had opened a possible wagon route . . . and occupied Camp Chelan early in the spring of 1880. The distance and great difficulties of the region and the present needlessness of this post at that point, was soon recognized, and late in 1880 I was ordered to examine the country about the mouth of the Spokane River with a view to carrying out my original recommendation. I then selected the site of the present Camp Spokane and recommended a post there of eight companies of infantry and cavalry in lieu of both Camp Chelan and Fort Colville.
>
> I should say here that in selecting the sites of both Chelan and Camp Spokane I was accompanied by Lt. Thomas W. Symons, Chief Engineer Officer of this Department, who fully concurred with me in the selection and joined in the recommendations of the same for Camp Spokane.[52]

Merriam went on to explain why he had strategically made the Spokane selection:

The reasons which influenced my recommendations: 1st, a few troops are most effective for protection of scattered settlers when occupying the smallest number of stations, provided these stations are within easy striking distance of all points exposed. 2nd, Camp Spokane is situated at a center of Indian tribes leading in all directions from the great fishing of the Spokane adjoining the site. . . . 3rd, Fort Colville is located on a site that would be untenable in case of hostilities. The settlers of Colville Valley number about eight hundred, and nearly all of mixed blood, having inter-married with the Indians for several generations, and living in peaceable and neighborly relations . . . and do not require a military post in their midst.[53]

In another report Merriam and Symons explained in a geographic and topographical sense why they recommended the Spokane River location:

In obedience to telegraphic instructions from the Department Commander we have selected a site for a military post on the south side of Spokane River, about one mile above its mouth.

The site is a level plateau, gravelly, and partly covered with open pine timber. It is four hundred feet above the river level and in extent is about three miles running parallel with the Spokane River. Its water supply would be stored from several large springs in the rolling hills back of the plateau. . . . Grazing facilities are unlimited and excellent. . . . The site can easily be reached by wagons from several directions. . . .

For economy and efficiency we would recommend the establishment of an eight company post on this site—six of infantry and two of cavalry—to take the place of the posts of Chelan and Colville.[54]

A very key geographic element at the Spokane River was its proximity to a favorite Indian salmon-fishing spot. Trails went off in many directions to Indian camps from this seasonal meeting place. It thus constituted an obvious transportation hub with easy contact routes to various tribes.[55]

Amid all these considerations of the location of posts or forts, Merriam received a new assignment of a more-permanent nature. By special field orders dated October 23, 1880, "Lieutenant Colonel Henry C. Merriam, 2nd Infantry, is released from duty at New Camp Chelan, W.T., and will at once proceed to Fort Colville, W.T., and assume command of that post."[56] It seems likely that he welcomed this respite from his site exploration activities with all their associated hardships. In addition, he could take Una and their children to a more-comfortable fort setting.

Before Merriam left Camp Chelan for Fort Colville, he prepared a "Memorandum of Recommendation" regarding the closure of Camp Chelan and the opening of a new camp at the mouth of the Spokane River. Like his reports on site explorations, these recommendations provide a great insight as to his thoroughness and mastery of details:

> 1st That fifty good four horse teams be hired by the day furnishing themselves and sent at once to Chelan. I believe these can be had at reasonable rates, a large number being about done with contracts on the N.P.R.R. or from Small and Putnam of Walla Walla. We shall have about two hundred loads to move and it will require about ten days for a round trip with trains.
>
> 2nd That J. Covington's (Virginia Bills) offer to Lt. Symons to make a good wagon road from his ranch to the site chosen for seven hundred dollars ($700) be accepted and be notified to do the work at once, this cost will be more than saved in the cost of moving by that route. He can do the work promptly by using Chinamen miners there at hand.
>
> 3rd The contractors for Chelan have signified their willingness to complete their contracts at the new site. A saving in time can be effected in this way perhaps, but if not the services and supplies should be procured by purchase in the open market to avoid delay, as time is the greatest element in the problem.
>
> 4th I will at once test the "Chelan" to determine whether she can be of service in moving our stores by water to mouth of Foster's Creek, and in case of failure will do what I can with troops to improve the hill south of the Columbia, some improvement at least can be made.[57]

Despite Merriam's obvious concern and involvement in closing Camp Chelan, it was left to Maj. Leslie Smith, 2nd Infantry, to establish the new Camp Spokane on October 21, 1880. Nevertheless, Merriam must have felt pleased, and somewhat vindicated, that his first recommendations on fort placements were beginning to fall into place.

The farther north into Washington Territory that Merriam moved in his site explorations and in his construction of camps, the more he came to deal with Indian leaders. All the Indian tribes in the region were on edge because of settler incursions into their reservation lands and continued efforts to reduce the size of their reservations. Obviously, they were interested in the location of new forts for many reasons. Furthermore, there was internal tribal friction over leadership and struggles between factions wanting peace and the wilder ones wanting war.

In 1879 Chief Moses, a Sinkiuse tribe member, and other Indians succeeded in negotiating a treaty with the secretary of the interior that established a huge reservation for his people. "This region was rich in agricultural, pastoral and mineral resources and contained rich deposits of gold and silver."[58] As a consequence, it readily attracted white settlers and prospectors. Complicating the friction in this Indian territory was a group of settlers who had established homes within the new reservation's boundaries before the 1879 treaty.

They were told that they had to leave their homesteads, and they loudly remonstrated against the treaty as depriving them of their property and rights. Some disobeyed orders to leave.

On September 11, 1879, General Howard sent Colonel Merriam a handwritten note about the Indian situation, particularly concerning Chief Moses, directing Merriam's actions with respect to the tribes. Howard was first upset that some officers had "the idea that this Government sustains Moses, overestimating him" in regard to other tribal leaders. The general continued, "[t]he Government has seen fit to try to control the wilder Indians" through Moses, and he wanted Merriam's "hearty cooperation" and not disobedience in the matter. He remarked that some men had "endeavored to sow dissension between Moses and other Indian leaders by implying they could supplant Moses as chief." Howard added, "Moses may not be equal to . . . other chiefs but he is recognized by this Govt. so beg of these officers to throw their influence in that direction." The general's backing of Chief Moses was clear: "Moses has kept his word with me. I want him sustained so far as practicable to enable him to fulfill the wishes of the Secretary and to carry out his engagements." In closing, Howard counseled Merriam, "Bind Moses to you as firmly as you can & exert all your influence for harmony among the Indian tribes." As for the signs of intrigue, "I think Moses is wise to exclude those wicked white men who have already undertaken to overthrow him and render futile the plans of this Government that we are required to carry out."[59]

While still commanding Camp Chelan, Merriam received further guidance (once again in personal form) from headquarters:

I am directed by the Department Commander to write to you the following instructions concerning Indian matters in your vicinity.

I. The white people, excepting those who have the right by rental, must leave the limits of the Indian Reservation.

II. Tell Moses that for all the tribes that recognize him as head chief, the military authorities will so recognize him.

III. The Department Commander and the military authorities will recognize him as head chief over those mentioned and as chief of the other tribes located between the Columbia and Camp Chelan and the British line.

IV. Secretary Schurz says that Moses mistakes in supposing that he has promised Moses money for improvements.

V. If you think that Moses has a just claim the General desires you to send it forward in writing with your recommendation and whatever the Secretary of the Interior replies shall be sent to Moses.

VI. The Department Commander made no promises about the post. He did not think he could put it at Chelan on account of the steep banks east of the river, but on your report the Department Commander recommended it and it was so ordered.

The General desires that you deal very kindly with Eenemosechie, for he has been a true friend, and try to allay his soreness about the post being unexpectedly located on his grounds.[60]

The Department of the Columbia's Indian strategy was to shore up Chief Moses as a leader and then to work through him to control the more-hostile factions. By all indications, Merriam sincerely supported this plan and found that he could work well with the chief. One example was how he defended Moses on occasion in what the colonel felt was incorrect information and alleged violations of agreements. Merriam rebutted intimations that the chief had tried to collect small bands of Indians on his reservation to make himself leader over them. Also, he corrected information about Moses having whites on the reservation, declaring that one or two white men were allowed to "pasture their stock" by "written contracts approved by General Howard." Merriam asserted that "Moses had not violated his compact with the Government in any particular." In addition, he declared that Moses "has not for a moment manifested a hostile disposition, although greatly humiliated and pained at the manifest bad faith of the Government towards him, as will be seen by comparing the Executive Orders of the two Presidents, Hayes and Arthur."[61] Merriam's sense of justice had come into play again, reinforced by a genuine sympathy for the Indians generally and for Chief Moses in particular.

Merriam's move to Fort Colville in October 1880 meant a return to happier times. He would once again be in command of a fort rather than a camp, his family would be with him, and Indian conflict had eased for the moment. The colonel would be able to stay in one place a bit longer than in his previous assignments, until September 1882. Fort Colville had been established in 1859 and was "located on the left side of Mill Creek, seven miles above its confluence with the Colville River." Like so many other military posts, it had been positioned there to control Indian tribes. It had also served as a base for the Northwest Boundary Commission. It was named for an official of the Hudson's Bay Company, which had been active in that part of the country. Una recalled that their time at Colville went quickly, and it was a pleasant stay. Adding to her pleasure was a visit by her younger sister Dora, who came all the way from Jamaica, bringing some personal treasures that Una had left behind so many years ago.[62]

During this time, railroad construction had advanced significantly but was still underway. The Northern Pacific Railroad, chartered by Congress in 1864, had been proposed as one of the main east–west lines, running from Lake Superior to a Puget Sound terminus. Meant to be completed by 1876, its construction had encountered many difficulties, but it gradually became a force in the development of eastern Washington, particularly under the aggressive, blunt-speaking leadership of Henry Villard. On June 15, 1881, the first Northern Pacific passenger train arrived at Spokane. Merriam did not specifically record what part he and his troops played in this progress—ostensibly they were to protect the surveyors and builders. But Villard, president of the Northern Pacific Railroad, had lavish praise for Merriam: "It affords me great pleasure to bear witness and my personal testimony to the all but inestimable value of the services you rendered to the Northern Pacific Railroad Company, while in command of the United States forces in Northern Idaho and Washington, during the survey and construction of the company's main line. It is not too much to say that but for your ceaseless vigilance and energetic action at critical moments, the work referred to could not have been carried on without great difficulty and expensive interruption from Indian depredations."[63] Merriam's calming work with the Indian leaders, earning their trust with his honesty and integrity, proved to be a godsend for the railroad company.

While Merriam continued to command Fort Colville, the establishment of a more-permanent post at the Spokane River progressed. General Howard decided to organize a group to reexamine the site because of the politicizing of the site selection. According to one of Spokane's newspapers, Howard "sent a board of examiners to make thorough inspection of the country about the mouth of the Spokane, which section has been recommended by Col. Merriam." The final result of this activity was fulfillment of the colonel's original recommendation—a large fort established at the Spokane River and closure of Fort Colville. Camp Spokane became Fort Spokane in 1882, and on September 20, 1882, an order signed by Merriam announced: "Complying with Par 2, SO 131, Headquarters, Department of the Columbia, this post [Fort Colville] is discontinued as a military station from this date. The command becomes a detachment in the field." Merriam in turn was now assigned to command Fort Spokane.[64]

Fort Spokane, by its strategic location, would hopefully keep a peaceful separation between the Spokane and Colville Indians, on reservations to the north and west, and the developing white settlements in farmlands to the south and east, including the city of Spokane Falls. The Spokane and Colville Indians had successfully farmed and ranched the region for generations, but the white settlers, prompted and aided by the Northern Pacific Railroad, worked to push the tribes north of the Columbia and Spokane Rivers. The Spokane fort, the last army frontier post established in the Northwest, thus would thrust an armed force between the natives and the settlers.

As Merriam transitioned from Fort Colville to Fort Spokane in the fall of 1882, construction of a permanent post was well underway. Major Smith, who had been in command of Camp Spokane, had secured civilian workers from Portland to build the permanent buildings; nevertheless, Merriam arrived while much remained to be done. It was not until the summer of 1884 that some twenty-five structures, including six barracks and a headquarters building, were completed.[65]

The colonel's most pressing concern at Fort Spokane became the renewed threat of Indian hostilities. He had informed Vancouver Barracks by telegraphic reports that several bands of Indians on Chief Moses's reservation were on the verge of war. The Indian leader Sussapkin, with a group of disgruntled followers, was at the center of the trouble. They were angered by recent presidential orders cutting off a fifteen-mile strip just south of the Canadian border of Chief Moses's reservation. Merriam's dispatches prompted a strong response by Brig. Gen. Frank Wheaton, the 2nd Infantry's former colonel now acting commander of the Department of the Columbia. He informed Merriam that he would reinforce the troops in his area, including establishing a summer camp of troops "on the Columbia River, at, or in the vicinity of Foster's Creek." This would serve "as an outpost to Fort Spokane," with Merriam as the overall commander. This reinforcement on the Columbia would back a movement of soldiers into the Okanogan country, if necessary. Wheaton added, "Should your efforts, seconded as it is supposed they will be by Chief Moses, fail to prevent actual hostilities by Sussapkin and his disaffected Indians, and a move against them becomes unavoidable, it must be made in force, and the Forts Coeur d'Alene and Lapwai garrisons will be added to the troops that will be soon in your country."[66]

In a letter to a newspaper editor, Merriam described how he had viewed the imminent threat of Indian warfare in the spring of 1883. He said that a "general Indian war" could have developed because "the disaffected from all the tribes from Umatilla to the Flathead country would have concentrated in hostile camp." He pinpointed the cause of the conflict as greedy white men who had hastened to stake out and seize Indian-cultivated farms in a fifteen-mile belt being withdrawn from their reservation by executive order. The actions of the settlers preceded an official notice to the Indians and conveyed an aura of intrigue and betrayal. "Nothing could be better calculated to arouse resentment and tempt hostilities, and it is within my official knowledge that Sus-sap-kin, Chief of the Western Okinakanes, had fixed upon the very day when he would have opened hostilities, had he not received protection in the possessing and cultivation of his farms at Toad's Coule."[67]

Merriam indicated that he took several steps to prevent the open warfare, including protecting Sussapkin's property. He reported to his headquarters about the situation and the need to assemble troops to project a strong deterrent force. He worked through Chief Moses to try to calm the Indians, taking him to confer with General Miles. Moses, according to Merriam, then went back to his people, then to Sussapkin to assure him that the colonel would use the army to protect his land while warning the settlers not to molest the Indians and their farms. Merriam also interposed soldiers between settlers and Chief Moses and his people as they traveled southward. "This combination has arrested hostilities and Moses is entitled to a full measure of credit for his part in carrying it into execution," wrote Merriam.[68]

General Miles, in his *Personal Recollections*, commended Merriam's actions with Chief Moses and the other Indians, saying, "Colonel Merriam, a very intelligent and judicious officer, of the Second United States Infantry, the commander of Fort Spokane, was assigned the duty of adjusting the causes of dispute." Miles added that the colonel had succeeded in keeping the peace by "rigidly excluding white settlers from any part of the Moses reservation south of the fifteen-mile limit of the strip" and then had ensured that the Indians with farms in the strip had the same land rights as the white men.[69]

Merriam's actions had averted another Indian war. He had skillfully used Chief Moses to counsel Indians bent on the warpath. He, like at times in the Rio Grande country, had aggressively and expeditiously marshaled an intimidating military force to dissuade disaffected warriors. Once again he gathered invaluable intelligence as to the developing situation on the reservations and correctly and promptly acted on what he learned. In one instance Merriam said that he gained "a great deal of valuable information concerning the tribes" from some Jesuit missionaries. The colonel did not underestimate the discontent always latent in the Indian tribes, which could break out in killings at any point, but maintained an evenhanded approach in working with tribal leaders that helped keep the peace. He basically earned their trust. While Merriam could rightfully take considerable credit for preventing an Indian war, he nevertheless insisted that Chief Moses was the key to maintaining the peace. He commented to one newspaper, "Whatever may have been his motive, you must admit that this region in both these years was spared from war mainly through his influence; for everybody knows he was offered every inducement by hostiles, and given every opportunity by the withdrawal of our troops to great distances in campaign; and whether he was governed by good will or good judgment he was equally entitled to credit."[70] As for the miners and the settlers, Merriam firmly sought to control and contain their intrusions, no doubt angering many. Yet these same settlers, miners, and railroadmen would eventually see a blessing in the absence of Indian war parties. Politicians, citizens, and boosters would later praise Merriam for helping eastern Washington Territory, especially Spokane, develop commercially.

Quite notable also was the confidence Merriam's commanders showed in his abilities as an explorer, fort builder, troop and fort commander, and Indian diplomat. General Wheaton ended up his long 1883 letter of directions for Merriam by declaring: "Fully appreciating the difficulties you may encounter in your endeavor to adjust difference between the whites and Indians near you, I have confidence that your experience and judgment will enable you to maintain, if it is practicable, peace and good order on the Moses reservation, and that you will make every effort to satisfactorily solve the intricate problems that are likely to arise in accomplishing that end."[71] His superiors had given him total command and control of the threatening situation in the spring of 1883, and Merriam would have wanted it no other way.

The time at Fort Spokane, from September 1882 to August 1885, proved to be happy years for the Merriams. Una recalled, "Many dear and lasting friendships were formed among the wives of officers of the regiment and staff stationed there." A third son, Charles Bailey, was born on August 27, 1885, at Fort Spokane. The three other Merriam children were growing and healthy. The colonel, an excellent horseman, taught them how to ride at a very early age. Also, he delighted in passing along his skills in ice skating and sledding, even fabricating his own bobsled. Merriam's favorite pastime, however, was billiards, and he constructed a game table that had a turning top that could transform into a large sewing surface for Una.[72]

Merriam's enterprising skills likewise came to the forefront. The city of Spokane was growing rapidly. "By 1889, the Northern Pacific officials recorded a local population of nearly fifteen thousand, representing a ten fold increase in six years." One resident declared, "The mines above here and the great wheat region a few miles south . . . seem to predict a future for the place." Merriam sensed that this business boom in Spokane meant investment opportunities. He put money into real estate, and a *Spokane Falls Chronicle* article later stated, "he has large property interests here."[73] He encouraged his father, a brother (Dr. Cyrus K. Merriam), and his older sister and her husband to emigrate to Spokane from Maine to take advantage of the thriving economy. Merriam became known in the city as not only a military officer but also a businessman.

On July 7, 1885, Merriam received word of his promotion to colonel, and due to the promotion and transfer of Col. John Gibbon to Vancouver Barracks, he was assigned to Fort Laramie, Wyoming Territory, to take command of the 7th Infantry Regiment there. The news of the promotion brought relief and celebration to the Merriam household. All knew that in those days promotions came only with a death, retirement, or promotion of an officer ahead of you, all based on the officers' dates of rank. The timing of a change of post, however, proved most inopportune. Because the birth of his third son was imminent, Merriam's assignment to Fort Laramie meant another transfer with either Una about to deliver or a separation while she and the baby recovered. Merriam evidently decided on the latter course, going on to Fort Laramie and then later returning to Fort Spokane to move his family.

Merriam had spent a very eventful eight years in the Pacific Northwest. During that time, he had greatly strengthened his reputation as a builder and commander of forts. While he was still at Fort Spokane, with construction continuing, General Sherman, commander of the US Army, made a "tour of inspection of the work in progress." At last Merriam could count on some on-the-spot, face-to-face, favorable recognition by Sherman to counterbalance those earlier questionable, more-negative incidents known by army headquarters and General Sherman in particular.

8

Fort Laramie

*Colonel Merriam had a sense of justice and fairness and was
never harsh in his dealings with either officers or enlisted men.*

BRIG. GEN. GEORGE W. McIVER, FEBRUARY 1943

Storied Fort Laramie began as a trading post as early as 1834. At one time
it was known as Fort William, after William Sublette, the enterprising fur
trader, and also Fort John, after John B. Sarpy, an officer of the company that
built the fort. But after the army purchased the post on June 26, 1849, the longstanding popular name Fort Laramie took hold. The Wyoming Territory trading post and evolving fort was located near the confluence of the Laramie and
the North Platte Rivers, a noted rendezvous point for Indians and traders. It
occupied a strategic location on the Oregon Trail, winding its long way to the
West Coast. The fort provided a way station for many travelers, such as gold
seekers headed for California, Montana, and the Black Hills; settlers looking
for new lands to farm; and Mormons seeking a religious sanctuary. It also provided protection against Indians for trail emigrants, the Pony Express, and the
telegraph lines. In the 1870s it became an important base for the campaigns
against the Sioux and the Cheyenne Indians. As a consequence, Fort Laramie
had been prominent for many decades and from time to time hosted many famous westerners.[1]

Henry Merriam left Fort Spokane on August 7, 1885, and arrived at this
old fort in the Department of the Platte on August 17. He would serve as commander not only of the post but also, and of great importance to him, would
command the 7th Infantry Regiment based there. Merriam believed that at this
point in his career, he needed to lead an entire regiment. The 7th Infantry not
only gave him a regimental command but also, because of the unit's noted history, offered him a prestigious one. The 7th Infantry was one of the oldest regiments in the US Army, tracing its origins back to the War of 1812. Later it would

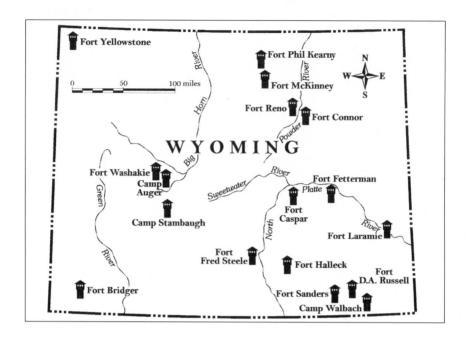

be recorded as the only regiment that served in every nineteenth- and twentieth-century war. In the West it had been heavily involved in the Indian Wars.[2]

In the weeks spanning August to October, Merriam spent time becoming familiar with his new regiment and Fort Laramie. Evidently he felt at ease with this new command and the new post as he requested a long leave in October, which was approved, to take his family back to the East Coast. First, however, he had to return to Fort Spokane to pick up Una and the children. Then ensued the lengthy rail trip to New York City, with Una once again traveling with an infant, three-month-old-son Charles. In New York Charles was baptized, and Una visited with her sister and family who resided in the city.[3]

Some army-officer rail travel was greatly assisted in those days by rail passes for themselves and family members. This represented a form of compensation for the likes of Colonel Merriam, who had done much to further railroad construction. The very long trips in the West would have been financially difficult for such families if not for these charitable contributions by the rail companies.

Merriam's leave lasted until February 1886, when the trip back to Fort Laramie began his new adventure. The travel to Cheyenne via the Union Pacific proved comparatively comfortable, a dining car was now included, but then it was a return to army wagons for the last leg to Fort Laramie, approximately 128 miles. The two-day trip necessitated a midway stop overnight at an "uncomfortable and unclean" ranch. Una and the colonel "spent the night protecting the children from what they told them were 'hives'; and much was their embarrassment in the morning when the children insisted upon recalling the night's horrors and the crawling 'hives' before the owner of the ranch and his wife."[4]

In addition to the rough wagon travel and midway stop from Cheyenne

Watercolor of Merriam's quarters at Fort Laramie, Wyoming.
Courtesy Friends of Historic Fort Logan.

to Fort Laramie, the family received an unhappy introduction to the Wyoming winds, which swept over the plains and sagebrush with "great force." At one point Colonel Merriam called on all his ingenuity to keep the family wagon from blowing over by placing a spare wagon tongue, loaded with a bag of heavy rocks, at right angles to the wagon and the wind to counterbalance the wind's force. This worked to keep the wagon on its wheels. Despite their many difficulties, the Merriam family arrived at Fort Laramie on February 18.[5]

An immediate joy of the Merriams was the commanding officer's quarters. It was a "four square, well proportioned, two storied house with adobe walls, a mansard roof, and wide, covered porches on three sides." This constituted the family's "first really ample home." The residence's appearance had been enhanced by lawns enclosed by white picket fences on which colorful clematis entwined in the summer. There were flowerbeds and a vegetable garden, with stables, chicken houses, and a pasture for animals in the back.[6]

The Merriams' new residence greatly facilitated hosting social gatherings at the post. Fort Laramie had always had many visitors, and Una would need to host receptions for Washington officials and officers from department headquarters. Because of the fort's relative isolation, she would be taxed with providing dinners from not always immediately available resources; canned food and some local produce usually had to suffice. Amazingly, the receptions seemed to go well. Special times demanded special efforts, such as the custom at Christmas to have frozen fresh oysters shipped all the way from the East Coast. Cans of oysters would then be buried in a snow bank until the appropriate time for feasting. "Dinners, Theatricals, Dances, Picnics, Horseback riding, Driving, Reading, and Music, in which all the officers and their families and guests joined," provided a social spice to the oftentimes mundane life at Fort Laramie. Church services, usually in the Merriam quarters, were led by Colonel Merriam or one of his officers, with Una or another wife accompanying the hymn singing.[7]

The Merriam children, as well as adults, could swim and fish in the Platte and Laramie Rivers and ice skate in winter. Colonel Merriam would flood a place on the parade grounds to provide ice skating for the smallest children. Horseback riding and picnics proved especially popular in summer. Some enterprising officers set up a tennis court, "marking the court by lines of weather bleached bones." A school provided instruction for the children, and a substantial library had been organized.[8]

One of the colonel's passions was marksmanship. He strongly believed that men in the army should be able to shoot and do so accurately. He always insisted that the soldiers in his regiment would learn the importance of their weapons and practice using them. As in his views about drill and discipline, he set high standards in the use of firearms. Indicative of Merriam's training program was a letter to him from the inspector of rifle practice for the Department of the Platte, who stated, "the program on efficiency in rifle practice is wonderful." During Merriam's time as commander of the 7th Infantry, his unit won the Nevada Trophy six times in the annual rifle competition of the entire army, some forty regiments. Merriam himself took great pride in his prowess on a firing range, participating in various army-sponsored competitions. A number of times he earned the right to wear the "Sharpshooter's Cross." A letter from a friend in 1887 reflects Merriam's competitiveness: "My dear Col—I was very glad to get your magnificent scores. I congratulated myself on their receipt that you were not in competition in our revolver matches."[9]

Fort Laramie was not only an old fort but also an aging one. As a consequence, Colonel Merriam spent much time and energy in never-ending repairs and improvements to its facilities. At the time of the colonel's arrival in 1885, there were sixty-five buildings. In that year a long list of recommended expenditures for facilities had been compiled, ranging from $1,145.62 for the bathhouse to $19,352.50 for the six company barracks. Sometimes requests for such funding were approved, but at other times they were flatly rejected.[10]

The sorry state of Fort Laramie's buildings was highlighted in repeated reports of the post surgeon. For example, Surgeon D. G. Caldwell stated on October 9, 1885: "The sanitary condition of the post is about as good as the character of the buildings will admit. The enlisted men's barracks except those occupied by 'C' and 'D' Companies are old, the roofs leaky and walls full of crevices which are particularly bad at the windows and doors. There is no sewage system and the pit system in use for enlisted men sinks is wholly unsatisfactory and does not meet sanitary requirements." Another medical report in January 1886 again complained about the condition of a barracks: "[T]he roof is in very bad order. Large cracks admit rain and snow to the ceiling and thence to the squad rooms and render it necessary for the men to move their bunks to the center of the room. In their present condition these barracks are not habitable."[11] Adding to the building problems were some weather-related disasters, such as a severe hail storm on August 1, 1888, that demolished windows on the storm side of buildings and destroyed the post gardens.

Fort improvements were greatly handicapped by mounting uncertainty about the future of the post. On February 9, 1886, Maj. Gen. John M. Schofield filed an ominous report:

> The fact that Elkhorn Valley railroad will pass Fort Laramie at a distance of forty-five miles, while Fort Robinson is immediately on that road, diminishes the value of the former and increases that of the latter post.
>
> Even if another railroad should hereafter be extended along the valley of the North Platte to and beyond Fort Laramie, Fort Robinson would still remain much the most important station because of its closer proximity to the Sioux reservation.
>
> Hence I suggest the construction of additional barracks and quarters at Fort Robinson and a corresponding reduction of garrison at Fort Laramie.
>
> It would manifestly be unwise to expend money in repair of old buildings at Laramie.[12]

Merriam added an equally negative report about Fort Laramie on September 4, 1886:

> The buildings at this post are nearly all very old structures of various materials, and plans, and generally inferior construction. With few exceptions they are in very bad condition, leaky, crumbling, and unsightly, as well as uncomfortable, requiring constant patching.
>
> Plans and estimates for new buildings, submitted in April '86 have not received favorable response. A small sum $2,000 dollars has been furnished for repairs during the current fiscal year. Even that sum could be applied more intelligently, with regard to the best interest of the service, if some light could be given respecting the probable permanency of occupation of the post.
>
> In view of new railroad construction, and the consequent distribution of troops it appears to me this post has lost its significance, as a military location, and that no considerable expenditure for construction or repair of buildings would be justified.[13]

This report clearly reflected Merriam's extensive experience in assessing locations for military posts, in constructing forts, and in working with tight budgets, as well as a growing appreciation that railroads brought a new dynamic in the movement of troops.

Merriam would remain frustrated with the lack of funding for Fort Laramie and the growing structure problems as the War Department and the army hesitated in taking any action. Several years would pass before the army made the decision to abandon the fort.

The garrison at the fort varied from time to time, but Merriam's command peaked at seven companies of the 7th Infantry Regiment, declining to five companies by the end of his assignment. The medical history of posts reported in January 1888 that the troop strength was fourteen officers and 175 enlisted men. A company, or part of a company, might be detailed to another location for a brief period. For example, in 1884–85, troops helped construct a sixty-seven-mile telegraph line from Fort Laramie to Fort Robinson, with soldier labor used to cut poles and perform other tasks. In July 1887, companies marched to Camp Pilot Butte, Wyoming, and back. The absence of units from the fort, however, was often balanced with the quartering of troopers moving through on assignment from one post to another.[14] The sheer number of men at Laramie would keep Merriam, as post and regimental commander, busy with administrative and training matters. Fortunately, he remained blessed with a capable staff.

Near the end of March 1887, Merriam took another lengthy leave of absence, this one extending until July 11. The purpose of the leave was almost totally business associated with the promotion of his knapsack. Una and the children would remain at Fort Laramie while the colonel journeyed to the East Coast. His real objective, however, was a voyage to Europe. In his words: "In 1887, I visited Europe for the purpose of patenting and distributing samples of my invention among the principal War Offices." Merriam had gotten enough favorable "feelers" about his knapsack, particularly from Paris and Vienna, that he felt a follow-up trip was justified. In fact he received a message from the US legation in Vienna on May 4, 1887, reporting: "The Technical and Administrative Military Committee, which is the one I presume you refer to, is a permanent one, and likely to be in session about the 20th of May. I am told by military men that a change of Knapsack is being considered and your early presence would be desirable."[15]

Prior to this European jaunt, Merriam had continually worked to enhance his infantry pack and to sell it to the US Army, with foreign marketing a later consideration. As previously noted, he had faced some setbacks in his efforts but remained undeterred. His backpack had come a long way from the days in 1875–76 when Una had helped cut and sew materials for the first models. Merriam confided that he first began thinking about the military knapsack when he was a company officer during the Civil War. "It frequently happened that I slept without food or blanket in consequence of the defect of the pack until I learned to have upon my own person and that of my servant, always when near the enemy, some small supply of food and a blanket." During his honeymoon trip to Europe with Una in 1874, he took note of the use of backpacks on the Continent. He later commented, "I commenced my experiments in 1875, after studying the methods of the Swiss mountain guards, the market women

THE

MERRIAM PACK

combines haversack and knapsack, serves for lightest or heaviest marching order. Un-rivalled for comfort and convenience.

Advertisement for Merriam Pack from printed brochures.

of Holland, and the Armies of Europe, in the previous year." From this humble beginning had evolved three US patents. The first (148,545), on June 13, 1876, covered basic knapsack configuration; the second (204,066), dated May 21, 1878, dealt with improvements in comfort and convenience; and the third (362,302), of May 3, 1887, addressed some simplification and wearer comfort.[16] Merriam remembered from his Civil War days the irksome backpacks and other equipment and how vendors sought to secure lucrative contracts in their manufacture. Obviously, he proved very astute in realizing that he needed patent protection if he was ever to be successful in selling his invention.

Merriam's innovative knapsack essentially sought to transfer some of the weight and pressure of the pack from the shoulders and back to the hips, utilizing two adjustable sticks extending from the pack to leather pockets on a waist belt. This shift of weight would thereby ease back discomfort, heat, respiration, and breathing problems of the soldiers. Although relatively small, it importantly would combine the army's current valise knapsack (for clothing and personal items) and the haversack (for rations) into one knapsack. A bedroll of blanket and tent/overcoat would be slung horseshoe-like over the top of the knapsack. Its average weight was approximately twenty pounds. He developed versions for "heavy marching order" and "light marching order."

Merriam knew the post–Civil War army was looking into alternative knapsacks and actually doing some experimentation. In 1868 an ordnance board convened to examine the army's personal equipment, and in the summer of 1869, a board of officers met at Fort Leavenworth to review arms and accouterments. A board in St. Louis in 1870 considered eleven patented knapsack models, moving six to further testing, but none were judged satisfactory. In November 1871 a five-member board in Washington discussed improvements in infantry equipment.[17] Therefore, the time seemed ripe for Merriam to propose that the army consider his knapsack.

On May 1, 1878, Merriam, at "Camp Coeur d'Alene," wrote a personal letter directly to General of the Army Sherman:

Having just read your letter to General Sheridan on the subject of Army equipment now published in the Army and Navy Journal, I am convinced that you are tired of discussion on the knapsack question and yet I cannot refrain from saying that I doubt if you have read the reports of line and medical officers which have been passing through the Adjutant General's Office to the Chief of Ordnance upon the merits of an equipment I have designed for infantry and artillery troops.

These reports are the results of actual trials made and witnessed, and express the opinions of more than twenty five companies of troops and their officers as well as a considerable number of medical officers upon its merits. . . . [T]he results have been universally in favor of my equipment. . . . I trust you may find time and be inclined to examine these reports. I fully believe that they will convince you, to use your own words, "that we are keeping pace with the times."

I have made my experiments at frontier stations with improvised materials and imperfect facilities for construction as they afforded, and consequently have labored under very great disadvantages. The results however are no less convincing; and those officers who like yourself, had become prejudiced against every form of knapsack, and in favor of the makeshift of our necessities during the war, have given me the strongest reports.[18]

Merriam wrote numerous letters to friends and important officers asking them to test his invention and then provide letters or comments in endorsements, which he regularly forwarded to the adjutant general of the army. The colonel had men under his command field test wearing the Merriam Pack under various conditions. He had printed brochures of testimonies of troops who had used the knapsack. He also arranged for the manufacture of model knapsacks. Since he was involved in what today might be called ergonomics, he particularly sought endorsements from medical personnel. Typical of what Merriam wanted and then used was the 1877 comments of the assistant surgeon at McPherson Barracks:

Many attempts have, heretofore, been made and have failed to design a knapsack, such as would obviate the objections, existing against those now in use. These objections are: that the pack causes an irksome pressure against the back, and that the straps, necessary to secure the knapsack in position, exert a constriction pressure upon the shoulders and breast. Indeed, these objections not only make the existing knapsack a source of discomfort and fatigue to the wearer, but that the knapsack has an injurious influence upon the health of the soldier by reason of its straps interfering with the circulation and respiration.

Having carefully examined your knapsack, I think that a thorough practical test will show that it obviates these objections.[19]

Most important to Merriam's efforts to get the army to adopt his knapsack was obtaining an official test of his pack. He had conducted many evaluations on his own and had been successful in having other commanders voluntarily use and report on the knapsack. Still, he needed to convince the army's senior leaders. On February 3, 1886, he again wrote to the adjutant general in Washington: "After years of study and experiment I have completed equipment for foot troops designed to take the place of the present blanket bag and haversack. It is supported upon a new principle and to be carried with less discomfort than any arrangement heretofore used in this country or elsewhere." Merriam then disclosed that during his previous leave, he had arranged the manufacture, at his own expense, of "one hundred samples of the equipment for general distribution among the dismounted troops of the army for trial against any other known method of carrying the supplies necessary for a soldier to have on his person in campaign." He enclosed a circular on the knapsack and offered to deliver the Merriam Pack wherever the army wanted.[20]

On February 11, 1886, Merriam received a reply, stating: "Referring to your letter of the 3rd instant enclosing a circular of a new equipment for foot troops invented by yourself and designed to take the place of the present clothing bag and haversack, I am instructed by the Lieutenant General Commanding the Army to request you to send the one hundred samples of this equipment." Perhaps Merriam believed this was the long-sought breakthrough. In April he sent the one hundred samples of his knapsack and at the same time requested a "competitive" trial at Fort Leavenworth. His request triggered an unexpected negative reaction by the army commander: "I am directed by the Lieutenant General Commanding the Army to inform you that the equipment will be tested by the Commanding Officer at Fort Leavenworth at such times as he in his discretion deems most opportune." Then followed a stinging rebuke. "I am also directed to say that you have not the right to make demand or choose the time or place for trial of your inventions, and that your communication not only betrays impatience, but assumes privilege which does not belong to you."[21] Once again Merriam's aggressiveness and persistence had resulted in a serious career wound. He would diplomatically back off but remain undaunted in his promotion of the Merriam Pack.

The colonel's problems in securing US Army adoption of his knapsack stemmed from a number of factors and a series of events. First, in the years immediately following the Civil War, the army had "over half a million double-bag knapsacks on hand," and this surplus negated contracting for new items. But this roadblock eased somewhat in 1870, when Quartermaster General Montgomery Meigs announced that the old surplus had been ruined and thus more knapsacks and haversacks had to be procured. Second, General Sherman had favored a British "brace system" pack when shown samples of knapsacks being considered by an evaluation board, which prejudiced decision making on the issue for sometime.[22] Third, Merriam's design was relatively complex due to having several parts, particularly the sticks, which caused some concern about troops losing these key components during a campaign. Fourth, Merriam had contracted for the manufacture of his pack by T. B. Peddie and Company of Newark, New Jersey, and some difficulties developed with the quality of materials. Later he would get squeezed by the manufacturer wanting to charge more than the army wanted to pay, particularly after some upgrades were made. Perhaps most significant, though, was that troops traditionally preferred no knapsack at all, and during the long marches in the West during the Indian Wars, they turned to using only a blanket roll slung across the body. Thus, despite Merriam's great efforts in getting endorsements regarding his pack, often repeated year after year, there was considerable built-in resistance of some units and of some leadership in accepting a new knapsack.

Merriam began to experience problems as well with the foreign marketing of his backpack. European sales looked most promising at first. Through contacts with US legations and embassies, he became aware that a number of European countries were considering new military equipment for infantry. He hired a firm in Paris, Brandon & Ses Fils, to obtain patents in London, Paris, Berlin, and Vienna. The colonel also established contacts in various capitals to help arrange interviews with European military personnel and then provided them samples of his Merriam Pack. Before Merriam left for Europe in 1887, there had been a steady stream of correspondence to Fort Laramie from individuals on the Continent whom he had engaged to help with contacts and sales. Early on, the correspondence and the information were encouraging. Typical was a 1887 letter from the US chargé d'affaires, Legation of the United States, in Madrid: "The sample of military knapsack mentioned by you was duly received. At the time of its receipt the Minister of War was absent on account of his health. . . . The knapsack has lately been delivered to him and he informs me that he will give immediate orders for its examination." But then difficulties and disappointments began to surface. While Merriam was in Paris, the French director of infantry informed him that their knapsack evaluation had determined that his invention was "ingenious" and possessed all the various advantages enumerated in the press articles; Merriam had appended newspaper comments and circulars to his sample backpack. Then came the sad news: "I cannot, nevertheless, to my great regret, make use of it in our army. The limited resources at our disposal make it absolutely necessary for us to use the established equipments for our numerous armies."[23]

After a demonstration of his knapsack for German authorities in Berlin, Merriam discovered that one Andreas Sohner of that city had filed for a patent based on the colonel's design. This resulted in Merriam having to file lengthy records of opposition to Sohner's application. Sohner had even filed an application for his patent in London, so the battle continued there. In Vienna, Merriam became embroiled in some European intrigue wherein he procured the services of an American dentist, Dr. E. M. Thomas, supposedly a professional acquainted with the "Imperial Family." The colonel agreed to give Thomas half of all royalties for his help in introducing him and his pack to the Austrian Army. Merriam's knapsack was shown and discussed with a manufacturer of such equipment in Vienna. Subsequent to his departure from the Austrian capital on May 25, 1887, Merriam received messages of encouragement, but then months after returning to Fort Laramie, he learned from Dr. Thomas "that although the Austrian Government highly approved of your invention, they on hearing the price demanded by you, thought it proper not to further weigh the question." Merriam never again received replies from Thomas to his letters. In 1889 Merriam remarked, "I learned of the adoption of the present Austrian Infantry Knapsack, and I saw at once from its description, as given in the newspapers, that it was only a modification of my invention—that it follows out the exact principles covered in my patents."[24] For the most part, Merriam's efforts to sell his knapsack to foreign armies had been thwarted. Also, it had been a very costly enterprise, judging from invoices forwarded from various foreign agents.

Merriam's return to Fort Laramie, after what he surely considered a disappointing trip abroad, turned even more discouraging and serious. Some of his officers at Fort Laramie had sent word that Una was gravely ill and that he should return at once. Not only was there concern for her condition, but there was also a worry about the attending physician's treatment. Una had developed a severe case of bronchitis that went on for some time and, even with the army doctor's care, seemed to get steadily worse. Upon the colonel's arrival, he dismissed the doctor and undertook treating Una himself. Before long, she regained her strength and health but, from that time forward, would be especially susceptible to recurrent bouts of bronchitis.[25]

In the spring of 1888, Una and Henry welcomed the birth of Katherine Maude, their fifth and last child, on April 29.[26] This meant the commanding officer's quarters at Fort Laramie would continue to be a lively place. As for the rest of the growing children, the fort and the surrounding area would continue to be their playground.

During this time at Fort Laramie, the Merriams had as a house guest the colonel's niece, Katherine Boyd, daughter of his oldest sister. She and Una became very close during her stay, and their fond association continued long afterward.

An epidemic of typhoid fever struck Fort Laramie in 1887, becoming one of Merriam's biggest challenges while he was post commander. The post surgeon reported in October that the epidemic was abating and that he had made a thorough sanitary inspection of all the post. He recommended, "During the present warm weather all privies at this post should be disinfected about once every two weeks, particular care being given to the sinks of the quarters in which cases of typhoid fever had existed." He also recommended "adoption of the earth closet system" and new sinks, declaring that "the grounds of this station having been poisoned for years by the objectionable system of privies" meant that "[t]he importance thereof of destroying this poison by disinfection or of rendering it incapable of development need not be enlarged on." Merriam endorsed the report and forwarded it to department headquarters but brought up the lack of permanency of the fort, he added, "It is also noted that any change of system now made would not remove the poisons already deposited in the site during the forty years of occupancy." In November the surgeon reported that "two new cases of typhoid fever appeared in the children of the garrison" and that the number of cases had totaled fifty-four, with one death. Thus the epidemic had continued despite carrying out the prescribed disinfections.[27]

The post surgeon suspected that the fort wells might have been contaminated and he asked for analysis of the well water, which came back negative. Despite this finding, he called for the digging of a new well in March 1888. This presented a dilemma for Merriam as he questioned the expense of a new well without "verified" contamination. In April 1888, after the quiet of the winter months, typhoid fever reappeared. Again the post surgeon forcefully called for a change in the fort's water supply and "system of sewage and water closets." A long series of letters and reports, with endorsements, ensued up and down the chain of command. Merriam, displaying unusual hesitancy in directly attacking the problem, believed that the new cases had developed from the hospital, so he concentrated his corrective actions there. Two enlisted men died on May 2 and 3. Throughout the summer, burning of refuse and care of sewage and sinks seemed to ease the epidemic. Later in the year, despite misgivings about the cost, the Department of the Platte authorized a new well. It was completed in November 1888 but was dug only about forty-five yards from the old one.[28]

On December 23, 1888, Merriam submitted the following information to the assistant adjutant general: "The work of removal of contents of old privy vaults and sinks directed in your letter of December 18th will begin tomorrow and weekly reports of progress will be rendered until the work is completed. Action would have been taken earlier under the suggestion contained in your letter of June 11, 1888, except for the advice of the Post Surgeon against attempting such work in warm weather. Yellow fever was developed by similar excavations at Jackson, Miss. during the current season according to the reports. The temperature has remained exceptionally warm at this Post for the season to date."[29] Several more cases of typhoid fever occurred up to the time Fort Laramie closed, but the actions taken forestalled another epidemic. Cases of scarlet fever, mumps, and whooping cough, involving the entire post population, also concerned Merriam and the post surgeon.

In the same December letter regarding the typhoid fever corrective actions, Merriam returned to his other major headache, the questionable future of Fort Laramie and its consequences on facilities and budget.

With regard to the language quoted from my endorsement of December 13, vis "the post should be rebuilt or promptly abandoned" it seems to me a sufficient explanation is found in the actual condition of most of the buildings at this Post, when considered in connection with the failure from year to year on the part of government to supply funds for their repair or reconstruction. In 1886, plans and estimates were made for new buildings to replace such as were deemed unfit to repair on the basis of a permanent six company post, as contemplated in the annual report of General Sherman for 1882. No action was taken. In the meantime railroad construction has reversed the problem of the region, giving permanency to Fort Robinson and Fort Niobrara, which were listed by Genl. Sherman as temporary posts to which situation the government has responded by ample funds for building up those posts, while almost nothing has been given this post for the extensive repairs needed. The logic of these events points irresistibly to the conclusion that the occupancy of this post is but temporary and argues against considerable expenditures of labor or money, beyond the actual and immediate requirement of the garrison.[30]

After noting Merriam's concerns and problems with fort administration, it would be a mistake to assume that military training and operations were pushed aside and ignored. In both 1888 and 1889, "camps of instruction" were held during the late summer and early fall as directed by the commander of the Department of the Platte. In both years the 7th Infantry marched to the encampments. In 1888 the camp of instruction was held at Old Fort Casper, Wyoming, a distance of approximately 225 miles from Fort Laramie. Preparations for such troop deployments would take months. For example, on March 14, 1888, Merriam wrote to headquarters asking five very specific questions about the movement, ranging from a discussion about shoes to "entrenching tools." In his typical mastery of detail, the colonel outlined the weight of items that he thought must accompany the troops, such as "3 axes, 3 spades 2 pick axes = 90 lbs." He then estimated that the total weight of 5,460 pounds would exceed in weight the capacity of the six-mule team to be furnished each company. To Merriam, such a detail of preparation had to be resolved.[31]

After the late-summer march from Fort Laramie, a camp of instruction was established "on the south bank of the North Platte River" near Casper on September 1, 1888. Companies B, C, D, E, and F, 7th Infantry, plus field staff, band, and the assistant surgeon deployed to the camp, joining units from other posts in the Department of the Platte. Individual organizations were responsible for conducting most of their own training. In the case of the Fort Laramie contingent, Merriam reported: "The schools for non-commissioned officers and morning drills were put in charge of Lt. Col. A. [Andrew] S. Burt, 7th Infantry, who prescribed the daily lessons in such a way as to have the drill an illustration of the lessons recited on the previous afternoon. In this way the entire school of the company and skirmishing, was covered in two weeks." Company schools covered outpost duty and field fortifications. Burt also conducted the NCO School of the Battalion, and Merriam held officer recitations, with emphasis on army regulations related to troops in campaign, guard duty, convoys, and School of the Battalion tactics and skirmishing. He later commented, "The recitations . . . were thorough and appeared to be well understood."[32] The camp of instruction also involved several organizations in some practical exercises in handling wounded, outpost duty, reconnaissance, signal instruction, and convoys. Units assigned to attacking and protecting convoys were judged as to effectiveness.

At the conclusion of the 1888 camp, the regiment arrived back at Fort Laramie on October 5. Merriam soon after filed a detailed, five-page report providing his observations and recommendations. Overall, he had positive views about what was accomplished and saw value in bringing together large numbers of soldiers.

> That the assembling of troops in large camps for instruction can be made of great practical benefit to the troops there can be no doubt. The long marches, and the drill of larger numbers together gives a freedom and "swing" to their movements under arms which cannot be obtained in ordering drill in garrison. The men move with the confidence of veterans, which takes Companies and Battalions from point to point in these maneuvers with promptness and precision. The assembling of officers and troops from different posts tends to bring into contrast the different methods pursued in different commands and the comparison and discussion naturally brings to notice and eliminates errors which would otherwise remain undiscovered.[33]

Merriam, however, with his consuming interest in discipline and his sharp eye on individual soldier equipment, expressed mild criticism about unit differences in troop accouterments, such as the "Blanket Bag." He contended that soldiers see one unit using equipment a certain way or of a certain kind while another employs wagons, and they wonder why their unit does not do the same. He considered this lack of standardization as prejudicial to good discipline. Merriam wrote: "Soldiers like other men, are reasoning beings, and when they are made uncomfortable without good reason, or a reasonable excuse, they are conscious of it, and cannot avoid a mental condition which is entirely inconsistent with discipline." Therefore he recommended that army regulations should spell out in exact detail "what soldiers shall wear and what they shall carry, and how, whether on their persons or in wagons."[34]

Merriam also expressed concern about the utilization of railroads and supply wagon trains and their effect on maneuvers. He recommended "that the marches be conducted as far as possible away from lines of railroads, the troops and wagon trains moving separately from point to point, the meeting points being not less than three days apart in order that the marches may be made somewhat similar to field maneuvers in actual war." Merriam no doubt appreciated the logistical benefits of the railroad and the wagon train, but he apparently worried that there was too much reliance on them to the detriment of battle tactics. The colonel wanted to "mimic war" in these maneuvers. He concluded his recommendations by stating that they were based on the theory "that in actual war large armies cannot have wagon trains in the immediate presence of the troops, when maneuvering against each other, even in the most favorable country, and that the period for which the battalion must be made self supporting will have to cover the time necessary for getting into positions, fighting a battle, and at least one day for pursuit or retreat. This period cannot be less than three days and would oftener extend to five days or more."[35]

In 1889 a similar encampment was ordered, and again the 7th Infantry participated. The site this time was Fort Robinson, Nebraska, in the northwestern part of the state. Practically all the troops of the Department of the Platte were involved, with the department commander, Brig. Gen. John R. Brooke, overseeing this camp of instruction. Besides six companies of the 7th Infantry, the 2nd, 8th, 16th, 17th, and 21st Infantry Regiments and the 9th Cavalry Regiment, with its black troops and white officers, were assembled. Although the regiments at this time were mostly understrength, the total number of men present was one of the largest deployed in one area since the Civil War. The end of the Indian Wars and the redefinition of the frontier meant a change in operations, and this camp was intended to once again address the need for practice in maneuvering large military forces.

General Brooke and most of the regimental commanders, like Merriam, had served in the Civil War. Since that conflict, they had spent many years in small operations against Indians and had become deeply absorbed in the details of commanding posts. One astute observer, a young second lieutenant, a participant at the time, commented: "Owing to these special conditions it came about that officers were rated not so much on their capacity as military tacticians and students as upon their ability to display to inspectors a smartly conducted review of the troops of the garrison and a well administered, clean looking post. Post administration had become the important thing and to that extent military standards had become perverted."[36]

This camp of instruction succeeded in reinstituting training in maneuvering large contingents of troops. Merriam must have welcomed this experience, but he did not file an extensive report as he had in the summer of 1888. It remained for another to report pertinent observations.

In attempting to direct the field exercises, under assumed war conditions, of a large body of troops composed of the three mobile arms of the service, these Civil War men were confronted with a somewhat new problem. Having served for many years at small widely separated stations, they had not been required or even encouraged to keep up with the developments in the science of war and it was not to be expected that a set of maneuvers conducted by them would be up to date. Naturally they fell back on their own early experience so that the ideas put into practice, the formations and the tactics used were much like those of the Civil War. Lacking a body of competent umpires, no reviews of the different exercises were undertaken for the purpose of pointing out mistakes and errors of judgment and each one of the participants was left to judge for himself. General Brooke, as the senior officer, was in position to see about everything that took place, but I never heard that he uttered a word either in the way of criticism or commendation.[37]

Did this criticism of former Civil War commanders having grown stale in their military science and thus falling behind the times apply to Colonel Merriam? Certainly the 1888 and 1889 camps of instruction had provided Merriam's first experience in large troop maneuvers in several decades. There were indications, however, that he was aware of changes in warfare and factors affecting combat. As previously noted, he saw railroads as an increasingly important element in the deployment of troops and the location of army posts. Interestingly, in his 1888 report he nevertheless warned of too great a reliance on trains in a campaign. Also, in his 1889 annual report from Fort Laramie, he revealed some points that he had observed about military developments in Europe:

> The equipment of our troops is in many respects faulty and incomplete to an extent, which in the aggregate must be admitted to unfit our Army for war with a civilized enemy. We have no standard or effective entrenching tools[,] an article conceded to be as essential to modern war as the rifle itself. Even our rifles and carbines, so reliable in their day, are fast becoming obsolete, in view of the great improvements being introduced into foreign armies. The times demand that all armies of civilized nations be furnished with magazine rifles of the smallest effective caliber. And that every item of the soldiers armament equipment and supply be reduced to the lightest weight and most comfortable adjustment to the end that his endurance may meet the vastly increased mobility demanded by the rapid firing and long range of modern arms. In all of these points we are far behind our neighbors across the Atlantic.[38]

These Merriam comments obviously reflected his interests in firearms and soldier equipment, but they likewise showed his cognizance of foreign developments. He demonstrated once again that he could couple his interests, awareness, and experience into a vision.

Besides the summer encampments, Merriam focused on drill and handling firearms during the Fort Laramie winter months. "The drill of the troops is exceptionally good and their skill in the use of their rifles is believed to be equal to any in service notwithstanding the large percentage of recruits joining shortly before the practice season," Merriam reported. He also claimed that "[d]iscipline and instruction of command are good in all respects," with schools for officers and noncommissioned officers addressing "tactics, guard duty, [and] target practice." Officers, the colonel stated, were required to give "at least one original lecture."[39]

As Merriam prepared this report for department headquarters in August 1889, he also described a sweeping change already begun. "On May 1st, 1889, Co. 'D' & 'F' 7th Infantry marched from this Post changing station to Fort Logan, Colorado, under Genl. Order No. 4 c.s. Hdqrs. Division of the Missouri." Fort Laramie would be closed. Far from being sad, Merriam wrote, "I renew my recommendation that this post be abandoned at the earliest possible date in the interest of economy and the morale of the garrison."[40] He now faced a relatively different task, closing a fort rather than establishing and building one. Also, he would be confronted with a divided command, with part of his regiment at Fort Logan and part at Fort Laramie.

Despite the movement of two 7th Infantry companies to Fort Logan in late spring, Colonel Merriam and the remainder of the regiment remained at Fort Laramie until October 1889. Since Fort Logan, near Denver, was under construction as a totally new fort, there was uncertainty as to when barracks construction would be completed to house the rest of the 7th's companies. Merriam had a report from Fort Logan that quarters might be completed by December 1, 1889. The colonel, however, telegraphed Department of the Platte headquarters on October 14, explaining: "As the matter stands, I think it best to take no action until I reach Fort Logan myself and examine the situation. We shall move to Bordeaux so as to take train for destination on the 19th inst."[41] Thus, Merriam and his family left Fort Laramie in mid-October 1889.

With the departure of the colonel and the regimental staff, Capt. Levi F. Burnett was left in command of the post. He reported to headquarters on December 14 that he had heard "unofficially" that the barracks for Companies C and E would be completed by December 20. When these companies departed, it would leave Captain Burnett, the post surgeon, and Lt. George W. McIver, acting as a quartermaster, as the only officers at Fort Laramie. In the process of shutting down the fort, Burnett requested that a detachment be sent to help with shipping property to the other forts. McIver would end up as the last officer at Fort Laramie, responsible for this disposal of property, which would not be completed until April 1890.

McIver, who would eventually retire as a brigadier general, had been assigned to the 7th Infantry in 1887 and thus served under Merriam for several years at Fort Laramie. Decades later he provided one of the rare written assessments of the colonel by a subordinate:

Col. and Mrs. Henry C. Merriam and family at Fort Laramie, 1888.
Courtesy Friends of Historic Fort Logan.

Colonel Merriam had a sense of justice and fairness and was never harsh in his dealings with either officers or enlisted men. As a matter of fact he was often very lenient. In the course of his service of more then ten years with the 7th Infantry only one officer was ever tried by Courts Martial. He was a very temperate man and his example in this respect had a very good influence on others. Having a wife and five children everyone admired his attitude towards them which was that of a kind and generous husband and father. He was an excellent post commander. Without the imposition of harsh and exacting rules, good order and good discipline prevailed in all the garrisons that he commanded. While close attention was given to the details of post administration, he never allowed anyone to forget that the purely military side of life in a garrison was of the first importance. He paid great attention to close order drills and formal parades and was himself a very good drill master. Under his direction the regiment became very proficient and officers and men came to have a great pride in making a good appearance. Like many other men who had served in the Civil War, his attitude towards drill and training was influenced by the impressions gained in that war. He could not see that the adoption of breech loading arms involved changes in the formations and tactics of infantry. For that reason he never took much interest in extended order drills and in minor tactics, so to a certain degree his regiment lacked training. He was, however, very modern in the matter of target practice in which he took a great interest.[42]

McIver also added that at that time he considered Merriam to be a relatively young colonel and an "active" and "vigorous" man in contrast to other officers, who had served many years and yet were still junior officers.

While Colonel Merriam seemed anxious to terminate his time at Fort Laramie, that apparently was not the case with his family. Una and the children all looked back fondly on their years at the old fort. As McIver remembered of that period: "I found the social life of the post very pleasant. There were more people to associate with than I had known before and the number was increased by occasional visitors." Even the isolation of Fort Laramie contributed, in some respects, to more togetherness among the garrison and residents. "Lacking the distractions of a nearby town, the people were inclined to depend on each other for amusement and recreation and a social atmosphere prevailed there I had never seen before and have never seen since." When the day came in October 1889 to leave Fort Laramie and journey to the railhead at Bordeaux, the children of the fort decided to keep an attachment to the post as long as possible. During the weeks of preparation for the move, they had collected all the pieces of string they could find, and after it was rolled into a ball, they fastened one end to a point of the fort and let it unwind as the wagons rolled on.[43]

9

X∿∿∿X

Fort Logan, Colorado

*With great satisfaction the Regimental Commander informs the
officers and enlisted men of his regiment that their instruction,
soldierly bearing, and appearance in the review and maneuvers
yesterday before the Lieutenant General of the Army received the
highest commendation of that officer and members of his staff.*

HENRY C. MERRIAM, JUNE 4, 1895

he Merriam family's move from Fort Laramie to Fort Logan, near Denver, Colorado, in October 1889 was one part of a three-part operation in the transfer of the 7th Infantry. The first elements of the regiment, Companies D and F, under the command of Capt. Constant Williams, departed Fort Laramie on May 1, marching more than two hundred miles to their new post. Colonel Merriam received word from a friend at Fort Logan: "Your two companies now en-route are expected here tomorrow evening [May 16], roads are muddy but weather fine." The same letter provided other important information for Merriam: "the 18th will never form any part of our permanent garrison, . . . indications point to your regiment coming as fast as quarters are provided." Reference was being made to two companies of the 18th Infantry that were already in place assisting in the planning and constructing of Fort Logan.[1]

The second part of the transfer operation involved relocating Colonel Merriam, regimental staff, medical personnel, regimental band, and officers' and noncommissioned officers' wives and families. This group had a much-easier travel, with the boarding of a train at the railhead at Bordeaux, thence to Cheyenne, and finally to Denver. Their autumn departure from Fort Laramie on October 19, 1889, many months after the first companies had transferred, likely stemmed from Merriam's growing concern about the approach of winter. Further delay in moving the staff and the families might put them amid hazardous weather. It appears that he would have preferred to have moved the remaining 7th Infantry companies, C and E, at this same time, but questions about the availability of quarters for those troops had not been resolved. Merriam reported to department headquarters on October 14, "My information from Capt. Campbell, A.Q.M. in charge of the construction at Fort Logan is to the effect that Quarters will be completed for those Companies by December 1st." The colonel believed that Companies C and E could then follow as "it would not be too late to move them in my judgment." Merriam told his commander that he would arrive at Fort Logan, assess the situation, and then report his recommendations.[2]

Companies C and E, 7th Infantry, still at Fort Laramie under the command of Captain Burnett, constituted the final portion of the regimental transfer operation. Burnett reported on December 11 that he had heard unofficially that quarters for the companies would be completed about December 20 and anticipated that an order to move might come at any moment. If one did not, he warned, "there are sufficient subsistence stores on hand at the post to supply the present garrison until January 10th." He requested authority to "obtain rations from Fort D. A. Russell" if the companies had to remain at Fort Laramie.[3]

Captain Burnett, Lieutenant McIver, and Companies C and E ended up spending a most lonely winter of 1889–90 at Fort Laramie. It was not clear whether this was a result of quarters not being ready at Fort Logan or a reluctance to order a midwinter movement. Perhaps both came into play. Not until the end of February 1890 did the remaining 7th Infantry units receive orders to travel to Fort Logan. On February 24 Captain Burnett wrote to the Union Pacific Railroad superintendent in Cheyenne stating that one officer and fifty-seven enlisted men expected to be able to leave Bordeaux on March 4, for which he requested arrangements of "two Immigrant Sleeping Cars and one Baggage Car." He further wanted to have those railcars "go with the regular passenger train to Cheyenne and have an engine ready there upon our arrival to take our cars right through to Denver and Fort Logan, and thus avoid delay and trouble at Cheyenne."[4]

While the regiment was at last coming together at Fort Logan, Lieutenant McIver was left to complete the disposal of army property and the shuttering of Fort Laramie. Some equipment, animals, and supplies were shipped to other regional posts, while some items were sold to the public. In December 1889, for example, Captain Burnett informed headquarters that "wire and insulators belonging to the telegraph line between this post and Bordeaux, Wyoming, was sold . . . at public auction for the sum of thirteen dollars and fifty cents." McIver and ten enlisted men worked on the fort's abandonment until early April 1890, then they too went to Fort Logan. McIver commented that his lonely isolation and the monotony of his work (packing, invoicing, and shipping) were broken only by his enjoyment of conversing with the old post trader, John Hunton. With a sense of the long history of Fort Laramie, McIver sadly concluded his last writing, saying the ending "somehow lacks the glamour and the romance associated with the more distant years."[5]

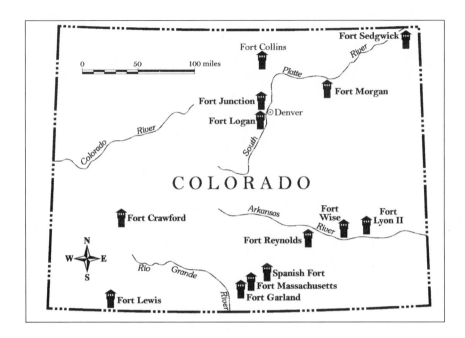

The 7th Infantry, under the command of Colonel Merriam, was now totally based at the new Fort Logan, some nine miles southwest of downtown Denver. Sensing that the US Army was in the process of closing many old historic frontier forts scattered throughout the West, some chamber of commerce men in Denver had vigorously campaigned to establish an army fort near their city. They promoted Denver's rail connections and its strategic location with respect to various Plains Indian tribes, the growing mining interests, and the rapid urban development in the region. Perhaps they were aware that these promotional themes coincided with some of the thinking about future deployment of forts and units by the army's senior leadership. The businessmen succeeded in getting Sen. Henry M. Teller to introduce legislation to authorize a fort. Congress approved the measure, and Pres. Grover Cleveland signed the authorization bill in February 1887. Denver entrepreneurs and other civic-minded men thereupon secured donations to purchase as many as 640 acres, which were then to be deeded by the state to the army.

Famed Civil War general Philip Sheridan came to Denver to review the proposed eleven sites for the fort in March 1887. Sheridan chose a sagebrush-covered, relatively flat ranchland near water from Bear Creek (to the north) and the South Platte River (to the east) and close by railroads. He thought it wise to locate the post nine miles from Denver's downtown, with troop behavior in mind. The general's choice was purchased, and the first soldiers from Kansas garrisons, largely the 18th Infantry, arrived in October. After first camping on a nearby ranch, they moved to the site, first called the "Camp near the City of Denver," on October 31, 1887, marking the beginning of what would later become Fort Logan.[6]

Commanding officer's quarters at Fort Logan, Colorado, 1891.
Courtesy Friends of Historic Fort Logan.

All during 1888 and into very late 1889, when Merriam arrived, the fort construction went on at a furious pace. In 1888 the Denver and Rio Grande Railroad built a spur line to the fort site. Workers were recruited from eastern states and were augmented by army labor. This new, more-urban western fort included architect-designed brick buildings artfully looped around a spacious parade ground. It was designed as a large fort, with ten barracks for six companies of infantry and four companies of cavalry. The buildings looked luxurious and gave an air of permanency that the Merriams had not seen in a very long time. Imagine what the colonel felt at seeing, and then using, all-new modern facilities after contending with the "crumbling," deteriorating buildings at Fort Laramie.

The Merriam family, Una, Carry (now fourteen), Henry (twelve), Cyrus (ten), Charles (four), and Maude (the baby), were unable to move into the large commanding officer's quarters as it was still under construction. They instead initially went into "another new and comfortable dwelling," which was probably one of the two field-officer houses flanking the commander's house. Niece Katherine Boyd had moved with them from Fort Laramie and in all respects was a member of the family. Despite the ongoing construction, preparation of sidewalks and roads, and the planting of trees and grass, the Merriams were soon settled. Numerous trips were made into Denver to obtain furnishings and for clothing for the growing children. Schools also had to be found. They decided to send daughter Carry back east to school. Una accompanied her to New

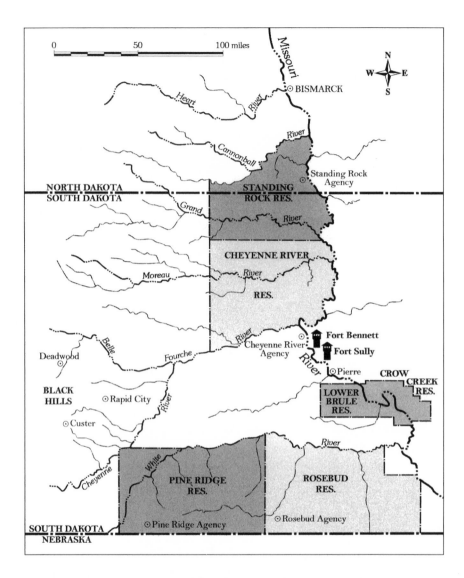

York, where she was enrolled in St. Catherine's Hall, a girls school. There she could be under the watchful eye of Una's sister, Mrs. Robert Lynch.[7]

In 1890 Colonel Merriam faced many problems regarding the completion of Fort Logan's construction. He likewise had a myriad of details to consider in getting his regiment accustomed to the new barracks buildings and other facilities. However demanding this was, nevertheless, it did not take long for the colonel to establish his noted drill proficiency. Because of the fort's proximity to Denver, Merriam made a point of cultivating ties with the city's civic, social, and business leaders. These people were invited to the fort for receptions and dancing, to observe drill and parades, and to listen to regimental-band concerts. The colonel, Una, and the children began to form important and lasting friendships in the Denver area.[8]

In December 1890 Merriam and the 7th Infantry received orders to board trains for South Dakota. Some of the Teton Sioux leadership in that state had embraced a growing and spreading religious belief in an Indian Messiah, ghost-shirt invulnerability to white bullets, and associated spirited dancing with trance-like visions. Various Indian agents near the Sioux reservations became frightened by the Indian unrest and worrisome uncontrolled activity. This in turn generated fear and concern by settlers and politicians, leading to a call for troops for protection. There was a great fear that a general Sioux uprising or war would develop. Maj. Gen. George Crook, who had been in command of the area, had recently died of a heart attack, and Major General Miles had taken over command. Although Miles hoped for a diplomatic solution, mainly by keeping the Indians on their reservations and, if need be, disarming them, he also intended to display an overwhelming military force of more than five thousand troops.[9]

On December 11 Merriam received a "My dear Colonel" personal letter from General Miles while he was at Pierre, South Dakota. Miles addressed an interesting subject with Merriam: "At a time when matters looked very serious in the Sioux country, and looked as if an Indian war was inevitable, I suggested the mounting of four Infantry regiments that I knew would do good service, in view of the fact that the Cavalry regiments had been consolidated and I understood were not to be filled up to their full strength. I do not know how you would like the idea of having your regiment mounted now under the circumstances, and I would like to hear from you on the subject." The general went on to say that this action might allow Merriam to hold his whole regiment together, being a "benefit to the regiment, and at the same time give you a good command." The colonel's reply seems to have been lost, but he was already in South Dakota, and apparently such a proposal could not be carried out as events began to unfold around the Sioux reservations.[10]

As part of the mobilizing of cavalry and infantry regiments at the South Dakota Sioux reservations, Merriam and six companies of the 7th Infantry left Denver by train on December 3. "Each soldier carried a blanket roll, haversack, canteen, and a big 'entrenchment' knife. In his belt were forty-four cartridges; on his shoulder was a forty-five caliber Springfield." The Fort Logan contingent arrived at the Missouri River near Fort Sully on December 7 and deployed south of the Sioux Cheyenne River Reservation near the confluence of the Cheyenne and Missouri Rivers. Merriam was directed to cross the Missouri and then proceed up the Cheyenne River. He was then expected to link up with troops of the 8th Cavalry and 3rd Infantry coming from the west.[11] All of this movement was part of Miles's strategy to completely box in the main Sioux tribal forces with US troops on all sides.

Chief Sitting Bull had been tragically killed on December 15 during an attempt to arrest him on the Standing Rock Reservation to the north. Merriam's regiment then had a new mission: to block the angry northern Sioux groups from moving south to link up with those at the Pine Ridge and

Colonel Merriam (seated, third from left) in South Dakota at the time of the Sioux Ghost Dance trouble in 1890. Courtesy National Archives.

Rosebud Reservations.[12] This action became even more important as there were reports that Big Foot and his Miniconjou band at the Cheyenne River Reservation were headed south. In fact Big Foot had escaped the troops poised to arrest him and had arrived at the valley of Wounded Knee Creek near the Pine Ridge Agency. This development would lead to the unintended clash on December 29 between Big Foot's group and the 7th Cavalry, under command of Col. James W. Forsyth, that became known as the infamous Wounded Knee Massacre.

Before the bloodshed at Wounded Knee, however, Merriam worked to deploy his regiment. A key factor was whether the troops and wagons could get across the swollen, icy, and in some places frozen Missouri River. The troops had made it to Fort Sully, South Dakota, where on December 16 Merriam received a telegram from Brig. Gen. Thomas H. Ruger, commander of the Department of Dakota:

> It has been the intention to direct that you proceed with your command across the Missouri River and to camp near the agency, this for the restraining effect the appearance of the force would have on the disaffected element of the Indians, and for any service that might be called for. The state of the river has been such, as reported, that

wagons could not be crossed on the ice, and order has not been given. It is desired that as great part of your command be crossed to Fort Bennett as may be practicable before the 22nd instant which is fixed for general issues to the Indians at the Agency. If it be not practicable to cross tentage but men may be by crossing on the ice or by boat, you may cross with some companies at least, provided proper clothing and ammunition, and temporary shelter my be had in the barracks there and by using all the available tentage.[13]

Merriam must have determined a river crossing could be made. On December 18 General Ruger sent the colonel further instructions. "I am glad to learn wagons and animals can be crossed." He went on to say, "Commanding Officers at Forts Sully and Bennett have been directed to obey your orders." Ruger stated that the 7th Infantry was "to stop the Sitting Bull fugitives or even young men at Cherry Creek from going to Pine Ridge." Also, Merriam was advised, "Have officers and others who know Cherry Creek Indians to go with you too and give them assurance that they will not be harmed if they stay quietly at home."[14] Thus Merriam was first to employ diplomacy, a course he always favored and in which he felt quite comfortable.

During the time Merriam was engaged in crossing the Missouri River and establishing camp at a place called Dupree's Ranch near the Cheyenne River, he asked Capt. J. H. Hurst, 12th Infantry, commanding Fort Bennett, not too far to the north, to contact the Cheyenne River Reservation Indians to calm them and keep them in place, thereby complying with Ruger's orders. Hurst sent Lt. Harry E. Hale on this mission on December 18. Hale found the Indian camps at Cheyenne City largely deserted, with many Indians having fled. On December 20, however, a party of forty-six Hunkpapa warriors arrived on scene, coming south from Sitting Bull's area. Hale believed that he could persuade this party to stay in place and possibly go to an agency, so he rushed back to inform Hurst of the situation. The captain, acting on his own, immediately returned with the lieutenant, accompanied by a sergeant and two interpreters, to council with the Indians. Hurst later filed a detailed report describing what ensued:

Believing that affairs at the Indian dancing camp at mouth of Cherry Creek, and at Big Foot's camp farther up the Cheyenne River, S.D., were assuming an alarming character, I ordered Lieut. Hale, 12th Infantry to proceed on the morning of December 18, 1890, rapidly to mouth of Cherry Creek and remain there or in that vicinity until further orders, observing, directing and reporting any movements that might occur. After promptly and frequently reporting the situation as he found it and the result of his observations he reported to me in person during the night of the 20th ultimo direct from Cherry Creek, that there were a large party of Sitting Bull's people just arrived on

Cherry Creek, many of them armed, but that he thought they could be induced to surrender and come into the Agency here.

At daylight next morning I started with him on his return to the Cherry Creek, accompanied by Sergeant Philip Gallagher, Co. "A" 12th Infantry, and two enlisted Indian Scouts who spoke English and acted as interpreters, for the purpose of disarming these Indians and bringing them into the post.

We arrived at mouth of Cherry Creek at 3:30 P.M. same day, distance from Bennett 52 miles. In a very brief interview with those Indians immediately upon my arrival, I told them what I had come to them for, and that as I was very tired and hungry, I would have a council with them after they had had a feast, for which I purchased two beeves and turned over to them.

Upon a hasty and close observation of these Indians, I believed I could induce them to come quietly into the post, and apparently paid no attention to them until they indicated that they were ready to talk, which they did about 8 P.M. At that hour I met their principal men and all in council, for which I had provided a liberal quantity of smoking tobacco. They told me that they had left Standing Rock Agency never to return; that their great chief and friend Sitting Bull had been killed without cause; and that they had come down to Cherry Creek to talk with their friends there and had found them suddenly gone, and that they had not yet fully decided upon their future course. I replied and said that I wanted them to believe and trust me, and that I wanted them to give up their arms to me that night and to return with me to Fort Bennett next morning, where they would be provided for and taken care of; that I could give them no promise as to their future disposition and could only assure them of present protection if they trusted me, but that if they chose to join Big Foot, who was only ten miles up the river, the result would be certain destruction of themselves and probably their families, and that I had nothing more to say to them.

They said they would soon tell me the result of their deliberations, and at mid-night they came in a body and delivered up to me all the guns they said they had, seventeen number, and twelve Winchester cartridges. I told them I was sure they were not acting honestly, and that they were not giving up all of their arms, but not being in a position to dictate measures, I quickly received such as they gave me— four guns were found secreted amongst their baggage on arrival at Bennett, making twenty-one guns taken from them.

Broke camp at daylight on the 22nd ultimo and camped that night at Dupree's Ranch, where we found Colonel Merriam's command also in camp.[15]

The encounter of Captain Hurst and Colonel Merriam at Dupree's Ranch may not have been all too friendly. Despite the fact that the captain had been successful in taking the Indians prisoner, there were indications that the colonel was not pleased that he had largely acted on his own initiative. Merriam ordered Hurst the next morning, the twenty-third, to "proceed immediately to Fort Bennett to resume command of the post, turning the Indians over to Lieut. Hale." According to Hurst, he appealed this order and asked to remain with the Indians, "for I feared the result of a sudden scare or panic among them, with Lieut. Hale absolutely alone." Merriam rejected the appeal and again ordered him to proceed to Fort Bennett. In his December 22 instructions to Hurst, Merriam had directed: "On arriving at Bennett I desire you to give all possible aid in obtaining teams and forwarding the remainder of the Infantry under Captain Sanno. If other teams are not available at once, the Agency teams should be used temporarily for that purpose instead of forwarding Indian prisoners, and for which there is now no need of haste."[16] Obviously, Merriam believed that with the Indians now prisoners, there was no urgency in getting them to Fort Bennett, and Captain Hurst would be more beneficial in aiding the movement of his regiment.

Merriam had received a telegram on December 21, 1890, from Department of Dakota headquarters, saying: "Action in respect to surrender of Sitting Bull Indians and securing their arms approved. The Big Foot people will not likely be difficult to attend to shortly."[17] Unfortunately, the command had misjudged the movement of Big Foot's followers, and they escaped containment to eventually arrive near the Pine Creek Agency for their fateful encounter at Wounded Knee.

On December 24 Lieutenant Hale and the Standing Rock Reservation Indians, augmented by some others, arrived at Fort Bennett, and the Indians "went immediately into camp by themselves on the river bottom below the post. The Cherry Creek Indians with them were allowed to go to the camp of their own people next day." The department commander ordered the Indians to move on to Fort Sully, where they arrived on December 30. The Fort Sully commander recorded 227 Indian military prisoners total: 81 men, 43 boys, 72 women, and 31 girls. Also with them were 148 ponies and four wagons.[18]

With the surrender of the Sitting Bull Indians and others, Merriam naturally believed that he had accomplished his mission. He was no doubt pleased with his role in a peaceable resolution of the difficulties with this part of the Sioux tribe. The colonel received favorable press too, with the *Denver Republican* reporting a statement by him, "I succeeded in obtaining the surrender of about 300 of the Sitting Bull Indians whom I sent back to Fort Sully as prisoners of war." Unfortunately for Merriam, Captain Hurst became aware of this publicity, which triggered the captain's long, detailed report, covered earlier, to the Department of Dakota commander. The question of proper credit for the surrender of the Indians became an issue between Hurst and Merriam and involved General Ruger, the department commander. Ruger wrote to Merriam on February 26, 1891, stating that he had ordered an investigation of the facts associated with the surrender "so no lack of justice to any one shall obtain." Merriam in reply wrote a March 1 personal letter to the general defending his position as deserving credit because of his overall command of the area, though acknowledging that Captain Hurst and Lieutenant Hale deserved recognition for their roles.[19] In time the issue died, but some hard feeling lingered.

After the terrible clash at Wounded Knee on December 29, 1890, General Miles began tightening his cordon of troops around the remaining Sioux ghost-dance participants. He had approximately 3,500 soldiers in the immediate formidable ring, with another 2,000 that could be called upon. In the early days of January 1891, Miles began contracting the area of operations, with great care taken to prevent any of the Sioux from escaping to their stronghold region north of the White River. Colonel Merriam and the 7th Infantry manned the north and east portions of the constricting ring, along the lower part of the Cheyenne River.

While Merriam was in his position and awaiting further movement orders, he became involved in another incident, one potentially serious enough to foment more Indian hostilities. On January 11 two Oglala Indian families, Few Tails and his wife Clown and One Feather and his wife Red Owl, were returning from a successful hunt with game-loaded wagons. As they journeyed toward Pine Ridge, they were ambushed by three white men. Few Tails was killed and his wife wounded and left for dead, while One Feather, although wounded, bolted with his wagon, wife, and daughters and managed to elude the attackers. On January 24, nearly two weeks later, One Feather and family appeared at the Rosebud Agency.

In the meantime, word of the attack and the death of Few Tails had reached Merriam, Miles, and the Indians. The Sioux believed that the attack had been made by soldiers. Merriam acted promptly to investigate, sending Lt. F. C. Marshall to the scene of the ambush. Marshall collected evidence and interviewed three Culbertson brothers who had fired on the two Indian families. They claimed the Indians had stolen horses and had fired on them. The lieutenant, however, found evidence to indicate that the Culbertsons had conducted an ambush and had in truth murdered Few Tails. He reported his findings back to Merriam, who in turn forwarded the report to the department commander and to General Miles.

Despite the fact that the Sioux had surrendered to General Miles on January 15, news of the assault and the death of Few Tails had created great excitement in the Indian camps, and General Miles worked diligently to persuade the Sioux to remain calm. Fortunately, Merriam's report of the investigation arrived, establishing that the deed had been committed by the Culbertson brothers and not soldiers, decidedly helping General Miles in his persuasive efforts. Later, Maj. J. Ford Kent conducted another investigation confirming Marshall's and Merriam's reports.[20]

Merriam, the prolific letter writer, also sent letters to friends and Civil War associates in Maine about operations in South Dakota, some of which were given to newspapers for publication. Former Civil War general I. S. Bangs in Waterville, Maine, a frequent correspondent, wrote on January 1, 1891: "I received your very interesting letter dated 'In the field, near Fort Sully, So. Dakota, Dec. 12th.' I need not tell you that it was very interesting to me and to the public here, as I took advantage of your offer and had it published in our local paper." Bangs added, "It seems too bad, Colonel, to try to win glory out of such an inglorious war." In another letter back to Merriam in February, Bangs acknowledged Merriam's comments about the duties of soldiers. "It is the most unfortunate thing for Col. Forsyth to have been placed under a cloud in this way." He noted the difficulty of diplomacy with respect to the Indians, wherein "the purpose was to avoid the enemy rather than engage them," and concluded, "Diplomacy and war are difficult to harmonize, particularly when in the field in midst of savages."[21]

Colonel Merriam had a harsh assessment of what transpired at Wounded Knee. He wrote to a friend his thoughts on the matter:

> No part of my Regiment, thank God, was engaged in this questionable combat, and it is by belief that had "Big Foot" been let alone till my arrival at his village, he would have been induced to surrender and go peacefully to his own agency, without bloodshed. You have doubtless read of the terrible fight and butchery which resulted. It is claimed the troops were placed in a position around the Indians (expecting to receive their surrender) so that when the combat commenced, they could not fire without shooting into their own ranks and that many of the dead Cavalry men were killed by their own comrades. General Miles has relieved Col. Forsyth of his command and is investigating his conduct. The affair is much mixed, at best, and has done great mischief amongst the doubtful chiefs, swelling the force of actual hostiles from hundreds to thousands. . . ."Big Foot" had about 125 warriors and 300 women and children. I believe it is conceded that about 70 guns had been surrendered before the fighting began, if so there could not have been many guns left for the Indians to fight with. This may explain why tomahawks and knives were used. The friendly Indians, and some of our scouts and Indian Police, now claim that the attack was made by the troops after Indians had turned over their arms, and that the soldiers had killed and wounded their own comrades. This cannot be true of course, but it is simply deplorable that there can be any question in the matter. General Miles is a wise and judicious officer, and the country may rely on his doing justice to all concerned in the investigation now going on.[22]

Some of Merriam's Civil War colleagues were more protective of the army in their views. General Bangs, for example, wrote, "Poor Col. Forsyth seems to have been made a victim, though I do not think the public condemns him." He further remarked, "We shall always have a lot of short haired women and long haired men cranks who will find fault with anything."[23]

Merriam also had strong feelings about Indian agencies and the men who ran them. "There is much to say on this question of Indian Agents. This is a weak point in our Government of the Indians. The Agents are noted for two things—their inefficiency and dishonesty."[24] The colonel's experience in the Pacific Northwest, at Fort Laramie, and then in South Dakota easily prompted such criticism.

Most of the 7th Infantry Regiment wrapped up its South Dakota campaign against the Sioux and took trains back to Fort Logan, arriving in late January 1891. Two companies that had remained behind at Fort Sully to guard the Indian prisoners did not leave until February 6, arriving at Fort Logan on February 10 after having been snowbound in Julesburg, Colorado, for twenty-four hours. Despite the horrible battle at Wounded Knee, Merriam and the regiment considered their expedition a great success. They had prevented Sitting Bull Indians from moving to Pine Ridge, had brought them into camp at Fort Sully, and had disarmed them, all of this accomplished peacefully. In addition, the deployment of the Fort Logan garrison by railroad had seemingly confirmed the wisdom of the army's strategy of closing small, scattered, and inefficient western forts and consolidating regiments at urban-type posts. Noteworthy also, a campaign had been conducted in midwinter in an area known for winds, snow, and bitter cold. Although Merriam had not been in actual combat, he had actively participated in the "biggest military operation in the United States since the Civil War."[25] It also enhanced his favorable standing with General Miles.

The publicity about Merriam and the 7th Regiment's actions in the Sioux uprising produced community accolades. The colonel became a heroic Indian fighter, at least in the eyes of various veterans organizations. In February 1891 he was asked to speak at Denver's "Sherman Memorial Exercises" at the First Congregational Church. Later that year a veterans organization asked him to serve as grand marshal at Denver's Memorial Day Parade.[26]

During the time that the 7th Infantry had been deployed to deal with the South Dakota Indian troubles, the wives had to manage on their own at Fort Logan. Una invited a new bride of one officer to stay at their quarters. One night, with nerves on edge, they heard disturbing noises in the house. Believing that they might have a burglar, Una with a pistol, the bride with a broom, and a nurse with a can of cayenne pepper descended the stairway in the darkened house only to discover the suspicious sounds came from a new family dog that had been locked in the basement.[27]

On February 9, 1891, a big family celebration occurred with the wedding of niece Katherine Boyd to Lt. William S. Graves at Fort Logan. Lieutenant Graves was a handsome young officer, fresh from West Point, and had quickly become romantically attached to Boyd. After some months of being engaged and after the regiment's return from South Dakota, the marriage took place.

Rare photo of Colonel Merriam (at right) on a horse at Fort Logan, probably taken during his final parade ceremony there. Courtesy Friends of Historic Fort Logan.

Perhaps it reminded Una and Henry of their own similar meeting and wedding at Fort Brown in Texas. Graves became a trusted associate of Colonel Merriam and would eventually rise to the rank of major general. The young couple quickly learned what army life entailed as Graves, bride, and his company soon after left for temporary duty at Rock Springs, Wyoming.[28]

After the 7th Infantry's return to Fort Logan, a serious influenza epidemic developed. There was much anxiety and turmoil, and a number of soldiers died. Colonel Merriam, no doubt, worried that he might have to deal with something similar to the Fort Laramie typhoid outbreak. Una received letters "by the different Soldiers Organizations thanking her for her sympathy and assistance during these trying days."[29]

In the summer of 1891, the Merriams made a trip to New York, where they joined Carry and spent some family time together at a cottage owned by Una's sister Dora on Shelter Island off Long Island.

Merriam continued his abiding emphasis on drill and ceremony of his regiment. The inspector general of the Department of the Platte, Maj. J. M. Bacon, visited Fort Logan from September 28 to October 3, 1891. In his inspection report he complimented Colonel Merriam, noting the "zeal, ability, and attainments of the Commanding Officer." He also called him "very energetic and efficient."[30]

In the years 1891 and 1892, Merriam became very "energetic" on another matter. He was much concerned that the ranks of his superiors were thinning through deaths and retirements and that some of his contemporaries were being promoted to brigadier general even though he outranked them. Never bashful nor reticent, Merriam determined that he needed to campaign for his promotion to brigadier general. In 1891 he launched a blitz of personal letters to friends, colleagues, and politicians asking for their support and recommendations for his advancement. In general, he received a most favorable response. On November 19 Merriam obtained a personal letter of endorsement regarding his promotion from Washington senator John B. Allen, which was strengthened by a petition from leading citizens of eastern Washington, particularly from Spokane. Another personal letter came from Texas governor J. S. Hogg on December 2, 1891. Also in December he secured a letter of support from the Minnesota governor. Letters from Wyoming congressmen soon followed with endorsements. Merchants in Laredo and Nuevo Laredo petitioned in his support. On November 24, 1891, Colorado governor John Routt wrote to the president recommending Merriam's promotion to brigadier general. Merriam asked for letters to go to the army leadership, the War Department, and the president. On December 28 his brother Lewis, who was in Washington, DC, wrote about his efforts in the capital on behalf of his promotion. The colonel's letter-writing campaign would continue for several years, but he obviously was mining support based on his experience and time in all of the various regions in which he had served.

Merriam also solicited assistance from his home state of Maine. The governor of Maine, Edwin C. Burleigh, and the commander of the state's Grand Army of the Republic each promised to write to the president. Burleigh later said that the president had acknowledged his request and that it had been forwarded to the secretary of war for consideration. A Maine senator wrote to the state's Civil War generals, Bangs and Chamberlain, saying: "Yours of Dec. 12 received. I am doing what I can to procure the Brigadier Generalship for Col. Merriam."

Some of the correspondence flowing to Merriam at Fort Logan took note of the fact that he was not a West Point graduate and that this probably affected his advancement efforts negatively. There may have been other factors working against him as well. Sen. F. M. Cockrell wrote Merriam these sobering words: "Knowing the feelings of President Cleveland in regard to outside influence on Army matters, I have been loth [sic] to take any part in Army appointments."[31]

Merriam evidently believed that his promotion efforts would be successful. In a letter to Senator Cockrell on August 20, 1891, he mentioned, "I have the support of Major Generals Howard and Miles and the governors of several states," as indeed he did.[32] His optimism exceeded reality, however, and his goal would not be attained for several more years. But like his marketing of his backpack, Merriam did not give up. There might be a lull in the campaign, but more letters and more pressure on political individuals would follow.

Merriam, the entrepreneur-businessman, received several waves of bad news from Spokane, Washington. The first came on August 4, 1889, with word about a disastrous fire that destroyed a great part of the city. The flames "burned 30 square blocks," and "for months thereafter, disposed residents dined on greasy over-priced ham and egg fare in dirty canvas tents alongside the Spokane River." Merriam's brother living there, Dr. Cyrus K. Merriam, evidently was hit hard.

There was no fire insurance. It was not clear whether Colonel Merriam's property investments in Spokane had included buildings, therefore the exact amount of his loss remains undetermined. Merriam also received the sad news that his father had died at Spokane. Only a few years later, in 1893, Spokane badly suffered from the panic of that year and the ensuing depression. Merriam's brother Cyrus, in Spokane at the time, wrote: "Dear Bro. Henry: . . . times are dull here and we property owners are being pinched as well as the others. Rents have tumbled and if no relief is to come to us . . . many who thought themselves very comfortably well off will be beggars or tramps." Cyrus offered to sell him "lots 11 & 12 . . . where Leonard and family have lived past 3 years." The colonel must have declined this offer as Cyrus wrote later, "I don't blame you for not wanting to purchase any more unproductive property here—while the present depression exists. . . . [M]uch shrewder speculators than I claim to be got caught by the financial cyclone." Despite this gloom, in only a short time Spokane boosterism again held sway, and "Spokane residents boasted of relief from the financial depression sooner than other cities."[33]

Colorado and Denver, of course, were likewise plunged into the 1893 panic and resulting depression. Barely six months into the downturn, nationally there had been eight thousand business failures, four hundred bank closures (mostly in the West and South), and over 150 bankrupt companies (including the Northern Pacific Railroad, which Merriam had aided). In Denver ten banks failed, unemployment became widespread, real-estate values declined precipitously, and foreclosures soared.[34] The panic subsided in the late summer of 1893, but the depressed economic conditions lasted for four years. Merriam must have been thankful that he was in the US Army and enjoyed the stability of job and salary.

The years of 1892 and 1893 proved relatively quiet for the Merriam family. Because of their upbringing and background, Henry and Una put great emphasis on education in the family. Daughter Carry was moved to a school in Cincinnati, and oldest son Henry was sent to Lawrenceville, New Jersey. The younger children, attending local schools, received assistance in their studies by a lady who came from New York.[35]

In 1893 Carry, then eighteen, was "introduced" in Denver society, and there was entertaining both at the fort and in the city. Both Una and Henry were invited to speak to city groups. Una presented a paper on Michelangelo to the literary-social Fortnightly Club, and her husband spoke to civic associations. The colonel wrote articles and commentaries. One article, published in Washington, DC, entitled "The Essentials of Infantry Tactics," prompted this response: "Your views agree so closely to the 'tactics' which I am now proposing, that it gave me great assurance in my work." In addition, the colonel wrote to the army adjutant general presenting his views on the "evolution in firearms" and the bayonet. In a letter to General Ruger, he offered comments about revisions to drill regulations.[36]

Merriam again returned with great intensity to the promotion of his knapsack. He had been encouraged when the army looked to be moving to a major test of the Merriam Pack at Fort Leavenworth. In 1892 the colonel received a letter from the War Department Ordnance Office, saying, "an award has been made to T. B. Peddie & Co., of Newark, N.J., for the manufacture of 500 Merriam equipments at $2.65 each, exclusive of royalty, to be delivered at Rock Island Arsenal within six weeks." In October 1893 Merriam informed the chief of ordnance: "I was notified from your office that troops at Fort Leavenworth, Omaha, Sheridan, and Snelling had been instructed to make a thorough trial of the Merriam Pack and Dodge Yoke in competition with each other and the Blanket Bag, then the regular equipment, and 'to make a full report of the relative merits of each system with a view to definitely adopting one of these devices.'" Over two years later, he still did not know the results, or at least he let army headquarters know that he had not received some official word. Showing his frustration, Merriam wrote to the adjutant general in February 1896: "I should like to know what result was reached in the tests ordered. This information is desired for my personal guidance in determining whether further expense and labor on my part are justified in endeavoring to give to the service a satisfactory equipment."[37] The Fort Leavenworth tests were found inconclusive, thus depriving him of the favorable result he had confidently expected.

Merriam believed he might achieve a breakthrough by another channel. He had been communicating with officials in several National Guard units. In 1886 he actually made a demonstration of the benefits of his design for the Pennsylvania National Guard, getting good reviews but no adoption orders. On May 10, 1892, Merriam received the good news from New Jersey that "on the recommendation of the State Military Board the Merriam Pack has been adopted for the use of the National Guard of this State in place of the knapsack now in use." A subsequent letter, however, stated that New Jersey did not have funds to buy any. In the next year he succeeded in getting the New York National Guard to give the Merriam Pack some trials. Again the colonel was able to obtain favorable comment that he could use in his marketing, one report reading: "The 'Merriam Pack' supplied to my company prior to the late tour of duty in camp and worn by them from station to the Camp of Instruction . . . were satisfactory in every respect; members of the company being unanimously enthusiastic at the use and comfort which this form of pack when properly adjusted, gives each man."[38] There were some criticisms, however, about the manufacturing quality of packs furnished by Peddie and Company. In addition, the 1893 depression and the lack of state funding meant there would be no purchasing of new knapsacks.

In 1894 Merriam managed an assignment to New York to advise and assist the summer National Guard camp of instruction at Peekskill. At the camp's conclusion, he filed a long report of his observations to Washington. Not surprisingly, he was quoted in newspapers as recommending that "more attention should be paid to regimental and brigade drill." During this time in New York, he demonstrated the utilization of the Merriam Pack and used his influence to try to secure its adoption. Despite positive comments from a number of units that tried the pack, Merriam was unsuccessful in securing purchase orders. The depression hard times, with a scarcity of funding, worked against his efforts. There also remained resistance from many officers to knapsacks in general. At one point Merriam challenged remarks by Lt. Col. G. V. Henry of the New York Guard, who reported, "Some have 'Merriam Packs' but in actual service I believe the old blanket roll would be preferred." In defense of his remark in the face of Merriam's questioning, the National Guard officer simply replied, "I base my opinion against men carrying anything but a 'blanket roll' upon my seeing hundreds of knapsacks thrown away."[39]

Merriam kept being encouraged by support from some senior officers. For example, Major General Howard, then commanding the Department of the East in New York, commented to Merriam: "It is certainly a little to be wondered that we cannot somehow look into an invention from one of our own officers with impartiality and a little strange that other nations are more favorable to an invention of one our number than are we ourselves. . . . I have always liked your 'pack' better than any I have seen."[40] But the army's top general, John M. Schofield, did not share Howard's views. In addition, there were hints in the official correspondence of resentment that "one of their own" was asking for a royalty for his invention.

During this same time in the 1890s, Merriam carried on a lively correspondence with the manufacturer of his knapsack, T. B. Peddie and Company of New Jersey. Production delays had to be resolved, and improvement in the quality of materials posed a continuing headache. Disputes developed over the cost of substitute leather, webbing, and sewing. On August 30, 1893, Merriam did record receiving "[r]oyalty on 805 Knapsacks $1.00 = $805." Later, in 1895, he noted a check for $1,377 representing the royalty on Merriam Packs purchased by the State of New York for its National Guard trials. Merriam's royalty had dropped to fifty cents per knapsack, however.[41] Considering expenses, time, and energy devoted to his backpack promotional efforts, Merriam was not getting rich.

The colonel continued to have men of the 7th Infantry conduct trials of his knapsack, then arranged for reports to be printed into circulars. A typical printed pamphlet in 1895 told about troops of the 2nd Battalion on a practice march of 210 miles. All of the soldiers carried the Merriam Pack and made representative comments about its "serviceability." Still another report, concerning a march to and from Colorado Springs, told an interesting tale of two privates of the 1st Battalion who "requested . . . permission to carry the pack and full equipment to the summit of Pike's Peak": "Private Bean starting from the 'Iron Springs Hotel,' Manitou, made the summit of Pike's Peak in five hours and thirty minutes. Private Doescher consumed about one hour longer, he having made more frequent halts upon the road to rest." The company commander added, "I have no complaint to make neither did I hear any made."[42] Without a doubt, Merriam rejoiced at hearing or seeing such reports, and he skillfully used them whenever he could. Despite repeated setbacks, he never felt defeated in his promotional efforts and continued to battle for US Army adoption.

Early in 1894, Fort Logan troops became involved in the strange case of Denver's City Hall War. Colorado governor Davis H. Waite had created a governmental crisis when he sought to remove two of his own appointees to the Denver City Fire and Police Board. Although the governor appeared at first to demand removal of the two men because they were not responding to his wishes, he brought charges that they were officially protecting gaming interests. The men denied the charge and refused to resign, and with the sympathy and support of the county sheriff and his deputies, they barricaded themselves in the Denver City Hall to resist any forced removal. They were sustained in their position by the assistance of the entire police force. Over 200 officers, with loaded rifles, fortified city hall. Governor Waite, in response, on March 14 ordered out the 1st Regiment of Colorado Infantry and the Chaffee Light Artillery, with two Gatling guns and two fieldpieces, and ordered them to surround city hall. The next day there was a real threat that a civil war would erupt if the troops forced an entrance to the building to eject the board members.

The governor hesitated to give an order to open fire. He had conversations and meetings with Maj. Gen. Alexander M. McCook, commander of the Department of the Colorado, headquartered in downtown Denver. The governor asked McCook to send federal troops to provide backup to the militia. The general in turn ordered Colonel Merriam to send the Fort Logan soldiers to the city. Merriam hastened to send five companies, about 300 regulars, from Fort Logan to Denver on the night of March 15. According to the *Denver Republican,* "within two hours and forty minutes nearly 300 armed troops of the regular army were landed at the Union Station to quell any disturbance." No doubt Merriam took great pride in his ability to respond so fast. McCook hoped that as the Fort Logan men marched down the streets, the crowds would disperse and the crisis would abruptly end. He publicly tried to adopt a neutral stance. "We are here to preserve the peace, gentlemen," he said to the press, "and recognize the rights or wrongs of no man. The merits of this trouble do not concern us. We have but the welfare of the people at heart." To the general's dismay, however, Governor Waite refused to withdraw the Colorado militia. The Fort Logan troops then camped on the west side of Union Station, and Merriam established his headquarters in a vacant room at the north end. At first the soldiers were excited and enthusiastic to have the boredom of garrison life disrupted, but reality set in when they realized that they would have to sleep on hardboards rather than their barracks bunks.[43] They would remain deployed at Union Station until the morning of March 18.

Meanwhile, the excitement of the citizenry was extremely high, with onlookers anticipating bloodshed at any moment. The people reportedly felt reassured by the presence of the US troops since they would certainly not be engaged in any attack but would more likely assist in truly keeping the peace.[44]

The crisis and standoff had alarmed prominent Denver citizens, including many businessmen in the chamber of commerce. They formed a "Committee of Safety," which met with the governor and, after protracted discussions, persuaded him to refer the whole matter to the Supreme Court. This defused the threat of violence. The Colorado militia units were withdrawn and the 7th Infantry companies quickly returned to Fort Logan in the morning of March 18, when the War Department became more fully aware of the nature of the conflict. While the federal troops never became directly embroiled in the city hall–governor conflict, it was significant in that it represented Merriam's first plunge into domestic troubles.

In this time of depression and serious national labor strife, with violent strikes and destruction of property, the mission of Fort Logan soldiers had taken a decided turn from keeping peace with Indians to maintaining order in the cities and industrial sites. The Denver City Hall War seemed to be the beginning, and even though troops avoided direct action, the deployment and presence of regular soldiers had influenced events. In July 1894 again five companies of the 7th Infantry were ordered to proceed to Trinidad, Colorado, and Raton, New Mexico, where railroads were shut down due to labor strife. The courts defined their mission "to enforce mandates of the U.S. Courts [and to] prevent obstruction of said property and transmission of U.S. Mails." The Pullman strike had reached Colorado, causing the interruption of rail traffic. Fort Logan troops were to protect property and get trains moving again. In the next month 7th Infantry's Company D was detailed to New Castle, Colorado, to back up militia ordered there for a labor disturbance.[45]

Following the events of the Denver City Hall War, the labor-related troop deployments, and Merriam's involvement with the New York National Guard encampment, the colonel's command of Fort Logan became even more complex. In 1894 the army closed Fort Bowie in Arizona and sent two troops of the 2nd Cavalry by train to Fort Logan. Not only did this mean a significant increase in fort population, but it also added many headaches associated with accommodating very different units in the garrison complement. In particular, a major concern now became the supply and maintenance of the cavalry's horses.

Another addition to the Fort Logan garrison was a twenty-four-man Signal Corps unit under the command of Capt. William Glassford. These men were responsible for an observation balloon that had been based at Fort Riley, Kansas, but was moved to Fort Logan in 1894. The unit recruited twenty-eight-year-old Ivy Baldwin, an aerialist, tight-rope walker, and experienced balloonist, as a sergeant to conduct most of the ascensions. In 1895 a big wind destroyed the French-built, hydrogen-filled balloon, and only through Captain Glassford's pleading did the Signal Corps make available $700 to purchase pongee silk to make a new one. Sergeant Baldwin and his wife sewed the silk, varnished it to be more airtight, and used the old rigging and basket to fashion a new craft. In 1898 the balloon, now called the "Santiago," was deployed to Cuba during the Spanish-American War. After its first few ascensions, primarily for artillery spotting, the balloon was shot down by Spanish troops and largely destroyed, ending any future ballooning at Fort Logan. Interestingly, Merriam never commented about these more-diverse elements affecting his command of Fort Logan.[46]

When Merriam received orders detailing him to the New York National Guard for the duration of the summer of 1894, he arranged for all the family to accompany him to the East Coast. During this family vacation, son Charles slipped off a streetcar, "was run over, dragged and terribly injured, one leg badly smashed." A local doctor advised that amputation was imperative, but Una and Charles refused such an operation. Fortunately, another physician (from New Hampshire) was nearby and came to Una's assistance. With skill and constant care, he succeeded in saving the young man's leg. As Charles recuperated, the family decided to spend some time on the Maine coast. When Colonel Merriam completed his assignment and rejoined them, they capped their eastern trip by sailing with Maine's most-prominent Civil War hero, Maj. Gen. Joshua L. Chamberlain, on his schooner to Portland.[47] Soon afterward they returned to Denver and Fort Logan.

Contributing to a busy 1894, Merriam got a taste of media problems similar to those of the twentieth and twenty-first century. The *Kansas City Times* reported on September 3 that some of the more recently constructed buildings at Fort Logan had structural deficiencies and were inadequate for their designated purpose. The article focused on a double barracks, the guardhouse, and the band quarters. After army headquarters became aware of the derogatory remarks, on September 11 officials requested, through the Department of the Colorado, a report from Merriam on the matter. The colonel prepared a five-page response by September 23. First, he pointed out that all construction was the domain and prerogative of the quartermaster, but he had offered some advice on the buildings that had not been accepted. He particularly noted that the location of the barracks in question was poor because of drainage. Merriam indicated that some of the newspaper facts were correct but went on to condemn the manner in which the information was gathered. He claimed in his report that the reporter had come on the fort surreptitiously. "I had no knowledge or suspicion that the *Kansas City Times* agent who visited this post about a month ago soliciting subscriptions, had any purpose beyond," said Merriam. He went on: "In conclusion I wish to say that I do not approve nor countenance newspaper criticism of any feature of army administration or discipline. They are seldom correct in point of fact, and still more seldom correct in their conclusions."[48]

Merriam informed his headquarters that just as he was preparing his response to the *Kansas City Times* article, a reporter of the *Denver Republican* had visited the post and was escorted around by a captain. The colonel attached a clipping of the resulting newspaper report to his reply and added, "It is certainly not nearer to the truth than the *Times* article, especially as viewed from the standpoint of economy, utility, and consistency."[49]

The highlight in 1895 at Fort Logan was the June visit of the commander of the US Army, Lieutenant General Schofield. As was to be expected, Merriam went all out to impress this high-ranking visitor, and he was successful. After the inspection Merriam immediately congratulated his men in a specially printed order:

> With great satisfaction the Regimental Commander informs the officers and enlisted men of his regiment that their instruction, soldierly bearing, and appearance in the review and maneuvers yesterday before the Lieutenant General of the Army received the highest commendation of that officer and members of his staff. Especially was the appearance and marching of the regiment in field dress and equipment commended; while the making of shelter tent camp in six minutes, and breaking camp, packing and forming for the march in three minutes and forty seconds was pronounced "wonderful" by the Lieutenant General, who personally kept the time.[50]

Not only was Merriam able to demonstrate his noted emphasis on drill proficiency, he likewise impressed the visitors with his other obsession, firing on the target range. The colonel made sure the inspectors were aware that the 7th Regiment had won the annual marksmanship trophy six times in seven years. In his comments to his men, Merriam declared this performance was the result of "careful study and constant, painstaking exercises, to which all officers and non-commissioned officers have given intelligent and earnest effort." His strong pat-on-the-back was coupled with a bit of rare humility, noting that their performances "are peace victories, yet they are true measures of efficiency for any possible service of which soldiers of the regiment may well be proud."[51] Perhaps no statements better encapsulated Merriam's thinking about what a peacetime army needed to do: remain disciplined with honed firing skills for whatever task loomed ahead.

Merriam received a letter from Schofield dated June 13, 1895, which expressed the general's appreciation for the "excellent condition of your command at the time of his recent visit to Fort Logan and of the great accuracy and promptness with which all the military exercises were performed." He added, "It was a great satisfaction . . . to find a military command in so complete a state of efficiency."[52] Merriam was delighted to receive these written remarks. They likely eased some of the tension that had existed between the two over the Merriam Pack.

Merriam's relatively long tenure as Fort Logan commander allowed him to more fully integrate post life with the surrounding communities. For example, athletic soldiers participated in city sports events. On one occasion, the newspaper in nearby Littleton reported that during the town's 1895 Fourth of July celebration, men from Fort Logan had won the 100-yard dash, 200-yard dash, "putting the shot," and the broad jump. Sports events were held on post too, and civilian competitors and spectators were invited. Representative was a sports program on a Saturday afternoon in June 1895 that included, besides many track events, mounted sports ("wrestling, mounted"), bicycle races, and a baseball game.[53] Besides the on-post drills and parades that attracted sightseers from Denver and surrounding towns, Merriam seized opportunities for his troops to participate in civic ceremonies. Such an event was Denver's Washington's Birthday parade in 1896. The following commendation received by Merriam from his superiors explained why he supported such activities:

> The Commanding General of the Department [of the Colorado] directs me to express to you his gratification at the fine display made by the troops of your command in the procession held in Denver, Colorado in honor of the birthday of Washington on the 22nd instant. It was a great pleasure to hear the universal praise of the United States troops by many distinguished persons who witnessed the parade.
>
> In this connection the General wishes to also refer, at this time, to the excellent appearance of the two battalions of the Seventh Infantry when at Colorado Springs last August, and he is glad to see that the garrison of Fort Logan is maintaining its high reputation amongst the people of this community.[54]

A military-civic social highlight occurred in May 1897 with the retirement of the Department of the Colorado commander, Major General Wheaton. Colonel Merriam became a key organizer in the planning for the elaborate farewell ceremony, calling upon his broad social contacts in Denver and throughout Colorado. A Denver newspaper described the upcoming event at Fort Logan as a "Grand Inspection and Review": "[I]t is expected that a large number of citizens of Denver will attend the parade. Special trains will be run from the Union depot to carry the sightseers." The general and his staff were to arrive at Fort Logan by a separate train and then given a special salute upon stepping off. The newspaper further outlined what would happen at the fort, with Merriam leading:

> Colonel Merriam and staff will be in waiting at the depot and the arriving officers will at once mount horses in waiting, the entire party proceeding up the broad roadways to the point of review. On either side of the road will be stationed at a distance of several yards apart a mounted escort and the military band will lead the procession as it slowly winds through the grounds. Then will follow the dress parade, inspection and review, at the close of which the general and his staff will be entertained by Colonel Merriam and officers of the post.[55]

This carefully planned ceremony reflects once again Merriam's mastery of detail. It also shows why Denverites would find attending such events attractive.

The colonel, as well as others, thoroughly understood the value of good public relations. One wonders also if Merriam, amid the pomp and circumstance, pondered his own ambitious quest for being a general, and if he would likewise be so honored sometime. The retirement of General Wheaton had another consequence on Colonel Merriam. He was ordered to the temporary command of the Department of the Colorado replacing Wheaton. During this short period, May 10 to May 27, 1897, he actually held the reins of a department commander.[56] It was not lost on him that this was a general's position. The fact that the Department of the Colorado was headquartered in Denver, however, meant that little transition effort was necessary.

Merriam continued his usual military training and exercises during the first part of 1897. For example, 7th Infantry troops would again spend part of the summer at rifle practice at the Broadmoor in Colorado Springs, for which preparations had to be made for the encampment.[57] Then came the joyful news— Merriam would be promoted to brigadier general on June 30, 1897. At long last, all his efforts at obtaining a general's star had come to fruition. He had accomplished one of the great goals in his life. Many military colleagues and civic, political, and business leaders who had earnestly tried to assist his promotion now deluged Merriam with congratulatory letters and messages. Una and the children joined in the celebration, knowing full well what this meant to Henry Merriam.

The promotion to brigadier general required a change of station. Merriam was to be assigned as commander of the Department of the Columbia, based at Vancouver Barracks. He likely saw this move as most positive. He would be a department commander, looking to a possible second star as major general. He would be returning to the Pacific Northwest, where he had spent so many years moving about, establishing and commanding various camps and forts. It was an area he knew well, and Vancouver Barracks was a good and comfortable post. To the Merriam family, however, this uprooting from Denver to the state of Washington and the Portland, Oregon, area was bittersweet. It meant severing close civic-social and educational ties and establishing new friends and schools.

Merriam's departure from Fort Logan also meant disrupting his social-civic network that he had carefully cultivated. His community standing was exemplified by an article that appeared in the *Army-Navy Register* of July 10, 1897: "General Henry C. Merriam was given the most imposing reception last week at Fort Logan ever given to any military officer in the State, as an expression of satisfaction felt by his friends over his recent promotion to the rank of Brigadier General. The reception was participated in by the officers of the Department of the Colorado, the National Guard, the Loyal Legion and Governor Adams and staff. The Governor and Col. Merriam received the guests, to the number of about 250."[58]

Colonel Merriam served as commander of Fort Logan for just short of eight years. It would be the longest tenure for any of that post's commanders. During his time there, a number of seemingly subtle yet profound changes occurred. In

1890, for instance, he was involved in one of the last Indian campaigns against the Sioux in South Dakota, but by the end of his tenure, he had an observation balloon on post, presaging the coming military airpower. Merriam began at Fort Logan as the age of the scattered, frontier Indian forts drew to a close and urban, rail-connected posts became the norm. The type of conflict facing the army shifted from fighting and keeping Indians on reservations to dealing with domestic violence and protecting property in a time of labor upheaval. Merriam dealt with post boredom, the peacetime bane of the military, by holding to his drill and discipline, but by the end of his time at Fort Logan, he plainly saw the same drill and ceremonies as furthering public relations and community involvement. During these almost eight years, significant transitions had taken place.

At the same time that changes were occurring, it is worthwhile to note that Merriam, the man, the military commander, remained rather consistent and the same. He was always the energetic person who so impressed his superiors and others with his self-initiative. Merriam consistently put great effort into letter writing, whether to promote his knapsack or to push his advancement in rank. He scarcely ever deviated from his emphasis on drill, discipline, and firing skills. And he managed to maintain regimental morale and pride by treating his officers and enlisted men with intelligence and care. Time after time he demonstrated his command of detail in various operations and his persistence in striving toward his goals. In his military command and in his family life, he remained a core of stability.

The conclusion of Merriam's Fort Logan command also meant the end of his long association with and responsibility for posts and forts. As a general, he would now command areas or regions. The scope of his capable administration had broadened tremendously. He welcomed this new and different challenge.

10

Department of the Columbia
Vancouver Barracks and Alaska

All officers here are enthusiastic in spite of the difficulties.

BRIG. GEN. HENRY C. MERRIAM, JANUARY 20, 1898

In the summer of 1897, the Merriam family hurriedly packed for the move from Fort Logan back to the Pacific Northwest and Vancouver Barracks. There was an air of excitement and eager anticipation to return to an area they knew well, a region of natural beauty, and a fine permanent post. They would be renewing some friendships made many years ago but still held in fond memory. The only negative was that just the name of Vancouver Barracks brought back images of the horrible nightmare of diphtheria that hit the family there during the winter of 1879–80.[1] Otherwise, General Merriam, Una, and the children viewed the move as a wonderful new assignment.

As part of the farewell to Fort Logan, General Merriam held his last "pass in review" with the 7th Infantry Regiment. His officers presented him a beautifully inscribed sword as a parting gesture. This was the third sword presented to Merriam during his military career, with ones awarded during the Civil War and at Laredo on the Rio Grande. After twelve years serving as commander of the 7th Infantry, this departure generated more emotion than most of his previous transfers. Perhaps feeling the separation from the unit and wanting to keep some ties, Merriam elected to take two 7th Infantry officers, Lt. William S. Graves and Lt. John B. Bennet, as aides.[2] Graves would accompany him to Vancouver Barracks, and Bennet would become an aide in 1899. Each would eventually profit greatly in his career from a long association with the general.

In addition to the change of station to Vancouver Barracks and the elevation of Merriam to brigadier general with command of the Department of the Columbia, the Merriams underwent another major upheaval. When the family left Fort Logan, daughter Carry remained for awhile in Denver and became engaged to George Bart Berger. With that news, Merriam, like a good father, wrote letters to Denver friends checking on Berger's character. Later in the year, Carry's fiancé visited Vancouver Barracks, and Merriam gave a somewhat pained approval of marriage in a letter dated October 22, 1897, fully realizing this meant breaking up the old tight family circle. Also, son Henry enrolled at Stanford University, and his third son, Charles, entered Portland Academy across the river in Oregon.[3] The Merriam children were maturing, and the immediate family faced a time of adjustment.

It did not take long for the Merriams to get settled after returning to the Pacific Northwest. Son Charles wrote on arriving at Vancouver Barracks that the houses provided there "were more elaborate than any previous house—the general's quarters were most comfortable." He went on to add that "on the parade ground were what seemed to us children huge evergreen trees with branches as large as ordinary trees . . . and walking among them in the evening . . . gave me a weird feeling of smallness, but great beauty."[4] Vancouver Barracks, like Fort Laramie, was an old fort. It first served as an outpost for the Hudson's Bay Company as early as 1824–25. Located on the north bank of the Columbia River, opposite Portland, Oregon, and some 124 miles from the mouth of the river, it occupied a commanding position. Not surprisingly, the first US troops to occupy the post in 1849 were part of the 1st Artillery. The military designated the location Fort Vancouver in 1853, and it was not until 1879 that it became Vancouver Barracks.[5] As headquarters for the Department of the Columbia, it had status as a beautifully positioned, permanent military installation, with fine officers' quarters.

One of the first actions of General Merriam was a tour of his new command. Commanders believed this obligatory travel established the new face with new troops and at the same time afforded the commander an opportunity to evaluate the status of various elements under his authority. Merriam's 1897 inspection visits in the Department of the Columbia were particularly enjoyable and enlightening as he returned to forts he had at one time established, including Fort Sherman (formerly Coeur d'Alene) and Fort Spokane. He was accompanied by Lieutenant Graves and two of his own sons, indicating that he saw this as a far-more-pleasant excursion than his pioneering ones in the late 1870s and early 1880s. Coincident with Merriam's new command, the Klondike gold rush developed. To the general this was totally unexpected, although he understood the history of mining runs in the West. The Department of the Columbia for some time had been responsible for military matters in Alaska. Nelson Miles, a previous department commander, had quietly tried to determine the army's role in the vast territory after the army's administration came to close in 1877, when the Treasury Department and the navy took jurisdiction.[6] Miles made a trip to southeastern Alaska in 1882 stating that he was inspecting an area he might have to defend. But he remained disturbed that so much of Alaska was unknown country. Consequently, he sent several army-led expeditions to explore river systems from the southern coastline into the interior. In 1883, for example, he ordered Lt. Frederick Schwatka, an 1871 West Point graduate, to

determine a route that could reach the Yukon River from Haines and Dyea at the head of the Lynn Canal of the southeast Alaskan Inside Passage.

Lieutenant Schwatka's expedition, comprising a map-making assistant, a medical officer, a civilian prospector, and three enlisted men, took a path from Dyea, up the Taiya River, over Chilkoot Pass to Bennett and Lindeman Lakes, and eventually to the Yukon River. This route was known by the native Tlingits as a trade trail and by some prospectors as a route to the interior. The later publicity given to the route by Schwatka's group greatly contributed to the selection of this path to the Klondike in 1897 and 1898. General Miles, however, ended up trying to explain why US Army personnel were mapping in a Canadian territory.[7]

A second exploratory expedition took place in 1884 when Miles ordered Capt. William R. Abercrombie to go up the Copper River from the Gulf of Alaska to better define that area, hopefully leading once again to the vast interior and up to the Yukon. Abercrombie proved unable to advance much beyond the lower Copper River, so later it remained for Lt. Henry Allen, General Miles's twenty-four-year-old aide from Kentucky, to lead two other men who documented the area of the upper Copper River and much of what is today the eastern part of Alaska.[8]

These pathfinder expeditions were important for several reasons. Foremost, they established routes for the flood of miners and adventurers anxious to penetrate to the Yukon and its gold deposits. They also indicated the interest of

General Miles in Alaska. This concern about the huge Alaska territory would come down on Merriam as the new Department of the Columbia commander, when Miles became general of the army and Merriam's boss. He no doubt believed that Merriam should be as interested in the Alaskan expeditions as he had been.

Perhaps Merriam had little choice but to become involved in the Klondike rush. In the first place, reports coming back from Canada's Dawson City and from Alaska indicated that there was a lot of gold. As early as 1893, new gold discoveries around Circle City, Alaska, caused a modest rush to that area. The excitement coming in 1897 from stories associated with the arrival of two steamships loaded with gold proved most potent in producing a run to the Klondike. The ship *Excelsior* docked in San Francisco reportedly with $400,000 in Yukon-Alaska gold, and around the same time the steamship *Portland* arrived in Seattle with supposedly $700,000 in gold. A "ton of gold" became an exciting rally cry at the time, prompting declarations that this was the biggest strike since California's discovery in the middle of the century. It was reported that "Western Union operators in Seattle transmitted 50,000 words of golden news in 48 hours of the *Portland*'s docking." This became very big news throughout the country. An auxiliary factor for a big mining rush, that apparently there was a lot of gold to be found, was the hangover of the 1893 panic and the lingering depression. The US government had once again put great emphasis on gold. Tossing aside populist William Jennings Bryan's cry about mankind crucified on a cross of gold, President McKinley made clear that there would be a gold standard for US currency. Gold then seemed of vital importance to restoring prosperity for the nation and a means of recouping individual and corporate financial losses. Still another element, perhaps less understood and faintly recognized, was the subtle belief of some that with the taming of the West, the end of Indian Wars, the settlement of vast areas, and the slowing of new mineral discoveries, the Alaska-Yukon strikes might be the last great frontier adventure. Despite reports of extreme hardships in the far north that could scarcely be imagined, such as mosquitoes that could "kill a naked man inside of an hour," the thrill of battling such conditions existed.[9]

Whatever entered the minds of those who hit the trails to the Klondike, the stampede was on. By the end of August 1897, "ten thousand fortune hunters" had arrived in the state of Washington, most in the Seattle-Tacoma area.[10] Thousands boarded ships, then clogged the two main avenues from Dyea over Chilkoot Pass or from Skagway over White Pass. Despite Canadian requirements at the border that each man had to cross with provisions for a hundred days, there were soon reports circulating that the flood of gold seekers would create a famine at Dawson and nearby camps. Furthermore, the trails themselves presented gruesome scenes of dead horses and dead trekkers. With the approach of fall in 1897, concern grew among federal officials and others about serious food shortages in the Klondike, which some called the "frozen truth." There were some accounts, and much conjecture, about miners having inadequate supplies to survive the harsh winter of 1897–98. Prices would be extremely high regardless, and some worried about the possibility of camp riots over potential famine conditions.

Pacific Northwest merchants added fuel to fears of a looming crisis. For example, on October 28, 1897, the Portland Chamber of Commerce reported: "[T]here will be great suffering, deprivation and even starvation among the miners and prospectors in the Alaska Gold Fields the coming winter, and it is thought a Relief Expedition to leave Portland, the natural gateway and point of supply and departure, about January 1st, 1898, with a few tons of flour, bacon, blankets, and fresh beef, to be sent over the passes and down the Yukon River to Dawson City by horses and sleds, would not only prove a great relief to the sufferers, but a great achievement."[11] Merriam was told to investigate the situation with the likelihood that an army-led relief expedition might be necessary. On December 16, 1897, he received a telegram from the adjutant general in Washington, DC, giving rather specific instructions:

Preliminary to sending supplies to the Yukon River via Dyea or the Copper River or both you are directed by the Secretary of War to send two or three competent officers to Dyea and vicinity to make a reconnaissance and report at the earliest possible day what in their judgment will be the best route in, whether cattle can be driven over the pass, whether there are boats running to the Copper River by which officers could go there and such further information as will be of service in fitting out these expeditions which must of necessity be on a large scale. It is not expected that the officers shall go over the passes but that they will obtain such information as they consider reliable. This unless you have the information already.[12]

General Merriam received another telegram that same day with more detailed instructions:

In anticipation of the authority of Congress to send food and relief to the miners in Alaska, the Major General Commanding directs that you ascertain where supplies can be purchased, where transportation by water can be procured and what numbers, also beef cattle. It would be better to get the latter from ranges in a cold climate. Obtain all information necessary for supplying and equipping one expedition from Dyea and the Dawson Trail. The other up the Copper River route to Belle Isle or Circle City and be prepared to organize and equip such expeditions as speedily as possible when funds and authority are granted. Due economy will be exercised and every effort made to render such expeditions successful.[13]

Clearly, Merriam experienced tremendous pressure. He was expected to collect as much information as possible, determine requirements for the relief, organize the expedition or expeditions, determine where to procure equipment and supplies, always keeping in mind controlling costs, and do all speedily. In typical fashion, the general methodically began collecting information about conditions on the passes and around Dawson City and what would be required to mount a relief column in the middle of winter.

Merriam interviewed a wide range of individuals who in some form or fashion were associated with the gold rush. He talked to Portland merchants; attendance at the annual banquet of the Commercial Club in Portland on October 9 afforded such an opportunity.[14] He sought out men who had made the trek over the passes to the Yukon and prospectors who could give a realistic counsel on the hardships that might be experienced. On December 17 J. F. Pratt of the US Coast and Geodetic Survey provided details on the Canadian disposition of men and supplies on the trail to Dawson City, highlighting the difficulties of the various routes. "It is estimated there are over 2400 dead horses strewn along the trail on the White Pass, 200 on the Chilkoot Pass," Pratt stated. "As to how long the provisions in the Klondike country will hold out, it is next to impossible to obtain satisfactory estimates," he concluded.[15] Merriam wrote a letter to the US Consulate in Victoria, British Columbia, soliciting information about the purported crisis and problems associated with any relief expedition. The general received a detailed response:

> Referring to yours 19th instant . . . I called the manager of the Hudson's Bay Company in this city without delay. Showed him your inquiries relative to the relief expedition to the Yukon mines . . . not very encouraging as regards the feasibility of an expedition this winter. . . .
>
> 1. In all winter expeditions to snow covered countries, dogs are necessary. One man to four dogs.
>
> 2. Sleds that carry 400 lbs. should be used.
>
> 3. Dogs can be bought of Hudson's Bay Co. and at their posts . . . usual price of good draught dog is about $25.
>
> 4. The best feed for draught dogs is dried fish . . . requires 3 or 4 lbs of dried fish—7 cents per lb.
>
> 5. No trouble so far to get all the Indians wanted—$2.50 per day and board.
>
> 6. The average Indian is better than the average white man for this work.
>
> 7. On good roads, 4 good dogs with good driver, can easily draw 400 lbs on one sled.
>
> 8. In December, 10 miles per day, February 15 miles per day. In March or April, 20 miles per day.
>
> 9. The manager declined to take responsibility of giving an outline of organization necessary to transport provisions from Dyea

or Skagway to Dawson City. He thinks it is impractical at this season. . . . He personally went over the trail from Dyea—involves four
mile ascent of mountains steeper than the average roof of a house,
and risk of frightful storms and avalanches . . . ascent by clinging
to holes chopped out of snow. Dogs would eat up all the provisions out
of Dyea before reaching Dawson City. He strongly advises go by Fort
Wrangel-Stickeen River. . . . [I]f any expedition goes by way of Dyea,
it should start before March.[16]

This consulate letter to Merriam once again demonstrates how thorough
Merriam approached any task, asking a multitude of questions and seeking
comprehensive details. It also highlights another Merriam characteristic. He
was always sincerely interested in the cost. Obviously this had been reinforced
by instructions from Washington. Merriam no doubt was preparing a relief-expedition budget and getting ready to warn the secretary of war and army headquarters what to expect in expedition expenses. All indications pointed to some
very high costs.

After Merriam's research on the status of provisions on the trails and at
Dawson City and equipment and personnel requirements of a relief expedition,
he apparently had serious misgivings about the whole idea of a relief effort. On
January 20, 1898, he sent a message, marked "personal," to the War Department: "I own that the exact truth is hard to find in the midst of so much rivalry
of business and local interests. When a local editorial explains the early rush already on for the Klondike, with the commercial boom it brings, by saying that
it results from a knowledge that the government will follow in their wake with
free supplies, on which they can fall back on in case of emergency, an insight is
given with the motives which largely control."[17] Despite his skepticism, the general continued to prepare for an army-led relief expedition. In his January letter
to the War Department, he provided the broad outline of his plans:

Part of the expedition will sail from Portland on or about February 1st, and balance from Seattle on or about the 5th. Probably the
Snow & Ice Transit Co. will take part of the supplies over Chilkoot Pass
and Dawson Trail to be followed up by the reindeer train on its arrival,
while the balance will be taken over Chilkoot and White Passes by our
pack train and tandem sleds, and down the lakes, possibly resorting to
boats at foot of Lake Labarge if the river is found still open there. It
is significant that the N. W. Police have been unable to get below Big
Salmon, using both horses and dogs. They began early in the autumn.
All officers here are enthusiastic in spite of the difficulties.[18]

The Merriam letter's reference to a "reindeer train" pertained to a proposal by noted Alaskan missionary Sheldon Jackson to import herds of reindeer and use them on trails for hauling provisions and also to be slaughtered for

food if necessary. In the summer of 1891, Jackson started the reindeer importation to Alaska and continued in succeeding years, with mixed results. Many animals died, but he proceeded to establish reindeer at a number of native mission schools. Reportedly, some prospectors claimed reindeer had more stamina than dogs and could forage for their own food along the trail. Jackson convinced the federal government that reindeer could be used in Klondike relief efforts. He arranged for a shipment of the animals, which was delivered to Captain Abercrombie at Chilkat. For reasons unclear, the attempt to use the reindeer ended in a fiasco. Many reindeer starved and died, and the relief herd was lost. Some alleged that the reindeer were sent without proper consultation and without preparation for feeding them. Even Una indicated that she felt great sadness about the episode, remarking, "This affair of the reindeer reflected no credit on those who originated the idea and profited by it."[19]

By late January 1898, Merriam's planning to carry out the relief expedition had progressed to the point where specific personnel were designated for the mission. Portland's *Morning Oregonian* on January 20 reported that the Yukon relief expedition would include eighty-seven men, consisting of "7 officers, 4 civilian clerks, 1 civilian laborer, 17 civilian packers, and 5 enlisted men packers, 50 enlisted men of the Fourteenth Infantry as an escort, 2 enlisted men of the hospital corps and 1 enlisted man, an acting quartermaster sergeant." Captain George Ruhlen was in overall command and in charge of transportation and quartermaster. Captain D. L. Brainerd would be in charge of commissary of subsistence and distribution of supplies.[20]

Merriam continued to solicit information about trail conditions and the status of provisions at the Yukon gold camps regardless of his developing plans to mount a relief effort by February. On December 26, 1897, he forwarded to Washington a "Synopsis of interview between Department Commander [Merriam] and Messrs Gardner and Dalton at Vancouver Barracks." These two men, who had just arrived back at Dyea on December 17, described the situation on the passes and offered their recommendations, including, "horses are the best and only animals suitable for transportation purposes over the Dyea or Skagway trails." This opinion conflicted with those who advocated the use of dogs. Most importantly, the two men interviewed did not see a food crisis. Gardner reported "Dawson as a very orderly town, that many people there have more than sufficient food to last till navigation opens on the Yukon next summer and that many have not enough; but that up to [the] time of leaving the food had not been collected with a view of its distribution to guard against shortages or possible starvation." Dalton, an experienced frontiersman involved in freighting over the passes, said "in his opinion there are not to exceed 4,000 people in Dawson and that 100,000 rations or 300,000 lbs. [of] food supplies will be sufficient to supply any deficiency in food in Dawson that may exist till navigation opens on [the] Yukon and boats can reach Dawson with food."[21]

Added to these opinions that a food shortage was not imminent, Merriam sent to Secretary of War Russell A. Alger a clipping from the *Morning*

Oregonian, which reported: "At least 40 miners have just arrived from Dawson City. . . . Each and every one of these gentlemen say there is absolutely no truth in the report that people will starve in Dawson City, and they say it is absolute foolishness on the part of the government to send in provisions where they are not needed. Within the past 15 days, over 100 men have arrived from Dawson, and without exception they give the same report. A portion even went so far to emphatically state that no one would even go hungry, as those without provisions have all left and those who remained have plenty."[22]

Merriam, in forwarding the article, wrote: "I enclose for you a clipping from the morning 'Oregonian' with a block marked in second column which summarizes the evidence of all recent arrivals from the Klondike. I have myself interviewed many of them and wired synopsis to the War Department." Cautious, he went on to state, "I write this to you personally because I do not know that it would be wise to express myself so freely for record and in absence of any instructions or request." At this point Merriam had concluded that the "frozen truth" was really that the merchants, not the miners, were profiting from the Klondike gold rush, and they saw further gain outfitting government relief efforts. His doubts about a starvation crisis had most certainly colored his reports to Washington. Even before the telling Portland newspaper article, on January 14 Merriam had received a War Department telegram instructing him to postpone any relief expedition to Alaska. Another newspaper at the time said, "The orders effect a temporary abandonment of the expedition, and it is understood they were based on the recent reports that there will be no starvation or suffering in the Yukon country that the relief expedition would relieve."[23]

Merriam must have experienced a profound release from the onerous burden of directing a wintertime rescue expedition to the Yukon. At the same time, however, he now faced canceling and redirecting Alaskan operations and issuing new orders to widespread personnel. Without hesitation, he immediately began considering further Alaskan exploratory assignments and determining next winter's provisioning requirements. On March 23, 1898, Merriam wrote to a friend, "I am, as you know, very busy over the outfitting and instructing of the exploratory expeditions into which the debris of the defunct relief expedition are being diverted." On March 6, 1898, Merriam wrote a personal letter to General Miles that explained in considerable detail his proposed routes of trail explorations, sending along a map of Alaska to clarify geographic points.[24] Merriam then received a telegram with instructions from Miles:

The design of the government in regard to the military expeditions and explorations in Alaska during the present season, the coming summer and preparations for next winter:

The command to be divided into three expeditions, 1st expedition No. 1 to proceed from Skagway or Dyea, along the Dalton Trail or down the valley of the Yukon to Dawson (medical supplies included). . . . The expedition will then proceed to discover and explore and mark a trail from the Yukon up Forty Mile Creek to the Tanana. . . . 2nd expedition, No. 2 will explore the valley of the Copper River or tributaries from its mouth to the Tanana River establishing a line of communication to the junction with the expedition No. 1 on the Tanana. 3rd expedition, No. 3 will start from some point on Cook's Inlet and endeavor to discover the most direct and practicable route from tidewater to the crossing of the trail from Copper River and Forty Mile Creek on the Tanana. . . . Authorized to enlist 150 Indians—75 to 100 men will be ample for this purpose.[25]

As in previous exploratory missions, General Miles emphasized establishing and mapping a trail from the Alaskan port of Valdez up the Copper River to the interior. In a letter to Merriam on February 4, 1898, he noted Captain Abercrombie's previous work up the Copper River, but he said, "Since the excitement has occurred in Alaska, I have urged that an expedition be sent up the Copper River." Part of Miles's interest in this route stemmed from the need to have an all-American trail avoiding the concern of always dealing with the Canadians over the passes from Dyea and Skagway. In April 1898 two exploring teams were outfitted, instructed, and sent to Alaska. Capt. E. F. Glenn, 25th Infantry, was named commander of one group, and trail veteran Captain Abercrombie, 2nd Infantry, was to lead the other. As expected, the two expeditions were to work routes during the Alaska summer and then return to Department of the Columbia headquarters in October and November. Upon completion of the field work during the 1898 summer, both leaders were ordered to report to the assistant secretary of war in Washington, where they would have better facilities for completing their maps and reports.[26]

In June Merriam wrote to the commander of Alaskan Exploratory Expedition No. 3, Captain Glenn, saying, "5 pack mules sent" and urging that the captain establish supply depots on the trail. Later in the month the general experienced trouble with the captain. He told Glenn that his comments about the expedition's medical officer were inexcusable and that his "request for authority to cache your supplies and abandon important and expensive work entrusted to you at your own request, is equally disappointing." Also in June, Merriam wrote to Captain Abercrombie, commanding Expedition No. 2, saying, "Arrangements have been made to ship supplies for your expedition to extend from June 30th to October 31st. . . . Five pack mules and one packer were shipped to you from Dyea, Alaska, in the latter part of May." He went on to address the captain's exploration of the Copper River and his need to "establish one or more supply depots—say from 100 to 150 miles apart."[27]

As in the case of Captain Glenn, Merriam soon felt the need to reprimand Abercrombie. He scolded the captain, saying: "[I]n abandoning your detachment on exploring duty on or near Copper River in Alaska and proceeding to Seattle, Washington, appears to have had no purpose except to request authority to buy 25 range ponies for use of your expedition. The request could have been made as well from your place of duty." The general went on to emphasize the importance of Expedition No. 2's mission "to fix upon the best route for connecting Valdez Inlet with the upper portion of Copper River, thus preparing the way for undertaking the extended explorations toward and beyond the Tanana." Apparently the independent decisions and actions of several expedition leaders did not meet with Merriam's approval. With respect to the better-known and more frequently used routes over Chilkoot and White Passes, the general merely noted that he was "sorry to receive a telegram directing action to protect the toll road through White Pass."[28]

In addition to the concerns about the exploratory teams, Merriam worried about wider logistical support for Alaskan army units and adequate provisioning for the mining camps for the next winter. Since resupply was mainly limited to the summer months, there was always a narrow window for planning and shipping. On July 7, 1898, he received a status report from Lt. W. P. Richardson at Fort St. Michael. At nearly the same time, he received a letter from the Alaska Commercial Company at St. Michael, warning, "you will remember at that time [referring to the previous winter] the trouble was averted by the presence there of Capt. Ray and Lieut. Richardson . . . will occur again this fall." Taking this information, Merriam informed Richardson at St. Michael that his reporting "raises question as to the best location for the troops in northern Alaska during the coming winter. I have ordered supplies for one more year to go forward to St. Michael from Seattle about the 20th of this month for double the number of your command, this in order to give you a small margin for the relief of destitute miners should any be encountered during the coming winter."[29]

Obviously, Merriam was hoping this would avoid the relief-expedition turmoil of the winter of 1897–98.

General Merriam's supervision of Alaskan operations was soon eclipsed by the onset of the Spanish-American War. People in the United States, long troubled by conditions in Cuba under Spanish rule, clamored for aggressive action to address the situation. The explosion and sinking of the battleship *Maine* in Havana harbor seemed to be the last straw. President McKinley, in response to the public outcry, sent a message to Congress on April 11, 1898, asking that the president be empowered to act against Spain. On April 25 McKinley requested that Congress declare war, and Congress responded with a resolution saying a state of war had existed since April 21. On April 12 Merriam had written General Miles, stating, "Cuban affairs now appear to be assuming a business basis, and I beg not to be overlooked in case of mobilization." Not surprisingly, Merriam welcomed an opportunity to have a combat command. But orders on April 15 directed him to assume temporary command of both the Department of California and the Department of the Columbia.[30] Merriam was to report to San Francisco, headquarters for the Department of California, no later than June 30. In the meantime, the army set in motion the stripping of

soldiers from posts throughout Merriam's two departments to process for transfer to Hawaii and the Philippines; Merriam's new command would also encom-
pass Hawaii. He had two immediate concerns: the coastal defense of the West
Coast in case of the appearance of a Spanish naval fleet, and the organization of
logistical support for developing Pacific operations.

General Merriam's relatively short tenure at Vancouver Barracks turned out
to be only a prelude to his entrance on a much larger stage, essentially command of the entire West Coast. While he was denied his expressed wish to become a combat commander in the Spanish-American War, his mission to logisti-
cally funnel men, military equipment, and supplies to the far-distant Philippines
from West Coast ports was a Herculean task. His considerable administrative
skills would be tested as never before.

In hindsight, General Merriam probably viewed his command of the
Department of the Columbia and his responsibilities for Alaskan matters
as valuable precursor experience for the much-wider-ranging military operations associated with the Spanish-American War. He now had a decidedly
broader perspective of military command than from his times at Fort Laramie
and Fort Logan. The multitude of detail considered with planning exploratory
expeditions into Alaska and the Klondike relief effort, almost entirely logistical operations, provided insight as to how to deliver men and materials to distant areas. With forthcoming West Coast support of military operations clear
across the Pacific Ocean in the Philippines, an unprecedented supply requirement, Merriam's command duties became ever more magnified.

11

The Spanish-American War

I hope you have not forgotten my personal assurance
that every local consideration should be subordinated
to meet the demands of your expedition.

MAJ. GEN. H. C. MERRIAM TO MAJ. GEN. WESLEY MERRITT, JANUARY 11, 1899

Despite General Merriam's desire to lead a combat force during the Spanish-American War, he received very different orders to go to the Presidio in San Francisco, there to assume combined command of the Department of California and Department of the Columbia, reporting no later than June 30, 1898. The rapid development of the war, particularly Commodore George Dewey's destruction of the Spanish Pacific fleet in Manila Bay on May 1, merely a few days after hostilities began, meant that Merriam needed to accelerate his arrival at the Presidio or he would fall behind in coping with the military matters in the Pacific arena. Marshalling an army to send to the Philippines became especially urgent. Monumental problems developed because the US Army was woefully unprepared to fight any war, especially one across the Pacific Ocean. The Presidio would become the key staging base for a Philippines campaign.

Although the navy approached a state of readiness by the time of the US declaration of war, the army was in dire straits. The army strength of approximately 25,000 officers and men was deployed across the entire country in small, scattered garrisons. Many senior officers, veterans of the Civil War and the Indian Wars, were in positions of authority by seniority and not necessarily performance and efficiency. There was no modern general staff to provide central planning and direction. Equipment problems had multiplied because of inadequate funding, magnified by the fiscal drought of the 1893 depression. Despite impatience in Congress to get on with the war, legislators had only appropriated $50 million for the armed forces in March and waited until April, after the declaration of war, before authorizing expansion of the regular army to 61,000 men. Initially, the War Department proposed expanding the regular force in a range of 75,000 to 100,000 soldiers, but the wave of volunteers, fueled by patriotic fervor, and the opposition of the National Guard forced a political reassessment. Congress and the McKinley administration finally agreed to a call of 125,000 men, with the National Guard able to come into service as units similar to the state-raised volunteer units of the Civil War.[1] This decision was not without critics, however. Some argued that use of the National Guard outside of state boundaries, particularly overseas and for a purpose not related to domestic issues, expanded the role of the National Guard far beyond what was originally intended. Others pointed out that the War Department lacked any central mobilization office to conduct such an expansion effort for the Regular Army, let alone for thousands of volunteers. Nevertheless, President McKinley, like Lincoln, called for 125,000 volunteer men. Congress passed the Mobilization Act, permitting the National Guard to volunteer and be mustered into federal service as units but then placed within a Regular Army organization. Getting these new men processed, outfitted, trained, and deployed to overseas locations would certainly take time, but speed was essential. Merriam would be in the middle of all this mobilization effort.

Merriam's new command, with greatly expanded responsibilities, brought one bit of good news. On May 4, 1898, President McKinley sent Merriam's name, along with a number of others, to the Senate for confirmation as major general for the burgeoning volunteer army. The Senate acted immediately on the president's nominations.[2] Wearing two stars had been one of Merriam's career goals, and he truly felt gratified by the promotion, even if it was viewed as a temporary one with the volunteer forces.

Soon after General Merriam's arrival at his new headquarters in San Francisco, he sent for Una and the children to join him, never to return to Vancouver Barracks. Moving to San Francisco allowed Una the opportunity to visit son Henry, who had been at Stanford for a year. He, however, took exams with the intention of entering the army. In short order Henry was commissioned a lieutenant in the coast artillery and assigned as an aide to Gen. Charles King, and not long thereafter, he was deployed to Hawaii and then to the Philippines. Son Charles, meanwhile, prepared to enter Stanford.[3]

Before leaving for San Francisco, General Merriam evidently had concerns about coastal defense in the Pacific Northwest, especially Puget Sound. Responding to Merriam's queries on the subject, he was told, "A regiment will be sent you for distribution to points on Puget Sound and Columbia River." With the army in the throes of organizing forces for action in Cuba and the Philippines, the message concluded, "It is difficult to find troops for this duty."[4]

At the Presidio in San Francisco, Merriam assumed "temporary" command on April 20, 1898, and immediately had his hands full. In the first place, his predecessor, Brig. Gen. William R. Shafter, was transferred east to command troops for action in Cuba and took a number of department staff members with him. Merriam was forced to rely on the remaining staff members until he could bring in new officers to man the positions, thus having to handle his heavy new responsibilities short handed for the time being. He later wrote to Maj. Gen. Wesley Merritt, who commanded the army's Philippine force, "Stripped of staff as this Department was by General Shafter's movement eastward in April, the duties of the few left were greatly multiplied, yet every subordinate has cheerfully and generously aided me in meeting the many emergencies incidental to forwarding an expedition to a region so remote and to meet conditions novel, in many respects, to our experience."[5]

Because San Francisco was such a great West Coast harbor, soldiers (regulars and volunteers) came to the Presidio for training and preparation for deployment to the Philippines. On May 6, 1898, a Department of California general order stated:

> An encampment will be established at the Presidio of San Francisco for the 14th U.S. Infantry and the Volunteer Forces of the States of California, Oregon and Washington.
>
> The California Volunteers will be sent to the camp by regiments and batteries as fast as practicable after having been mustered into the service of the United States, and the other troops immediately upon their arrival in San Francisco.[6]

The 14th Infantry Regiment came from Vancouver Barracks, and the band and Companies C, D, E, and F departed that post on May 7 en route to San Francisco. Other elements of that regiment departed Vancouver on May 21. Some of these units had just been recalled from Alaska duty and were quickly redeployed for Philippines assignment. The 4th Cavalry from Fort Walla Walla was another Regular Army regiment designated for the Philippines. Like the 14th Infantry, it would assemble at the Presidio before deployment. As the regular troops left, hurriedly mustered volunteer units were assigned to Vancouver Barracks and other posts to replace them. For example, volunteers from Tacoma arrived at Vancouver Barracks on May 25. Some Regular Army troops had boarded ships and left the Presidio as early as May 1898, but volunteer units from the states of Utah, Washington, Montana, Wyoming, Idaho, Colorado, and as far away as Iowa, Pennsylvania, South and North Dakota, Tennessee, and Kansas soon poured into the San Francisco area. Some 80,000 men traveled through the Presidio from the war's beginning to 1900 on their way to and from the Philippine Islands.[7]

At the Presidio, tent camps had to be set up to handle the flow of men. One of the first was called Camp Merritt, and the second one, near the eastern border of the Presidio, was called Camp Merriam, after the new Department of California commanding officer. According to one newspaper report of May 5, datelined San Francisco, General Merriam ordered Col. Louis T. Morris, commanding the Presidio, to plan for the encampment of 6,000 volunteer troops.[8] All kinds of services, including hospital care, had to be provided. The dampness associated with the tent camps, particularly Camp Merritt, caused considerable sickness, necessitating improved medical facilities (the beginning of Lettermen Hospital). Support of the many volunteer units in their combat training became paramount. In addition, new buildings and many improvements became necessary at this old California military post. Merriam and his staff were besieged with all the details of shifting men and materials throughout the West Coast and the day-to-day demands of the mobilization effort at the Presidio.

The rush to get men and equipment to the Philippines, coupled with the first experience in deploying an army overseas, led to much confusion and inefficiency. The planning for the movement out of San Francisco had not been going well when Merriam arrived. For one thing, the establishment of an ocean-transport system proved difficult and frustrating, entailing extensive coordination with the navy and commercial shipping. During the period from May 15 to December 18, 1898, thirty-one different ships were involved in the Pacific transport.[9] In a relatively brief time, however, Merriam managed to bring order and efficiency to the departure of men and supplies from the Presidio and ultimately from San Francisco harbor. His efforts were aided by the powerful influence of the army's adjutant general, Henry C. Corbin, in Washington to allow more individual initiative by commanders. The magnitude of Merriam's responsibilities continued to increase rapidly. The War Department on May 11 allocated over 10,000 troops to General Merritt's Philippines forces. By May 22 this contingent was expanded to 20,000 men.[10] Merriam, perhaps believing that his efforts had not been properly recognized, wrote to Merritt on January 11, 1899, stating:

> In your recent statement before the Board of Investigation, as reported in the press, you were kind enough to say that the troops in your command in the Philippine Expedition were well fed and in all respects well outfitted and supplied.
>
> Inferentially, this is an acknowledgement that the work done on this coast during your campaign has been satisfactory to you. For this I cordially thank you.
>
> I hope you have not forgotten my personal assurance that every local consideration should be subordinated to meet the demands of your expedition.[11]

On January 17, 1899, General Merritt replied: "My Dear General: I have received your communication of January 11th, 1899, and have taken the liberty of forwarding your official communication to the Adjutant General in Washington, with a strong endorsement commending your services and those of your staff, and especially recommending again Major Rathbone for promotion."[12]

Major problems at various camps began to come to light soon after the war began. Centralized planning for fielding, equipping, and training a great volunteer army did not exist. As a consequence, some camps had equipment, while others suffered with very little. Most serious was the need for weapons and ammunition. There were also shortages of basic items, such as uniforms, tents, and personal equipment like canteens and mess kits. Camp commanders and quartermaster officers were forced to improvise. The unprepared status of National Guard units exacerbated the situation and at the same time tended to feed back to the general public the problems and conditions of the camps. The Presidio fared better than most, including the camp established at Tampa Bay, Florida, serving troops for the Cuban expedition.

Merriam had another new element of his command, the addition of Hawaii, while in charge of both the Department of California and the Department of the Columbia. Obviously, the Hawaiian Islands, and especially Pearl Harbor, were strategically important as a refueling and resupply stopover point on the long route to the Philippines. After Congress passed the resolution for annexation of Hawaii in July 1898, the US military presence in the islands became more organized. In September, Department of California general orders established the Military District of Hawaii and placed it under the command of Brig. Gen. Charles King at Honolulu. That fall Merriam made an official visit to Hawaii, spending several weeks there, accompanied by his son Charles. On the general's ship were also men and nurses headed for the Philippine Islands. In addition, former Texas governor J. S. Hogg, who had written letters of support for Merriam's promotion, was on board. This allowed Merriam to cultivate the ex-governor's friendship and political support.[13]

As oldest son Lt. Henry Merriam, junior aide-de-camp to General King, passed through Hawaii on his way to the Philippines, he became involved in an embarrassing incident. The young officer had accompanied another lieutenant, designated as provost marshal, into a Hawaiian town following payday with a dozen mounted soldiers with orders to arrest any soldiers if they created a disturbance. The lieutenant, acting as provost, had a "fracas with a merchant sailor," with a crowd of onlookers unfriendly to the officers. The streets were ordered cleared, and the senior lieutenant rode off in pursuit of a gang of sailors, leaving the woefully inexperienced Lieutenant Merriam behind. Young Merriam reportedly tried to disperse crowds by saying that he was evoking martial law (something he could not do). Word of this reached General King, who hurriedly dispatched a captain to investigate, ensure peace, and bring in the two lieutenants. After an investigation and a report to General Merriam, and with orders for the young officers to proceed on to Manila, the matter was dropped. No doubt the matter, involving troop discipline in Hawaii and specifically his oldest son, proved most embarrassing to General Merriam, an officer who took great pride in the exercise of discipline. Lieutenant Merriam, just beginning his military duty, fortunately escaped serious repercussions. The younger Merriam had another Hawaiian involvement important to the general and to his mother—he became engaged to Alice Lishman of Honolulu.[14]

Merriam family, circa 1898. Seated, l. to r.: Charles, Henry Clay, Una, Henry.
Standing: Cyrus and Maude. Courtesy Berger Family Collection.

General Merriam, Una, and members of the family attentively read the casualty lists of the 7th Infantry, published as a result of its action in Cuba. They were saddened and distressed at reading names they knew all too well.[15]

Although Merriam's mobilization responsibilities at the Presidio and Hawaii had begun at a furious pace, they were relatively short lived. The navy's stunning successes against the Spanish fleets and the army's quick progress in campaigns in Cuba, Puerto Rico, and the Philippines resulted in a virtually complete US victory by August 1898. After months of diplomatic posturing, the United States and Spain signed a peace treaty on December 10, 1898, closing the Spanish-American War. While the war in the Philippine Islands transitioned from combat against the Spanish to a more-prolonged struggle against Philippine natives (until 1902), the so-called Philippine Insurrection, the US Army began reverting to a peacetime organization and the demobilization of the volunteers. The process accelerated, in part, because of the high incidence of disease in the army, especially typhoid, malaria, and yellow fever.

General Merritt, who had commanded the VIII Corps in the Philippines, returned to the United States at first to aid in an investigation of the war's problems, then to assist with peace negotiations. He eventually was assigned to command the Department of the East, headquartered at Governor's Island, New York City. Major General Shafter returned from action in Cuba and on January 19, 1899, resumed command of the Department of California.[16] With these key command changes, General Merriam was assigned to command the Department of Colorado, with headquarters in Denver. The end of the Spanish-American War, the return of National Guard units to their respective states, and the release of the great numbers of volunteers also meant the end of the "temporary" rank of major general for many officers, including Henry Merriam.

The quick military victories in the Spanish-American War, the "Splendid Little War," made General Merriam's time on the large West Coast stage a very limited one, lasting approximately nine months. During that time, however, he had amply reinforced his reputation as an excellent administrator. In a comparative sense, the general's more-quiet and less-troubled camp administration at the Presidio profited by the lurid details of major problems associated with camps in the East supporting the Cuban expedition. He had once again demonstrated that he could keep superb focus on accomplishing the mission at hand, this time on the largest scope he personally had ever faced, and while holding one of the largest commands of the US Army at the time. To Merriam's great credit, he and his staff provided the necessary mobilization and logistical support for the Pacific operations in a way that was without precedent. The United States never before had attempted deploying an army overseas. The distances involved in crossing the Pacific to the Philippines, vastly complicating ocean shipping, constituted a daunting new task. Merriam, through his intelligence, mastery of multiple details, and tireless energy, proved up to the challenge.

One aspect of Merriam's role in the Spanish-American War was not to his liking. The general always remained proud of his military skills and accomplishments. He would have greatly preferred to have led a combat force, as in the case of General Shafter in Cuba and General Merritt in the Philippines. But in his role as logistical commander and military administrator, Merriam did not receive much national attention. Even in the army as a whole, his role and accomplishments were not well recognized. He certainly would have wished otherwise. In addition, he reverted to the rank of brigadier general, so another campaign to attain a permanent promotion to major general loomed.

12

Department of the Colorado and
the Idaho Mining Riots

*In all things connected with this affair, I have
simply done my duty; I am content.*

BRIG. GEN. HENRY C. MERRIAM, "IN REFLECTION ON IDAHO RIOTS"

eneral Merriam probably felt a let down with his assignment to lead the Department of the Colorado. After all, he had just been in command of the West Coast and Hawaii for the US Army during the Spanish-American War and had been responsible for ensuring men and equipment continued to flow to the Philippine Islands to support combat there. He had been headquartered at the prestigious Presidio and at a large American city, San Francisco. The excitement and exhilaration of wartime had abruptly subsided. Yet considering other possibilities of a new assignment, the return to Colorado and the city of Denver was welcomed. The Merriam family would be back in very familiar country because of their long and generally pleasant tenure at Fort Logan. Also, daughter Carry, engaged to George Berger of Denver, would be close by and once again a part of family gatherings. The Merriams would be able to renew valued friendships in the state and in Denver. In the family's view, there were many positives in General Merriam's new assignment to command the Department of the Colorado.

The Department of the Colorado had been established in 1893, with its headquarters in Denver. It encompassed a vast western area, including the states of Colorado, Utah, and Wyoming (excepting Yellowstone National Park) as well as the territories of Arizona and New Mexico. Within its authority were eleven major forts and a few minor posts. At the time of Merriam's arrival at the end of January 1899, the command had some ninety officers and 3,377 men; department headquarters had ten officers. There was a mix of units, infantry and cavalry regiments, along with Indian scouts, agencies, and agents. The great distances between forts and the length and breadth of the department geographically created imposing problems of communications and span of control.

General Merriam, Una, and family (Cyrus and Maude) arrived in Denver on January 30 and enjoyed accommodations at the Brown Palace Hotel until another suitable residence could be found. The *Denver Evening Post* commented upon Merriam's return to the city: "The general is well known in Denver . . . a member of the Denver Club and very popular with all who knew him. The commander has a splendid figure, with gray hair and mustache."[1] The general felt at ease getting back to familiar Denver, but almost immediately he became involved in controversy.

Several Denver newspapers were anxious to interview Merriam since he had been widely known, and they were interested in probing his views about the war and its aftermath. The *Denver Evening Post*, on January 30, 1899, had carried a report from a Los Angeles newspaper's interview with Merriam that he had "discussed freely the policy of the government toward the Philippines." In answer to a reporter's question of what to do with the islands, the California paper quoted Merriam as saying: "I would let them alone. We have no responsibility as to the people of the islands. Should I be asked if I would let Spain resume her authority over the people there I would say 'yes' if she could do so. I think expansion will lead this nation into most serious complications with other countries."[2]

The next day both the *Denver Evening Post* and the *Rocky Mountain News* ran their accounts of a Merriam interview in which he strongly denied having made the earlier reported Los Angeles comments: "The general takes exception to such gross misrepresentation. He also finds much other language in the interview to be decidedly erroneous." The papers reported Merriam as saying, with respect to the Philippines question: "I don't think it proper to express an opinion. It is the business of the soldier to obey orders and not discuss the policy of the nation." Nevertheless, Merriam went on to say in the interview:

Assuming that the possession and retention of these islands is decided upon, it makes us responsible for the behavior of 10,000,000 people of whom we know little, except that they are half savage. The islands are in a climate not congenial to American soldiers or citizens; they are surrounded by countries unfriendly both to us and to our style of Government. History shows that some races have rapidly developed character, while others are very slow. The races from which the Filipinos sprang are none of them distinguished for intelligence or civilized tendencies. They are a mixture of Malay, Chinese, and Hindu. Friends of expansion might find encouragement in the history of England in India, and there are undoubtedly many people in favor of expansion, but I would not say that these are in the majority. I have never said that I thought the United States should return the islands to Spain.[3]

This rather remarkable statement reflects a strong racial bias, a subject that always seemed to be treated circumspectly and much suppressed in Merriam's published opinions. It also evidently put him at odds with President McKinley regarding taking the Philippines.

Also, according to one newspaper, Merriam had an opinion about postwar expansion and reorganization of the Regular Army.

> That, of course is a matter which Congress must decide. The Departments of the Columbia, Dakota and Missouri were depleted by the large drafts for troops for foreign service. If the bill before Congress to increase the standing army becomes law, these departments will be regarrisoned. Another purported statement in that erroneous interview was that I saw no need for a larger army. Years ago I expressed myself in favor of an increased army and my views have not altered. It is not of the first importance that the posts in these three departments be regarrisoned, that is not because of the danger of immediate Indian depredations. The Indians are quiet now, and the necessity for a large army is not immediate on that account. However, that is a question of military policy, everything depends on the temper of Congress. If this body desires the retention of territory captured, it will be necessary for it to furnish men and money.[4]

To Merriam, and his vision, the establishment of an American overseas empire as a result of the Spanish-American War clearly brought a need for a larger US military. The nation could not just return to the army's peacetime size and structure.

The general came down strongly on still another postwar issue, involving arms and ammunition: "Yes, the question of the adoption of one caliber of small arms for the army and another for the navy—thirty caliber for army and twenty-three caliber for the navy—I regard as a serious error. . . . This is one of the most important questions that has arisen for some time, and I hope to see it settled promptly so that the same ammunition can be used by both army and navy."[5] Not surprisingly, considering Merriam's longtime interest in marksmanship, he saw an imperative need to have ammunition standardization in the nation's armed forces.

Despite stepping into issues about the disposition of the Philippines and army expansion, with the reported conflicting opinions, Merriam probably felt his command of the Department of the Colorado would be peaceful. Within a few months, however, a series of events would plunge him into a most stressful time, one of the worst he had ever experienced. The general scarcely could get familiar with his new headquarters and his new command before these issues developed.

The first upheaval for Merriam occurred with orders for him to assume temporary command of the Department of the Missouri in addition to his command of the Department of the Colorado. Thus, on March 31, 1899, Merriam again became commander of two large army departments simultaneously. This developed from the retirement of the Department of the Missouri's commander, Brig. Gen. Edwin V. Sumner. At first, Merriam remained at Denver, "occasionally visiting" department headquarters in Omaha. During the months of February and March, however, he stayed in Omaha. The major task facing him in the Department of the Missouri was preparing and moving various units for service in the Philippines. This "involved much labor, including all the detailed minutiae connected with complete reorganization," Merriam reported, adding: "In fact, this work was almost as great as organizing new commands, old character disappearing with the extensive changes brought about by loss incident to the Cuban campaign; by the discharge of war recruits; and by the weeding out by discharge or transfer of men unsuited to service in the tropics." The high number of new men, "awkward and undrilled," who also had to be clothed and equipped, "occupied all the time of the officers concerned, so that little time in the way of the regular course of routine work could be accomplished."[6]

The second event complicating Merriam's anticipated peacetime life occurred on April 5. Daughter Carry married George Bart Berger at St. John's Cathedral in Denver. This was a pleasurable change, though also a stressful one for the Merriam family.[7]

A far more serious disruption took place on April 30, 1899, when General Merriam received the following telegrammed order: "The Governor of Idaho reports an insurrection beyond the power of the State to control existing in Shoshone county of that State. The Acting Secretary of War directs that you report at once to the capital of that State and after conference with the authorities thence you go to the seat of action, calling to your aid such troops as may be most convenient regardless of department lines. Department commanders will be notified. You will take with you the necessary staff officers. The travel is necessary to the public service. By Command of Major General Miles."[8] This startling order, detailing General Merriam to emergency action in the Department of the Columbia territory, must have shocked Merriam, already nearly overwhelmed by his responsibilities in two vast departments.

Apparently this assignment came about because the president, the War Department, and General Miles did not believe that they could encumber General Shafter with this task, given his important role in administering the shipment of men and equipment in support of continuing operations in the Philippines. But why Merriam? While the answer to that question remains open to some conjecture, several points seem telling. Most apparent, Merriam, with his principal headquarters in Denver, was geographically the closest to the scene of action, but there were likely other factors involved.[9] There was an appreciation at the highest level for Merriam's performance as commander of the Department of California and the Department of the Columbia during the Spanish-American War. He was identified as familiar with the Coeur d'Alene area of Idaho through his establishment of the fort there that later became Fort Sherman. Also, there

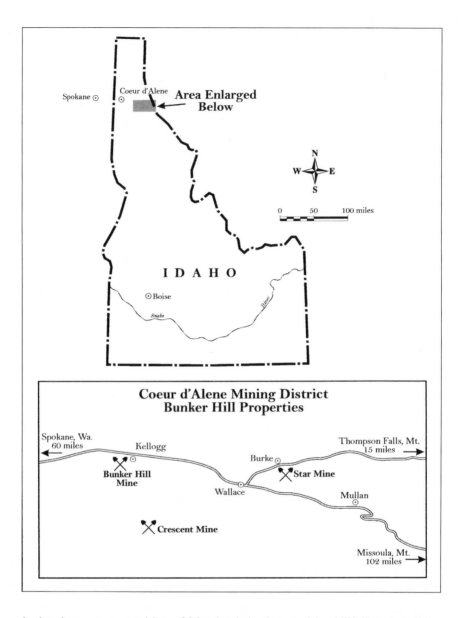

had to be some recognition of Merriam's background in skillfully using diplomacy in the problems with the Pacific Northwest Indians and earlier at Laredo with the Mexican revolutionaries. The Idaho situation would demand a forceful and decisive commander, though one who could truly work with the civil authorities.

There had been unrest and some violence in the Coeur d'Alene mining district for many years. In 1892 and in 1894, federal troops had been requested and sent to maintain order. In 1892 the federal troop intervention essentially caused the failure of a miner's strike, and when peace was restored, nonunion miners were mostly employed. Bitterness between the owners and miners continued.

In 1894, railroad strikes in the nation generated sympathetic labor strife on the Northern Pacific Railroad and among the Coeur d'Alene miners. On July 3 of that year, a witness in a trial against union miners was killed by masked men. Significantly, area law-enforcement officers did not act. Governor McConnell requested that President Cleveland provide troops, which he did on the ninth. The army regulars remained until September, when they were finally withdrawn. These two federal military interventions set significant precedents, aided mine management for the most part, angered the miners' unions, and did little to resolve tensions between workers and owners and their supervisors. A historian of this period aptly observed, "On the industrial front, Mountain West radicals stood out from their counterparts in other regions of the country in their willingness to confront employers and in the extent to which they were willing to engage in violence."[10]

After 1894, labor leaders continued organizing the Idaho miners, and a more-powerful union, the Western Federation of Miners (WFM), emerged and grew in strength. By 1899 the WFM had been successful in organizing workers at all the Coeur d'Alene lead and silver mines, with the exception of the Bunker Hill and Sullivan Mining Company, the mining district's biggest operation, located in an area called Wardner, later Kellogg. For years the company had bitterly battled against WFM efforts to unionize its workforce, refusing to recognize or bargain with the union. During this period, the primary union drive was to obtain recognition and thus be allowed to collectively bargain for labor contracts. If that could be achieved, so the unions reasoned, wages, working hours, and conditions would then be negotiated. Furthermore, the WFM's strength would be greatly enhanced if it could get the Bunker Hill Company included with the other unionized mines.

In April 1899, with the Idaho National Guard still involved overseas in combat in the Philippines, the union decided to violently settle its longstanding grievances with the company. There was a strong sentiment of finally exacting revenge. On April 29 the union actions began. The *Idaho State Tribune,* the official paper of the WFM in Wallace, Idaho, graphically described how events unfolded:

> Saturday last witnessed what might properly be considered the close of a seven years war. . . . About 10:30 a man on horseback came galloping down Bank Street from Canyon creek and halting in front of the Tribune office said, 'They are coming,' and passed on at a rapid rate. Five minutes later the whistle of the Northern Pacific engine pulling the train from Burke and Gem resounded with its usual regularity. . . . [O]n its nine freight and ore cars were packed one thousand men half of whom were masked and armed with Winchester rifles. The streets of Wallace took on an air of excitement and before the train proceeded to Wardner with its human freight on its mission of destruction armed men walked the streets in quest of an abundant

supply of ammunition. It was evident to all that some of the scenes of 1892 were to be repeated and this time the Bunker Hill & Sullivan Mining Company at Wardner, twelve miles below Wallace, was to be the victim of a forceful demonstration on part of the organized miners of the Coeur d'Alenes.[11]

The union men had commandeered the train, and after arriving at Wardner at 1:00 p.m., they set about placing "under the mill 3000 pounds of dynamite." The union newspaper reported, "All the details were managed with the discipline and precision of a perfectly trained military organization." Confronted by such a show of union force, some sixty mill guards and employees fled, along with the especially hated mine supervisor, Fred Burbidge. By 2:30 everything was set, and the detonation of the explosives completely destroyed the company's huge $250,000 concentrator. The force of the explosion was heard twenty miles away. The office, books, and papers of the company and a nearby boarding house, as well as Burbidge's home, were reduced to splinters and smoldering ashes. The union paper's headline read, "Work of Destruction Complete."[12]

As could be expected, the reaction in other quarters was one of shock, anger, and dismay. The anti-union weekly *Wardner News* of May 6 led off its account of the destruction of the Bunker Hill concentrator by writing, "The Coeur d'Alene miner's unions have at last broken their record of crime by an outrage so atrocious that the whole country stands aghast at the recital of the horrible details." The paper went on to say, as it described the event, "that such an iniquitous violation of the law would be attempted, even by the Coeur d'Alene miners' unions, hardened in crime and blood as they were, surpassed common belief."[13]

Immediately after the successful dynamiting of the mill, a shooting occurred. A Frisco miner was killed, allegedly by a Bunker Hill Company "scab," and a mill employee was shot and later died at a Spokane hospital. Despite the deaths, the union men celebrated with shouts and rifle fire, then retired back to their respective communities via the hijacked train.

Noted as accompanying the union miners in their attack on the Bunker Hill mill was the Populist Shoshone County sheriff James D. Young. The miners had twice helped elect him, and his sympathies were clear. The inclusion of the sheriff in the trainload of union men, the size of the union force, the tremendous property damage, and the killings prompted Idaho governor Frank Steunenberg to send an urgent request to President McKinley to intervene with a strong military force of five hundred regulars. The governor stated that the legislature was not in session and could not promptly reconvene to take any action. He and others believed that a dangerous conspiracy and violent labor insurrection had developed, a conclusion certainly strengthened by input from Bunker Hill Company leaders. Of course, precedents had been established by the federal military interventions in 1892 and 1894.

In Washington, President McKinley agreed to Steunenberg's appeal for federal intervention. Deploying five hundred regular troops to the Coeur d'Alenes was no easy matter, however. Because of the overseas commitments of the army in Cuba, Puerto Rico, and the Philippines, regulars in the United States were severely reduced and spread throughout the country. Furthermore, it was difficult to come up with senior commanders, as the combining of several departments indicated. The selection of General Merriam to lead the army in Idaho and the orders directing him to draw on troops without regard to department boundaries reflect the army's difficult status.

Washington officials believed it was urgent that Merriam get to Idaho and take command of the troubled area. The need for speed was evident in subsequent telegrams sent to the general on April 30. General Miles in one message said: "Acting Secretary of War directs that you give all necessary orders for movement of troops and supplies. Acknowledge receipt." In another, he stated, "Reference to telegrams of even date relative to insurrection in Idaho, you will understand the necessity of moving with as little delay as possible." Washington wanted to make sure that Merriam responded immediately.[14]

General Merriam, accompanied by his aide Lt. J. B. Bennet, managed to leave Denver at 6:30 p.m. on that same day, April 30, 1899. In the meantime he had wired Governor Steunenberg, asking, "Are troops needed now or is it too late?" The governor, ill with the flu, quickly replied, "While there is apparent calm today, troops are surely needed and must be sent in at once." By the evening of May 1, Merriam and the ailing Steunenberg met at Glenn's Ferry, Idaho, seventy-five miles southeast of Boise, to assess the status of the mining district. The governor and the general's discussion, with aides present, took place in the smoking room of Merriam's sleeper car as the train sped toward Boise. Merriam reported to Washington, "Conference with Governor discloses usual difficulties of dealing with riots and conspiracies." He recorded that "after hastily talking over the situation with the Governor and taking into account the number of rioters, their armament and ability for offering resistance, etc., I sent orders by telegraph from the train directing the troops at Spokane, Walla Walla, Vancouver, and Boise to proceed at once by rail, cavalry dismounted, to Wardner, thence to go into camp and maintain order." Early the next morning, May 2, Merriam sent orders for "troops from Harrison, Assinniboine, Russell, and Douglas to concentrate at Mullan." Thus General Merriam had soldiers coming from both west and east. He reported to army headquarters that he planned to go to Wardner that same night. Merriam conveyed to Washington what he might be up against. "Number of union miners in district about fifteen hundred; number armed and active in riots about one thousand."[15]

Merriam had some qualms about legal ramifications of the federal intervention in this domestic disturbance. He indicated that in further conversation with the governor while awaiting the train, Steunenberg seemed to be in doubt about declaring martial law. Merriam believed suspected rioters should be and could be controlled from escaping the district by checking trains leaving the area. On May 2, 1899, he wired army headquarters in cipher: "Troops concentrating at Wardner and Mullan will control outlets from mining camps. If not disapproved, I will direct to scrutinize travel outward and detain suspected passengers. This is martial law, but no other course likely to secure rioters." The next day a message from Brig. Gen. H. C. Corbin, the army's adjutant general, stated: "Your cipher message received. Submitted by the Acting Secretary of War to the President and I am instructed to say your action is approved."[16]

In remarkably quick time, troops coming primarily from the forts to the west arrived at Wardner. Also arriving on the scene was Governor Steunenberg's personal representative, Idaho state auditor Bartlett Sinclair, who had practiced law in the East before arriving in Idaho in 1890 and was familiar with northern Idaho by having resided for a time in Bonner's Ferry. The next day, after Merriam arrived at Wardner on the night of May 2, he received the following message from Capt. J. B. Batchelor, of Merriam's old black 24th Infantry Regiment, who commanded one of the first army units to reach the mining town: "I arrived here yesterday, two P.M. and encamped. Situation quiet at present. Much apprehension apparent. Search for arms now in progress, which I am protecting. Arrests contemplated which Sinclair thinks may lead to resistance. Walla Walla troop not in yet."[17] A brief time later Merriam notified Washington that there was no organized resistance on the part of the miners.

After consulting with Sinclair, according to one newspaper account, Merriam "established stringent military rule," which included mass arrests since so many union men had been involved in the destruction of the Wardner mill. The newspaper claimed, for example, that "Merriam had every man in Burke, 243 men in all," captured and placed under arrest without bail. "Before the soldiers came a non-union miner could not remain in Burke. He was run down the canyon at the point of a revolver. General Merriam reversed that condition." The total number of arrests varied greatly in the published accounts. One conservative estimate was 700 men, with one account stating there were 1,600 arrested.[18]

Merriam's plan to arrest miners fleeing the mining district via train appeared to be collapsing based on several reports from troop commanders. One stated: "It is reported that 150 rioters are making their way to Thompson Falls [Montana] and others to Belknap and other points. . . . Troops enroute might be directed to these points." Another message from a commander at Mullan carried similar news: "Many miners reported going into Missoula from this point; some have already arrived there. Others near there, tramping along railroad. It might be well to see if civil authorities at that point will act. I can do nothing there from here."[19]

Also on that busy May 3, a message from Governor Steunenberg in Boise eased many of Merriam's legal concerns. "My representative informs me that rioters are fleeing towards Spokane. Have all trains stopped and suspicious persons returned. Martial law declared." Six infantry companies continued to arrive at Wardner and Mullan, and a substantial force was concentrating that eventually would total about five hundred soldiers. Merriam now passed along the governor's orders to his men: "Arrest all persons attempting to leave mining region of Coeur d'Alene unless fully satisfied that they are not implicated in the riots. Martial law has been declared in Shoshone County, Idaho."[20]

The attempt to arrest any fleeing union miners now involved the adjoining states of Washington and Montana. Reports of men escaping on foot and arriving in Missoula led to requests from Governor Steunenberg to Montana governor Robert Smith to assist in arresting and returning the fugitives to Idaho. Merriam sent word to Capt. Henry G. Lyon, a West Point graduate commanding Company D, 24th Infantry, at Thompson Falls, Montana, to provide an escort for the prisoners: "Governor of Montana has ordered Sheriff of Missoula County to make arrests of fugitives. Return with the prisoners you have . . . delaying in Missoula long enough to permit your deputies and Missoula sheriff to make arrests there." Captain Lyon and his detachment of sixty-five black troops reported arresting a "ringleader" by the name of Eric Anderson. Other arrests were made at Thompson Falls.[21]

Apparently this operation did not go smoothly or exactly as planned. Friction developed between Idaho officers and Montana civil authorities and with the military officers operating in Montana. In addition, Montana miners' unions began blasting Governor Smith and his police for their role in aiding Idaho against the rioters, whereupon Governor Smith reconsidered the arresting actions in Montana. On May 12, 1899, he wrote to Merriam warning that Montana civil authorities had to be respected and emphasized that, although the state had responded as requested, "no part of Montana is acting under martial law." The general replied that his orders to his officers were "to avoid the slightest discourtesy towards the civil authorities of Montana" and that, he believed after review, they had acted properly. The Montana governor wrote to Merriam once again on May 17, saying, "Your letter with copies of telegrams disclosed that at all times you recognized the proper civil authorities."[22] With that, Merriam was able to show sensitivity to military-civil relationships and to diplomatically end the military's friction with Montana officials.

The arrests of suspected miners involved in the crimes of the April 29 mill's destruction continued daily in the mining camps by Idaho deputies escorted by troops. At first, many of those arrested were brought to a large, two-story building (later labeled the "bull pen") that had been used as a merchant's warehouse. For heat, the men had to have outdoor campfires, and hay had to be provided for sleeping. Food was brought in, and Merriam reported, "By daily inspections I satisfied myself that the prisoners were being furnished abundant food and well-prepared." The miners, however, complained forcefully and bitterly about their food, health conditions, and overall treatment. By May 5 the number of prisoners, approximately 150, exceeded the "bull pen's" capacity. About 200 men were then quartered in boxcars sidetracked at the Wardner station. Again, hay was provided for bedding. Merriam remembered that while the boxcar arrangement was not ideal, at least the miners did not have to sleep on the ground like his guarding troops.[23] By May 9, workers aided by prisoners began building a primitive new "bull pen" on higher ground.

There was extremely slow progress in charging men with crimes and releasing those having minimal or no involvement in the incident. Holding so many prisoners was developing into a crisis, and labor unions throughout the country brought increasing attention to the condition of the arrested miners. Even a racial element entered the picture as miners lodged complaints that they had been subjected to indignities, abusive language, and harassment by black soldiers of the 24th Infantry, then on guard duty. Realizing the explosiveness of the prisoner situation, Merriam wrote to Governor Steunenberg on May 11: "I am still holding nearly four hundred prisoners in a barn and box cars, all are very uncomfortable and with unsanitary conditions which will soon become intolerable. Something must be done to hurry preliminary examinations and release those not prima facie guilty. It is impossible to make this large number of prisoners reasonably comfortable here without time and expense. Can you not personally inspect the situation at once and bring help?"[24] Steunenberg did arrive in Wardner, and the prisoner problem eased somewhat but nevertheless lingered. Merriam began letting miner families provide bunks, stoves, and clothing to make the prolonged incarcerations more humane.

Merriam next faced another problem of far reaching consequences. On May 8 State Auditor Sinclair, representing the governor, informed Merriam that all mine owners had been told that under martial law they were forbidden to employ miners unless they possessed permits from state authorities. A proclamation was drawn up to announce this requirement, and it appeared in Spokane newspapers. Merriam proposed to Sinclair the inclusion of a paragraph that would make granting work permits conditioned on applicants denying participation in the riots and renouncing membership in any society that "has incited, encouraged, or approved of said riots." He claimed that he thought this revision would enable an "innocent member of an innocent union" to better obtain the work permits. Merriam consented to put his name at the bottom of the proclamation, indicating that he had "Examined and Approved."[25]

This proclamation, posted throughout the Coeur d'Alene district and published in newspapers, created a storm of controversy that spread nationally. Labor unions and pro-labor publications seized on the work permits as union busting and illegal. They denounced Steunenberg and charged that the army was indorsing his anti-labor actions. They focused on General Merriam as a "labor persecutor" and demanded his recall. The WFM alleged that Merriam was the real architect of the oath and work-permit system. Adding more fuel to the fire were purported Merriam remarks made to Wardner merchants on May 5, which quoted him as saying: "Since the trouble largely originates in hostile organizations of men known as labor unions, I should suggest a law making the formation of such unions or kindred societies a crime. Surely history furnishes argument sufficiently in favor of such a course."[26]

Merriam denied having made such a remark, but it was widely publicized and believed. The drumbeat of vilification of Merriam continued for many months. Newspapers, particularly in the region, kept the Coeur d'Alene martial-law situation on front pages. The pro-union *Idaho State Tribune* of Wallace declared: "arrests still continue," "Innocent Men Thrown into Bull Pen Who Were Never Miners," and "Many Prisoners Ill from Exposure." The *Spokane Spokesman Review* of May 14 ran headlines of "Martial Law Is Denounced" and "Declares the Coeur d'Alene Organization Has Been Abused." Labor unions throughout the West, and then in all parts of the nation, began passing protest resolutions. On May 11 the Spokane Falls Typographical Union and on May 20 the Western Labor Union in Butte, Montana, made resolutions deploring the Coeur d'Alene activities. A resolution of the Anaconda Typographical Union in Anaconda, Montana, on May 17 denounced the "actions of General Merriam and Governor Smith." Even Samuel Gompers, president of the American Federation of Labor, made a point of condemning the general's procedures in Idaho. In the AFL publication *American Federationist* of July 1899, Gompers, in a rebuttal to a *Denver Times* defense of Merriam, denied abusing the general but went on to state, "The ordinary citizen will conclude that either General Merriam at Wardner declared the Miner's Union a criminal organization, and aided and abetted in an effort to destroy it, or his denial yesterday lacks the element of truth."[27]

The public clamor, particularly originating from the labor unions, caught President McKinley's attention. On May 29 General Merriam received an alarming telegram: "It is charged in resolution by the Western Labor Union under date of May twentieth just received by the President that owners of mines in Coeur d'Alene district are denied the right of employing any man unless he first makes affidavit that he is a non-union miner and that the Army sent to aid the state authorities to preserve the peace and protect property is being used to enforce the alleged order. The statement must be the result of some misunderstanding which should be properly corrected. The President wishes a statement of facts at once. By order of the Secretary of War." The next day Merriam, onboard a train in Nevada, replied rather defensively: "Resolutions referred to in your telegram are at fault, like most others on the subject. State authorities require miners to obtain permits but no affidavits are required. Men must sign a paper denying participation in the crimes of April 29, also denying membership in any society which incite or approve these crimes and promise to obey the law. Troops are taking no part in this unless keeping the peace does so. Every mine owner I have seen strongly approves."[28] The general believed that his actions, including those associated with the work-permit system, were correctly and legally in support of Governor Steunenberg's declaration of martial law. No doubt influenced by the governor and other state officials, and mindful of previous military interventions in 1892 and 1894, Merriam concluded that firm action was necessary to end labor troubles and violence once and for all.

What Merriam believed, however, was not totally acceptable in Washington. There was concern that the army intervention, as directed by Merriam, had overstepped legal bounds by having troops act as virtual posses for civil authorities, sometimes without the necessary approval, in making arrests of miners. Then the general's "approved" work-permit system seemed to further project the army into uncertain and contentious legal areas regarding employment. The McKinley administration, acting through Secretary of War R. A. Alger, attempted to pull back from this confrontation with labor. On May 31 Merriam was directed: "You will instruct Major Smith, commanding at Wallace, that he is to use the United States troops to aid the State authorities to suppress rioting and to maintain peace and order. These were your original instructions. The army must have nothing whatever to do with enforcing rules for the government of miners or miner's unions. That is a matter for the local authorities to deal with." The comment about "original instructions" stung Merriam. It seemed to imply that the general had erred in his judgment and aggressive actions against the miners and unions and had violated orders. Merriam responded, "It was not intended that the troops under my command should assume any part whatever in carrying into effect these or any other rules affecting laborers or labor in the state of Idaho, nor have they done so in the remotest degree."[29] He argued that he was merely supporting Idaho's actions on work permits.

Merriam was hurt and angered about the "original instructions" comment. He resorted to mail to ask the War Department testily what were the "original instructions" that he must have missed and requested a copy sent to him. The general declared in his report on the Idaho assignment that he never received an answer to this request. In the meantime this message with its rebuke had been made public, and Merriam felt that he had been stabbed in the back.[30]

The general began efforts to extricate himself and the US troops from their seemingly thankless hardship conditions and physically demanding duty of guarding prisoners and supporting Idaho authorities on arrests. By May 12 Merriam sent an optimistic telegram to the adjutant general in Washington: "Number of prisoners reduced to four hundred and fifty and am relieving troops needed in connection with shipment to Manila, leaving one battalion Twenty-fourth Infantry here, under Capt. Leavell. All is progressing satisfactorily and many miners returning to work under necessary restrictions by state authority. I think I may return to Denver Monday, if approved, and not return unless later complications arise. Governor will be here tomorrow and will hurry forward investigation and prosecution. I hope he will be able to release half the men still held." Merriam received a quick reply to his message, directing him to remain at Wardner until he had talked with Steunenberg. Four days later, however, after consultation with the governor, Merriam told Washington that Steunenberg "deems it necessary to place troops at Burke and Mullan." Significantly, Merriam reported, from "present indications troops may be required for six months or more." Idaho officials and the mine owners were anxious to retain federal troops in the district as long as possible. With this somber forecast, the general asked Washington to send two troops of cavalry from Fort Robinson or Fort Meade with supplies for one month.[31] Thus Merriam's hopes for leaving and at least reducing the number of deployed troops had collapsed.

The reason for this abrupt change became clear in a wire Merriam sent to Washington the next day, May 17. In it he reported: "Union miners now refusing work under conditions deemed by state authorities necessary to insure good order. This seems partly due to sympathy and support given by kindred unions in other states. Result is large numbers of idle and sullen men in the mining centers, Mullan, Burke, and Wallace." Merriam added that the "mounted troops asked for in yesterday's telegram would have a restraining effect."[32] An important cause of this turn of events was the May 18 deadline for workers to obtain their work permits. Many were now refusing to do so, and as a consequence mines had to close for lack of laborers. Even the non-union men were now idled, swelling the ranks of disgruntled miners.

In face of the mounting criticism, emanating particularly from national unions and sympathetic press articles, Merriam tried to reassure army headquarters and the War Department that progress was being made and that he was acting wholly in concert with the state. In his telegram of May 16, he said, "referring to press criticism, I have made no orders. My action limited strictly to support of state authorities." Then in a May 17 telegram, Merriam expressed confidence in the current course of action: "The Governor's course appears to be judicious and his prompt support necessary to arrest lawlessness and crime, which has obtained in this county for several years. With troops placed order will be preserved. Trials will go on, witnesses can testify under the feeling of security. Well disposed miners will return to work and the turbulent element gradually disappear."[33]

By May 25, Merriam relayed to Washington his upbeat opinion that the "acute stage of disorders is passed." The general indicated, "Some miners accepting permits to work and others leaving the district." The cavalry units he had requested had arrived and were already patrolling the district and relieving guards at the magazines containing explosives. Merriam declared that civil functions were being restored and that the trials of prisoners were proceeding. The Populist sheriff and Populist county commissioners had been removed from office. He also reported that the number of prisoners was down to 330 and the "sanitary condition is beyond complaint." Overall, "conditions here steadily improving." With this positive progress report, Merriam told Washington that he planned to leave Wardner, go to Vancouver Barracks to confer about supplies and expenditures, and then proceed on to Denver to his department headquarters. The commander of the 1st Cavalry, Maj. Allen Smith, would be left in charge in Idaho.[34]

Washington approved Merriam's desire and intention to leave Idaho and return to Colorado. The general departed on May 25, leaving instructions to Major Smith reminding him of the sensitive nature of the army's role: "The troops are here by order of the President to aid the State Executive in maintaining order and restoring the state government to its legitimate functions." Then, with an obvious eye on the persistent criticism, he added, "To this end we are exercising the extraordinary powers which obtain under martial law, but we must not forget the necessity of using this power with great care and moderation, to the end that while exacting prompt submission of all persons to all measures needful to the object we have in hand, we may not overdo it to the annoyance of the innocent or even to the needless distress of those who may have offended." Reflecting one of Merriam's long-held beliefs, he continued, "Constant vigilance and prompt actions may sometimes prevent or nip in the bud tendencies which might otherwise lead to serious conditions." Finally, Merriam expressed confidence in Major Smith's abilities and the current situation. "The acute stage has passed," Merriam remarked, "and the game is now merely one of waiting till the civil officers and courts can be set up and resume their functions, and the local industries, lately paralyzed by mob violence, shall have time to reorganize and resume operations."[35]

Thus the general finally succeeded in getting away from Idaho, but in no way had he escaped the personal attacks that stemmed from his command there.

Merriam's assessment that the Idaho intervention was "steadily progressing" did not seem totally convincing to Washington. On June 5 army headquarters asked the general whether those who had participated in the insurrection and who had been arrested by military authorities "have yet been surrendered to the civil authorities?" Behind that question was a concern about when troops could be reduced or withdrawn. Merriam replied: "[M]ilitary guard may be necessary for several months, pending restoration of civil tribunals almost completely disorganized and demoralized by complicity or sympathy with the rioters. The Governor is making all possible haste and says he will continue martial law till the work in hand is fully done."[36] Later in June the general called on Fort Riley, Kansas, to supply fifty more enlisted men for service in Idaho. Any reduction in troop strength did not seem imminent.

Merriam continued to fend off personal attacks and criticism from many quarters. On August 24, 1899, he felt it necessary to write to army headquarters to rebut some of the charges lodged in the press:

> As to the colored troops, during the entire period I did not observe a single act or hear a word of rudeness or severity on the part of a soldier towards prisoners, nor did I hear of any misconduct or of a complaint. My observation includes the prisoners confined in box cars.
>
> In view of the above facts, I am compelled to believe these complaints to be wholly unfounded, that they are only a part of a conspiracy to get sympathy and support from the public, from kindred unions, and even from the President of the United States. It is incredible that so many outrages would have happened at Wardner in the very presence of so many officers and come to the light only in the form of affidavits long afterwards laid before the President in Washington. . . . [A]ffidavits are hand-written. . . . [T]hey have

been conducted by a few leaders, whose skill in self-concealment is proverbial.[37]

The role of black soldiers at the Coeur d'Alene mining communities remained controversial. While some people viewed the deployment of the black 24th Infantry Regiment as an intentional effort to avoid any fraternization of troops with the white miners, it was more likely they were geographically the most readily available soldiers. Although the regiment's companies were scattered at several forts, they were still at points that could reach the Coeur d'Alene areas in an expeditious manner. Some of the miner animosity toward the black men may have come from resentment of the part played by 25th Infantry black troops during the federal intervention of 1892. The miners viewed the soldiers then, as they did in 1899, as tools of the mining companies.[38]

As the weeks and months passed, and with the approach of fall and winter, government and military leaders became increasingly concerned about the continued presence of federal troops in the Coeur d'Alenes. Both soldiers and prisoners dreaded spending more time in such dreary living conditions soon to be compounded by bitter cold. On September 7, 1899, Merriam wrote to the adjutant general warning that "the lateness of the season requires that our troops still on duty in the Coeur d'Alene mining region be returned to their stations or provided with winter quarters. There are still in their custody nearly two hundred state prisoners." On September 12 Captain Graves, one of Merriam's aides, wrote from Omaha informing him, "Sinclair considers presence of troops in district necessary for morale effect, if no other." Graves reported, however, that Major Smith "believes all troops can be removed by first of October." He relayed Smith's judgment that mines were "running full handed and believe to be protected by own watchmen" and that the state had "material at its disposal so it can no longer demand troops."[39]

Following on the heels of this information came reports from Wardner that there had been an attempted escape from the "bull pen." The prisoners had been recaptured but refused to cooperate with military orders, whereupon the captain in charge had placed them on bread and water for eight days. In addition, a sergeant of the 1st Cavalry was charged with accepting a bribe in a release of prisoners.[40] The bread-and-water punishment prompted a renewed outcry about the treatment of the miners and the conditions at the mining district. Ed Boyce, head of the WFM, on September 27 sent a protest to President McKinley, claiming the miners were in such misery as to contemplate suicide. McKinley believed that he needed to act and, through his new secretary of war, Elihu Root, asked for explanation from Governor Steunenberg and General Merriam. Steunenberg dismissed the union chief's complaints as baseless, while Merriam defended the captain of the prison guard as applying appropriate punishment.

The September episodes and the furor that resulted caused renewed efforts to terminate the federal intervention. On October 11 Merriam wrote to Adjutant General Corbin, stating, "Governor of Idaho now at Boise . . . wires as follows 'Just returned from Shoshone county and am more convinced than ever that withdrawal of troops would be disastrous if not criminal.'" In a tone of resignation, Merriam added, "In view of the foregoing I will give orders to have all troops made as comfortable as possible in tents."[41]

Secretary of War Root became impatient with the reported continued need for troops. He told Steunenberg that he should look to state resources for providing civilian guards and to speed trials and release prisoners. He then informed both the governor and General Merriam that the "War Department directs troops be withdrawn from custody of civil prisoners October twentieth." This deadline thoroughly alarmed Governor Steunenberg, and he immediately sought to change it, going to Washington to personally make his appeal known to the president and the secretary of war. Steunenberg succeeded in getting an agreement to hold withdrawal of troops from prisoner guard duty until the end of October. It was anticipated that an Idaho National Guard unit would be available at that time to take over from the regulars. Shortly afterward, almost all of the remaining prisoners were released. In the trials that did take place, only eleven miners were convicted.[42]

Although some army regulars were relieved of Idaho duty and returned to their assigned posts, others remained in the district to support the total restoration of civil authority. The remaining force consisted primarily of a troop of the 1st Cavalry from Fort Robinson and dismounted troops from the 6th Cavalry from Fort Riley. These men had to plan for spending the winter months in northern Idaho, mostly at Osburn and Wallace. On December 7, 1899, Merriam wired sad news to Major Smith at Wallace: "Secretary of War will not authorize further buildings for your command. Make your men comfortable as possible with floored tents and stoves."[43] The following spring, in May 1900, a 7th Infantry company relieved the cavalry units. Some soldiers remained in the Coeur d'Alene district until martial law ended on April 11, 1901.

The uproar over the handling of the miners following the destruction of the Bunker Hill mill and the declaration of martial law became highly political and culminated in a congressional investigation. In February 1900, members of the House Military Affairs Committee went to the Coeur d'Alene mining areas to interview participants, including Merriam and other army officers, mine officials, Idaho leaders, and labor bosses. After months of examining witnesses and conducting hearings, a Republican majority report and a Democratic minority report were issued in June 1900. The two partisan reports differed sharply, with the Republicans striving to protect the McKinley administration and the Democrats seeking to make political hay with negative findings. The Republicans claimed that the federal intervention was legal and proper as an insurrection certainly had been underway, with the involvement of the sheriff and county officials. As to Merriam, they maintained that he and the army had not crossed legal boundaries in helping make arrests and guarding prisoners, these actions being essential in the absence of Idaho National Guard units. General Merriam, they argued, had demonstrated proper concern for the rights and welfare of the arrested miners and was not hell-bent on destroying the labor unions as labor leaders had contended. He was merely attempting to bring order and justice to crimes of sabotage and murder.

After examining some fourteen specific charges against Merriam, the Republican majority report concluded:

> The evidence presented to your committee completely vindicates General Merriam, and shows conclusively that there was no animosity to organized labor on the part of the military in performance of their duty.
>
> Brig. Gen. H. C. Merriam and the officers and men under him are to be commended for their wisdom, prudence, and soldierly behavior during the turbulent days of riot and insurrection in Idaho, and the result of this investigation is a complete exoneration and vindication of their conduct.[44]

In contrast, the Democratic report challenged the idea that an insurrection had even occurred. The miners had quietly retired after the mill destruction, they contended, and legal processes had progressed without hindrance. They specifically faulted Merriam for his cozy support of Steunenberg, the governor's declaration of martial law, and the work-permit system that impinged on the miners' civil rights. The Democratic-minority report concluded: "To summarize, the undersigned are satisfied from the evidence adduced before the committee that General Merriam was wholly mistaken as to his powers and duties; that he was ignorant of the laws of his country; that he failed to distinguish the difference between military law and martial law; and that his conduct has resulted in the gravest injuries to the liberty of the citizen and the rights of individuals."[45]

President McKinley accepted the Republican findings. While this largely calmed the public and political strife over the federal intervention in Idaho, unions and labor leaders continued to believe and to claim that Merriam had joined state officials in trying to destroy the mining unions and that the army had unfairly and illegally aided the mine owners. But businessmen and many public figures viewed Merriam as a stalwart upholder of law and order and protector of property.

The federal intervention in Idaho in the 1899 Coeur d'Alene insurrection had a number of consequences. First, General Merriam had received so much bad publicity that he could well believe his military career had been irreparably damaged. The hatred directed toward him worried his family and created concerns for his safety. Second, law and order was restored to the mining region, although it took far longer than anyone anticipated. Third, the actions taken by the state and the army decidedly hurt union efforts in the region. Fourth, Merriam's command and his support of state-declared martial law raised new legal questions about US Army involvement in domestic disturbances. Fifth, the success of the intervention spurred the growth of more-radical union membership, at least in the short term. Sixth, some members of Congress, angered by the army's role, argued for army reforms and against its expansion. Seventh, sadly, Governor Steunenberg would be assassinated on December 30, 1905. A subsequent investigation, indictment of big-labor leaders like Bill Haywood, and a sensational trial would keep the Idaho mining troubles in the news for years to come.

Merriam's role in the Coeur d'Alene intervention has remained controversial. Some writers looking back over the events claim the general was naive, did not know the law and regulations governing such domestic disturbances, and blindly followed the lead of Steunenberg and Sinclair in their union-busting efforts. It has been alleged that he blundered in confusion.[46] Yet the foregoing recitation of the historic events appears to refute these claims. As has been noted, Merriam had been involved in earlier domestic troubles, including the railway strikes and in the Denver City Hall War. Because of his long interest in and reading of law, he probably understood the legal aspects of the intervention far better than the average high-ranking officer. His close association with and support of Governor Steunenberg came from his strong desire to do everything necessary to restore law and order. The general sincerely believed that Steunenberg was on the right course. Far from being confused, Merriam's messages to Washington and to his troops, keeping them informed of his actions and decisions, were direct and clear. In his typical fashion, he was highly motivated to act speedily and forcefully.

Perhaps Merriam could be faulted for acting so quickly and aggressively that proper civil procedures were not followed timely and to the letter in all cases. He believed that if he did not make arrests and confine the many offenders, they would escape prosecution and again return to violent actions at another time. This fault was compounded by the perception that the general was far from neutral in this labor conflict. As a person who highly valued discipline, Merriam disliked unions because they caused disorders, destruction, loss of life, and loss of property—this he had trouble tolerating. He viewed Steunenberg's battle against the WFM as a righteous cause and had trouble conveying a neutral stance.

To Merriam's credit, however, as the Republican congressional report concluded, Merriam employed the army with moderation, with no heavy-handed disregard of judicial processes and miners' civil rights. When Merriam returned to Denver after testifying in Washington during the congressional investigation, he was quoted in the newspaper as saying, "In all things connected with this affair, I have simply done my duty, and I am content."[47]

13

Toward Retirement

The government, country, and the administration are very greatly indebted to him for the great intelligence and good judgment which he displayed during the Coeur d'Alene troubles.

REP. C. E. LITTLEFIELD TO PRES. THEODORE ROOSEVELT, NOVEMBER 5, 1901

When General Merriam returned from his tumultuous time in Idaho to his command of the Department of the Colorado at Denver, he likely considered that he would not have to face Indian problems, at least of any importance. This proved to be an illusion. Shortly after reaching Denver, the general had reports of renewed friction between whites and the Indians in western Colorado and eastern Utah. In the late summer of 1899, Merriam responded to Ute unrest over food provisions being inadequate and of poor quality by sending Col. Thomas McGregor, 9th Cavalry, from Fort Grant, Arizona Territory, to the reservation lands to investigate complaints. Merriam then reported to the adjutant general on August 12, 1899: "It seems to me the food being issued to these Indians (to all of the three tribes, as I understand it) is entirely inadequate for such families of them as have not taken to farming." He warned that hunger would likely "drive them to their old hunting grounds in Colorado and get them into trouble."[1]

In September 1899 some Colorado citizens charged that the Utes had illegally invaded western Colorado game preserves. Investigations proved these claims false. The *Denver Times* of September 22 reported that General Merriam "takes the side of the Indians in an interview, and has a number of supporters." The newspaper quoted Merriam as saying, "In his opinion, the red man has been sorely imposed upon by the state of Colorado and deserves to hunt where he pleases." He added: "The government does not give them any more than they absolutely need to sustain life, and in many cases not that much, and they simply desire to hunt for food. . . . The state laws are such as to keep the poor Indian from the game preserves, and allow, it might be said, promiscuous slaughter of game by Eastern sportsmen who are likely to spend money and advertise the state."[2] These public comments by Merriam took considerable courage as many Colorado citizens at the time still believed in the saying, "the only good Indian is a dead Indian."

The Utes, having been forced off much of their traditional lands in Colorado, had long been unhappy with reservation life and with efforts to change them into farmers, plowing the soil, or livestock ranchers. The white pressure had eventually resulted in the 1879 Ute murder of Indian Agent Nathan Meeker in western Colorado and the subsequent deployment of US regulars to suppress a much-feared Ute insurrection. Chief Ouray had helped calm this situation, but because of his death in August 1890, he was not available for a like effort with the continued friction with the Utes.[3] In 1896 Maj. James F. Randlett, acting US Indian agent at the Uintah and Ouray Agency in Utah, warned that white mineral claims on the Uncompahgre Reservation could lead to serious trouble. Of more-immediate concern to Merriam was a Ute complaint about an agent's allowing white sheepmen to graze their animals on Ute reservation land. In November 1899, for example, the general sent word to Washington that an investigation of the Ute charges by a 9th Cavalry captain from Fort Duchesne, Utah, determined that "the late disturbance controverts the agent's claim that only unused lands were included in the grazing." Once again, Merriam cast blame on Indian agents for troubles. In his report on the sheep-grazing issue, he declared, "It is unreasonable, if not impossible, to expect these savages to keep the peace and be won over to civilization if such irritating agencies and methods are permitted to arouse their native propensities." A short time later Merriam wrote: "Failure to investigate and correct this wrong [permission to graze sheep on the Ute reservation] led to violence and bloodshed later in the year. The ounce of prevention is sometimes possible in managing Indians as well as white men."[4]

Troubles with the Utes continued to the end of Merriam's command of the Department of the Colorado. In late 1900 and early 1901, Indian unrest centered around the detention of a Ute leader, Black Hawk. On January 15, 1901, Merriam received the following report from Maj. M. B. Hughes, 9th Cavalry, at Fort Duchesne, Utah:

> [T]he headmen of the three tribes located in the reservation came to the post wishing to state certain grievances. When made to understand that the CO [commanding officer] was not empowered to act with authority in such cases, they said they wished an interpreter might be sent out to investigate their grievances connected with the running of the agency, and particularly in regard to the late trouble at White Rocks Agency which resulted in the arrest of Black Hawk. . . . That they wished the investigation to be made openly at a place other than the agency—Fort Duchesne—and that the Post Commander, or some

other officer, may be present at the inquiry. . . . They also called attention to the fact that Black Hawk had been in the guard house since
December 13, 1900, without a hearing.

The Fort Duchesne commander added, "if this matter were laid before the authorities and the Indians given a hearing, I believe it would be in the best interest of the service as they think they are not fairly treated." Merriam sent this report on to Washington, indicating that he supported Major Hughes in the Black
Hawk matter. This resulted in a telegram from army headquarters on January
18, 1901, directing the release of Black Hawk.[5]

While seemingly never free of dealing with Indian complaints, whether in
Colorado, Utah, New Mexico, or Arizona, fortunately for Merriam, they never
escalated into a crisis. Merriam's dealings with the Utes demonstrated once
again his evenhanded thinking and actions with respect to Indians and emphasized his continued condemnation of Indian agents and their practices.

One might assume that Merriam's pressure agenda, involving his command
of two army departments, the Idaho assignment dealing with labor strife, and
the Ute Indian unrest, left him little time for considering other issues. But that
was not the case. Merriam managed to find time to pursue his long personal
crusade to secure the US Army's adoption of his knapsack. In March 1900 he
sent a letter to the War Department's Board of Ordnance and Fortifications,
"inviting attention to the demonstrated value in service of the Merriam Pack."
The board extended an invitation for Merriam to attend one of their meetings,
whereupon the general journeyed to Washington and appeared before the board,
exhibited a sample pack, and "explained the special advantages of the device for
carrying the soldier's equipments." On April 5 the board met, then informed
Merriam on April 9 that they were recommending that the chief of ordnance
"purchase one thousand of the Merriam packs," which would then be issued to
ten different regiments for "practical trial" in lieu of the current equipment. Reports would then be considered by the board as to the pack's merits.[6]

This may have been exciting news for Merriam. But like so many previous tests and trials, this latest one failed to bring about any adoption. As late
as 1906, long after the general had retired, he was still receiving reports about
efforts involving his knapsack. A letter from the army's chief of artillery in the
War Department dated March 30, 1906, proved particularly revealing as to what
Merriam faced:

My report went in on the 12th of January. It was very voluminous. . . . It
wound up with a strong recommendation of the Merriam pack. . . . I
am told unofficially that the General Staff (from which I was relieved
December 1st) has recommended the issue of 1800 of these, 200 in
each of nine divisions, for trial during the coming summer brigade
camps and on the marches to and from these camps. . . . I made a
strong point in my report that no test possible in time of peace could

compare with the 7th Infantry's approval of the pack after a use of nine or ten years in peace and war, but apparently this point was not received at its proper worth. . . . [P]lease be careful to avoid bringing me into the matter unofficially. I understand that the present Chief of Staff has not lost some of his admiration for the wretched blanket roll and I have been told that he is indignant at the general tenor of my report.[7]

For years Merriam worked with Ridabock and Company of New York, a "military and band equipment" firm, to fabricate his backpack. In 1901 he and the company sold the packs for three dollars, with a royalty of sixty-three cents. In May 1906 Merriam tried to eliminate a perceived hurdle in securing army adoption by waiving his royalty. On June 2, 1906, he received a letter from the War Department's chief of ordnance thanking him for his consent to manufacture "a certain number of Merriam Packs free of royalty."[8]

Despite all of Merriam's efforts, the numerous tests and trials, and the support of many army units and influential individuals, he never succeeded in getting the US Army to adopt the knapsack as a piece of army equipment. It remained a life's failure that he found difficult to accept.

After the general's return to Denver from Idaho, a semblance of normalcy returned to the Merriam family. Nevertheless, for the remainder of 1898 and all of 1899, there was continued family concern for the general's safety because of the publicly expressed hatred toward him by labor unions. After all, the violent minded in the labor movement had carried out assassinations. Also, there was much anxiety regarding oldest son Henry, who remained in the Philippines combat area. There was some comfort that his service as a general's aide did not put him in immediate frontline danger. Still, there was no assurance of safety in the guerrilla-type warfare of the Philippine Insurrection.

By the summer of 1900, the army was still in the throes of finally deciding issues regarding its future strength and organization. On July 24, 1900, the War Department wrote to Merriam, saying, "The Secretary of War desires to have your views in writing on the subject of army legislation for the coming winter." Significantly, he had earned enough respect in Washington that he was asked to submit his thoughts and recommendations. In reply the general, never reluctant to offer his opinions, took a conservative stance. His views were summed up in his statement, "I do not favor breaking up the regimental organization."[9]

Also with the summer season, more-quiet times ensued for the family. Una was active in the Denver Fortnightly Club. There was occasion for a nostalgic visit by Cyrus and Maude to Fort Laramie. Cyrus had fond memories of his time there, though Maude was only an infant then. They found the abandoned Fort Laramie in sad shape. "The adobe walls of their old home still stood, roof, windows, porches gone." Upon their return to Denver, the siblings eagerly shared their visit with the rest of the family. On December 4, 1900, General Merriam's responsibilities eased considerably when Brig. Gen. Fitzhugh Lee took command of the Department of the Missouri, coming from the Department of Western Cuba, and relieved Merriam of making periodic trips to Omaha. On December 27, 1900, General Merriam and Una welcomed their first grandchild, Merriam Bart Berger, a son born in Denver to Carry and George Berger. Early in 1901 Lt. Henry Merriam returned from duty in the Philippines and became an aide to his father. The family had come together again in Denver with the exception of son Charles, who remained at Stanford University.[10]

Merriam's successful experience in simultaneously commanding two large army departments brought him another such tenure on March 2, 1901. He was abruptly assigned command again over the Department of the Missouri in addition to his ongoing command of the Department of the Colorado. His dual command would continue until August 13, 1901, when he relinquished command of the Missouri department to Brig. Gen. John C. Bates.[11]

As General Merriam approached the mandatory retirement age of sixty-five on November 13, 1901, he faced yet one more culminating battle in his thirty-eight-year army career. It had long been one of his goals to retire as a major general. At that time the rank was the highest that could be attained through peacetime army promotions. Furthermore, the army did reward high-ranking officers of honorable service at retirement with the two stars. Merriam's last battle over promotion, however, became a most difficult and complicated one.

It should be noted that Merriam strongly believed that he deserved this final promotion, which fueled his determination to reach this goal. In the army's date-of-rank system, he placed near the top, but his advancement depended on the retirements of those above him in seniority. The age limitation, though, left him with little time to accomplish his objective.

In the aftermath of the Spanish-American War in 1898, Merriam considered his chances of becoming a major general as excellent. After all, he had President McKinley in his corner. Merriam had an interview with the president on April 11, 1901, and he quoted McKinley as saying, "General Wheaton will retire and make way for you at an early day." Merriam reported this conversation to General Corbin, the army adjutant general, and Corbin replied: "If the President wants a vacancy for you he has only to touch a button. I have in my desk Wheaton's offer to retire if promoted." Corbin promised to remind the president of his intention to promote Merriam and apparently did so on several occasions. McKinley also told Secretary of War Root and others of his promise to Merriam.[12]

Merriam's position with the promised presidential assistance unexpectedly crumbled with the shooting of McKinley on September 6, 1901, and his death eight days later. At that time Brig. Gen. Lloyd Wheaton decided that he was not ready to retire. Although the new president, Theodore Roosevelt, had been informed by Corbin of McKinley's intention to promote Merriam, the new president had different ideas about promotion to general rank of officers near their

General Merriam after retirement, with Una, at home in Maine.
Courtesy Berger Family Collection.

retirement age. He believed this was bad policy, concerned that this system con-tributed to old officers in senior leadership and failed to provide an incentive for younger officers to remain vigorous and efficient.

Thus Merriam's hoped-for major-general promotion became ensnarled in a series of unfortunate events. There was no time left to maneuver. By age, Henry Merriam retired on November 13, 1901, as a brigadier general. His long mili-tary career had come to an end, he having by all appearances lost his final battle. Surprisingly, however, he was not yet defeated.

Over the years, Merriam had fought tenaciously and aggressively to secure promotions, enlisting the help of any politician or fellow army officer he could think of. He again began writing letters asking for support in rectifying his fail-ure to retire as a major general, a grave injustice in his eyes. Merriam even had printed a long summary of his army service, at the end detailing the promises of McKinley and the complicating circumstances involving the retirement of Gen-eral Wheaton. He went to Washington and spoke with various congressmen, po-litical leaders, and army and War Department personnel. In an amazing turn of events, Merriam's notoriety in the Coeur d'Alene labor strife actually helped his promotion case. Some members of Congress, mostly Republicans, believed that he deserved the promotion because of his courageous actions in suppressing labor violence. Also, they felt that Merriam had borne the hostile shots of the Democrats and labor unions, thus deserving the thanks of the Republican Party.

Merriam also appealed for assistance from the Maine congressional delegation and from Maine friends, such as ex-Civil War general Joshua Chamberlain. An example, resulting from Merriam's efforts, was a letter of November 1901 from Rep. C. E. Littlefield of Maine to President Roosevelt: "I believe that the government, country, and the administration are very greatly indebted to him for the great intelligence and good judgment which he displayed as the officer in charge of the United States troops during the Coeur d'Alene troubles, and later in the courageous and intelligent manner in which he stood by the official acts which it was his duty to perform through a very warm and searching Congressional investigation. I believe that the country, and especially the administration is under obligation to him therefore."[13] Merriam additionally sought help from Colorado officials and other friends and politicians in that state to lobby Congress and the president on his behalf.

Merriam's campaign proved remarkably successful, defying conventional wisdom. On February 2, 1903, a unanimous vote of both houses of Congress approved "[a]n act to authorize the President to appoint Brigadier General H. C. Merriam to the grade of major general in the United States Army and place him on the retired list."[14] President Roosevelt accepted this action and Merriam had won his final battle and attained a major goal.

After retiring in November 1901, General Merriam and family remained in Denver until 1902, then moved to the East Coast, eventually choosing a retirement home near Portland, Maine. He remained active in civic affairs until the last two years of his life, when he became very ill. Henry C. Merriam died on November 18, 1912, at Portland and was subsequently buried at Arlington Cemetery in Washington. Una, his beloved wife and faithful companion, who significantly complemented Merriam's character and career endeavors, died many years later in 1938 at the age of eighty-nine.

14

Who Was Maj. Gen. Henry C. Merriam?

*The images of men's wit and knowledge, remain in books. . . . They
generate still, and cast their seeds in the minds of others, provoking
and causing infinite actions and opinions in succeeding ages.*

FRANCIS BACON

Maj. Gen. Henry Clay Merriam was the quintessential military man of
nineteenth-century American western history. After his Civil War experience, he traveled along the Santa Fe Trail to Fort Bayard, New Mexico; thence
down the Rio Grande to Brownsville, Texas; back across country to the Pacific
Northwest and Vancouver Barracks; then to eastern Washington, California, and
finally Denver. By his extensive travel, crisscrossing the great American West, he
became truly acquainted with this vast region. He knew its geography firsthand
and that of Alaska secondhand.

Merriam not only knew the West but also participated in important aspects
of its engaging history. He had long confrontations with the continent's first
people, the Indians. He fought against some of military history's finest horse
soldiers in the Plains Indians. In the Southwest he faced the Apaches and in
the Pacific Northwest the Nez Perce and Bannocks. He played a part in the army's response to the Sioux uprising that resulted in tragedy at Wounded Knee.
Merriam respected his Indian adversaries while still regarding them as uncivi-
lized and capable of horrible crimes of violence. He came to blame most Indian wars on relentless white intrusion on Indian lands. On occasion, Merriam
defended the Indians, such as Chief Moses and his people and the Utes. Yet he
condemned Indian agents and their practices.

As an explorer, Merriam contributed to the knowledge and understanding of the West. Like the fur traders and military exploring expeditions that preceded him, he surveyed areas in Texas near the Rio Grande and in eastern Washington. Sometimes virtually traveling alone as in Washington's Lake Chelan area

or with small groups, he had a good eye for selecting key lake and river junctions that offered a means for controlling the movements of Indians and settlers. He filed reports and made recommendations in vastly different regions as to the best and most strategic points for forts and troop garrisons.

Merriam stood out as a builder and administrator of western forts, such a significant element in the region's development. His extensive experience down the Rio Grande to Brownsville prepared him well for his later establishment of Pacific Northwest forts at Coeur d'Alene and Spokane. He adeptly employed skills learned in the Maine lumber industry in the layout and construction of army posts. As he dealt with the myriad details in securing resources to build a fort, he always was concerned with the financial aspects of each operation, the age-old problem of keeping within the army's tight budgets. Additionally, from the time of the Civil War, Merriam clearly understood what was necessary to command fort garrisons. He knew the multitude of problems associated with soldiers' health, building maintenance, control of supplies, ensuring discipline, and sustaining morale, as at Fort Laramie and Fort Logan. The tedium of life in isolated western forts made this no easy matter. Merriam bit by bit built a reputation as a superb military administrator and post commander. This would later translate into his trusted leadership of much-larger commands as in the Departments of California, the Columbia, the Missouri, and the Colorado and his crucial logistical management at San Francisco's Presidio during the Spanish-American War.

His long experience in command of black troops, dating from the operations culminating in the Battle of Fort Blakeley during the Civil War to duty along the Rio Grande, occupied a significant portion of Merriam's total army career. He quickly established an excellent reputation in dealing with black soldiers at a time when such commands were often shunned. At various times, from the Blakeley campaign to the Coeur d'Alene miners riots, Merriam defended black troops against what he believed were unjust claims about their behavior. He trusted his men, many uneducated ex-slaves, as in the conflict against the Mexican revolutionaries, and they responded in kind. Strangely, Merriam always seemed especially careful in expressing his personal opinions about black soldiers in his writings, most of the time apparently avoiding revealing any deep thoughts or feelings about his experience. This contrasted with his comments about Indians and Filipinos, which were sometimes racial in nature.

Besides being involved in the Indian Wars, western exploration, commanding black soldiers, and fort building, Merriam had a role in other key aspects of the history of the West. He played a small part in railroad expansion. His military protection of Northern Pacific Railroad's lines, for example, merited an expression of appreciation by the company's executives. In addition, he and his family extensively used the railroads in their many travels. Merriam grasped the strategic importance of the railroad on the movement of troops and thus on the location of forts.

He could not escape the influence of mining in the West as he contended repeatedly with the pressure of white mining claims on Indian lands and the resulting disruptions of peace with the affected tribes. He unexpectedly had to plan a rescue effort for Alaskan Klondike gold rushers, then was ordered to restore law and order when miners in the Coeur d'Alene district resorted to violence against mill owners. Indeed, episodes revolving around western mining provided extraordinary challenges for Merriam.

Westward expansion, however, also provided opportunities for Merriam. He was an entrepreneur. Wherever he went or was assigned, he viewed the settlers advancing westward as creating business possibilities, particularly in real estate. He thought Spokane offered such advantages that he had encouraged most of his family in Maine to move there. In Denver and other places, he cast a keen eye for ways to invest. Merriam's longtime promotion of his knapsack represented a glaring example of his entrepreneurial character.

Perhaps as part of his business acumen, he remained a salesman and promoter throughout his life. His favorite sales device was letter writing, which was largely the accepted media of the time. Merriam was prolific in this regard. He corresponded with friends and military associates, at times promoting his backpack, and at other times earnestly soliciting support for a promotion or an assignment. Once he made a contact or an acquaintance, Merriam took advantage of the same to help in future lobbying for an issue, and he was remarkably successful. Letters of support flowed from Laredo on the Rio Grande to congressmen from Maine. To fortify his sales efforts, Merriam from time to time would have tracts professionally printed, many times in promoting his knapsack. In the case of the Merriam Pack, however, he never succeeded in securing army adoption, though not for lack of trying.

While letters remained his greatest strength, Merriam was a skilled communicator. He was sought as a speaker for holidays, veterans' meetings, and civic occasions, particularly in Denver. Evidence indicates that he liked being interviewed by and quoted in newspapers. Even so, he had difficulty from time to time by allegedly being misquoted or making an ill-considered comment. Merriam was a man of strong opinions, and he was not hesitant in expressing them, which sometimes even threatened his army career. On several occasions he took up his pen to express his ideas about military tactics and strategy.

Despite being firm in his opinions and aggressively advancing them, Merriam had success as a diplomat. His experience at Fort McIntosh and Laredo, involving conflict with Mexican revolutionaries, was a remarkable instance of forcefully protecting US interests while gingerly avoiding international crisis along the Rio Grande border. He was particularly adept at collecting and assessing pertinent intelligence. In the Nuevo Laredo situation, Merriam possibly knew more about the chaotic developments in Mexico than the Mexican authorities across the river. While his overall philosophy was rooted in the belief that diplomatic ventures had to be backed by force, military or otherwise, he was fully capable of conciliatory gestures when deemed appropriate and effective. In the Pacific Northwest Merriam's work with Chief Moses demonstrated his ability to extend the olive branch at times and then show the power of the sword on other occasions. Also, he showed skill in using key leaders in Mexico and in the Indian tribes to further his objective of maintaining peace.

As has been frequently mentioned, from childhood, through college, and throughout his army career, Merriam believed in discipline. This trait began with his tremendous self-discipline, but in turn he expected those around him and subordinates below him to be disciplined. For example, he took note in his writings of fellow officers who became drunken and inattentive to duty. His command of various forts illustrated his emphasis on high standards of discipline in post life. This probably contributed to his notable success in commanding black troops. Merriam's zeal for discipline translated into a drive to restore or maintain law and order. His actions in the Coeur d'Alene riots were fully an example of his abhorrence of such chaotic conditions in which killings occurred and property was destroyed by mobs.

The harsh characteristics of being opinionated and possessing a drive for discipline were softened considerably by an underlying compassionate spirit that surfaced periodically. Merriam entered adult life, through his family circle in Maine, with a strong Christian moral compass. In turn, he became a caring family man, always concerned about his wife and children. In a military career with many and varied assignments away from his family, he endured long periods of separation from Una and children. At some points during his time in the West, Merriam found these separations intolerable and sought to change his assignments. Beyond the family, he had instances where he felt and acted on real humanitarian concerns. In the case of the arrested Coeur d'Alene miners and their harsh living conditions, Merriam warned his superiors that the imprisonment of the miners was becoming impossible, taking the initiative by allowing family members to provide additional food, stoves, clothing, and cots.

As one probes the character of Henry Merriam, certain traits stand out. Clearly, he was a man of courage and steadfast integrity. The Battle of Fort Blakeley established his physical bravery. Multiple times later he would unhesitatingly confront an adversary, whether Indian, Mexican, or rioting American. His courage took other forms too, including speaking his mind to newspapers and challenging his superiors in Washington. Merriam never tried to mask who he truly was or what he sincerely believed. He made decisions and approached events in a most straightforward manner.

Merriam's style of leadership was also revealing. First of all, his handsome physical presence conveyed dignity and an aura of calm that came from an even temperament. Although he at times tended to project an uncomfortable certitude, a belief that he was right, this never became overbearing or autocratic. Tempering this was an innate curiosity, by which he would seek to determine what others were thinking, as witnessed by his interest in Southern reactions to the Union occupation at the end of the Civil War. This led to an openness for input from those around him. Unlike some other generals, this quality kept his exercise of authority from becoming arrogant. In addition, since Merriam abhorred duplicity and deviousness, people knew where he stood. They also respected his hard work. In general, men liked serving under Merriam.

This officer from Maine was not perfect by any means, and his persistence could become at times stubbornness. While basically he was most congenial, making friends easily, he could prove irritating, as witnessed by his pushes for and the reactions to the Merriam Pack in Europe and with the US Army. Merriam was a practical man. His writings did not reveal philosophical reminiscing or deep thinking even in very personal documents. His thoughts concentrated on the immediate situation. Consequently, his actions proved most revealing about the inner man.

Merriam's education, his intelligence, and above all his high energy propelled him forward in his military career. His superiors, virtually without exception, praised his initiative in military matters and rewarded his good judgment. Also, he developed a well-deserved reputation as a master of details. Whether dealing with building a fort, planning Alaskan expeditions, or supporting martial law in a civil disturbance, he assessed the details involved and directed specific actions based on his understanding of the multitude of variables. These attributes helped him overcome a definite disadvantage of not being a West Point graduate in the post–Civil War army.

He was not a complicated man. In the current age, when people are talked about as "finding themselves," trying to determine who they are and where they are headed, Merriam was the exact opposite. From the very beginning of his life, he knew who he was and where he wanted to go. It did not take long, for example, for him to decide that he wanted to remain in the army after his discharge from volunteer service following the Civil War. This tremendous self-confidence and energetic drive toward his goals greatly helped his rise to near the top rank in his military career. Throughout his time in the army, Merriam watched carefully the steps he needed to take in advancing his career, what promotions needed to come and when, and who above him was being reassigned, retired, or promoted. He was always aware of what was happening around him.

With these attributes, Merriam could have been, and certainly preferred to have been, a leader of campaigns against hostile Indians in the West or a commander of fighting forces in the Spanish-American War. He might have been a warrior in the model of Ranald Mackenzie or George Crook. His fate and his great contribution to western history, however, was to be a builder and commander of strategically located military posts, often difficult, isolated, and forlorn places. The notable breadth of Merriam's post–Civil War experience in establishing and commanding forts, ranging geographically from the mouth of the Rio Grande in Texas to Vancouver Barracks in the Pacific Northwest, marked him as a remarkable leader in the rapidly changing American West. While the nation's attention tended to focus on the Indian fighter, Merriam superbly represented the stabilizing force so important in the region's development. Like a number of other relatively unknown leaders, he explored regions;

selected points to plant the military guidon; aided and protected the advancement of the railroads and telegraphic lines; brokered peace between settlers, miners, and natives; and actually invested in growing cities.

Likewise, Merriam's steadily expanding western army career, going from command of the small Fort McIntosh at Laredo on the Rio Grande to combined command of the Departments of California and of the Columbia, with headquarters at the Presidio in cosmopolitan San Francisco, provided another illuminating example of the stabilizing role of the military in the progression of western development. By his retirement at the turn of the century, Merriam was thoroughly involved in bustling urban centers such as Denver. In a way the journey of his life mirrored the "civilizing" of the West.

Another aspect of Merriam's contribution in western development was his attitude about the continued advancement of civilization. Through his upbringing, classical education, and travels in Europe, Merriam highly valued the civilized attainments he saw and read about. In 1876 he made a point of visiting the Centennial Exposition in Philadelphia. Like many of his age, he considered civilized advancements as inevitable. Nevertheless, he held remarkably tolerant views of blacks and Indians. He might not consider them to be equal to whites at the time, but there was promise for the future. Merriam would refer to the Indians as "savages," capable of the most horrible acts, but he would often turn and defend them if they showed signs of accepting "civilized" reservation life. His lack of toleration for labor unions, as in the destructive Coeur d'Alene miners' riots, reflected his view that they were disruptive of proper civilized behavior and decorum. Merriam firmly believed he and his army were in the vanguard of advancing law and order.

Writers have said that some notable historic figures were "creatures of the time," that "Time called him forth, the Time did everything, he nothing."[1] Such was not the case with Henry Clay Merriam. He became a shaper of the "Time," and therein resides his importance, perhaps not on the grand, sweeping scale of some, but in a step-by-step fashion. Merriam could not be defined as the type of heroic, "event-making man" like George Washington or Winston Churchill. But he emerges as an "eventful" man, establishing a model of leadership and decision making, confronting harsh and violent conditions with sacrifice and courage.

Finally, Merriam believed that he had a place in history. Like other leaders in American history, he carefully saved his many papers about his life and career, thinking they would tell his story someday and perhaps that of the country he served. He strongly felt that he mattered and sincerely wanted to make a contribution to the nation's progress. In that, he succeeded. Maj. Gen. Henry Clay Merriam had a most exemplary role as a military officer in the late-nineteenth-century history of the American West, thereby revealing both what the West was like at the time, and how it was changing.

APPENDIX

At various times, particularly during the Civil War, Merriam held higher brevet ranks.

1862	Aug. 29	Appointed Captain, 20th Maine Infantry
1862–63	Sept. 1862–June 1863	20th Maine Infantry, Army of the Potomac, participated in the Battles of Antietam (Sept 17), Shepherdstown (Sept 19), and Fredericksburg (Dec 11–15)
1863–65	Mar. 1863–Oct. 1865	80th, 85th, 73rd US Colored Troops in Department of the Gulf, participating in the siege of Port Hudson, La. (1863) and the campaign against Mobile, Ala. (Mar.–Apr. 1865)
1866–67	Oct. 1866–Mar. 1867	Recruiting Service, Missouri
1867	Mar.–June 1867	With 38th Infantry, Fort Harker, Kans.
1867–69	June 1867–Sept. 1869	En route with troops to and at Fort Bayard, N.Mex. Terr.
1869–71	Sept. 1869–May 1871	At Fort Bliss, Tex.
1871–72	May 1871–Jan. 1872	At Fort McKavett, Tex.
1872	Jan.–Mar. 1872	On Leave
1872	Mar.–Dec. 1872	At Fort Duncan, Tex.
1872–73	Dec. 1872–Mar. 1873	At Fort Ringgold, Tex.
1873	Mar.–Dec. 1873	Commanding troops patrolling Rio Grande frontier
1873–74	Dec. 1873–June 1874	At Fort Brown, Tex.
1874	June–Dec. 1874	On Leave
1874–76	Dec. 1874–Mar. 1876	At Fort Brown, Tex.
1876	Mar.–Oct. 1876	Commanding Fort McIntosh, Tex.
1876–77	Oct. 1876–June 1877	McPherson Barracks, Atlanta, Ga.
1877	June–July 1877	On Leave
1877–78	July 1877–Apr. 1878	With 2nd Infantry at Fort Lapwai, Idaho Terr.
1878–79	Apr. 1878–Sept. 1879	At Fort Coeur d'Alene, Idaho Terr.
1879–80	Sept. 1879–Jan. 1880	At Camp Chelan, Wash. Terr.
1880	Jan.–May 1880	Detached service at Vancouver Barracks, Wash. Terr.
1880	May–Oct. 1880	With 2nd Infantry, Camp Chelan, Wash. Terr.
1880–82	Oct. 1880–Sept. 1882	At Fort Colville, Wash. Terr.
1882–85	Sept. 1882–Aug. 1885	At Fort Spokane, Wash. Terr.
1885	Aug.–Oct. 1885	Commanding 7th Infantry, Fort Laramie, Wyo. Terr.
1885–86	Oct. 1885–Feb. 1886	On Leave
1886–87	Feb. 1886–Mar. 1887	Commanding 7th Infantry, Fort Laramie, Wyo. Terr.

1887	Mar to July 1887	On Leave
1887–89	July 1887–Oct. 1889	Commanding 7th Infantry, Fort Laramie, Wyo. Terr., and Fort Logan, Colo.
1889–94	Oct. 1889–June 1894	Commanding 7th Infantry, Fort Logan, Colo.
1894	June–Aug. 1894	With New York National Guard
1894–97	Aug. 1894–July 1897	Commanding 7th Infantry, Fort Logan, Colo. (Also commanding Department of the Colorado, May 10–27, 1897)
1897–99	July 1897–Jan. 1899	Commanding Department of the Columbia, Vancouver Barracks, Wash.
1898–99	Apr. 1898–June 1899	Commanding Department of the Columbia and Department of California, Presidio, San Francisco, Calif.
1899–1901	Jan. 1899–Nov. 1901	Commanding Department of the Colorado, Denver, Colo. (Also commanding Department of the Missouri, Mar. 31, 1899–Dec. 4, 1900, and Mar. 2–Aug. 13, 1901)
1901	Nov. 13	Retired from active service

NOTES

PREFACE

1. *Denver Post,* July 20, 2008, 12E.

CHAPTER 1

Epigraph. War Department, *Medals of Honor Circular,* 85 (copy in Merriam Papers, Fort Laramie Archives). Also see *War of the Rebellion: A Compilation of the Official Records of the Union and Confederate Armies,* 128 vols. (Washington, DC: GPO, 1880–1901), ser. 1, 49(1):313: "Medals of Honor, Merriam, Henry C. Lieutenant-Colonel 73rd U.S. Colored Troops, April 9, 1865, Distinguished gallantry at the assault and capture of Fort Blakely, Ala." (Note that the fort's name is variously spelled as "Blakely" or "Blakeley.")

1. Henry C. Merriam, "The Capture of Mobile" (paper presented to the Maine Military Order of the Loyal Legion of the United States, May 3, 1905), Merriam Papers, Fort Laramie Archives.

2. Lt. Col. H. C. Merriam to Acting Assistant Adjutant General, 1st Brigade, 1st Division, Blakely [*sic*], Ala., Apr. 10, 1865, Merriam Papers, Special Collections, McFarlin Library, University of Tulsa. This letter constitutes Merriam's after-action report and is hereafter cited as Merriam, Blakeley Report.

3. Merriam, "Capture of Mobile."

4. Brig. Gen. William A. Pile, Official Report 82, Apr. 13, 1865, *War of the Rebellion,* 49(1):288–89. General Andrews was commander of the Second Division, XIII Corps.

5. Merriam, "Capture of Mobile," 13.

6. Ibid., 18.

7. Merriam, Blakeley Report. Louis A. Snaer, Company B, 73rd USCT, was the only black officer on the battlefield that day. "Snaer was considered a free person of color in New Orleans upon his joining the Louisiana Native Guards in 1862." See Camille Corte, "History of 73rd U.S.C.T.," Historic Blakeley State Park, http://www.blakeleypark.com/73rdusct.htm.

8. Merriam, "Capture of Mobile," 19.

9. Merriam, Blakeley Report; Merriam, "Capture of Mobile," 19; Henry C. Merriam, Civil War Diary, Apr. 9, 1865, in private collection.

10. Merriam, Civil War Diary, Apr. 10, 1865; Merriam, Blakeley Report.

11. Some reports indicated that 3,000 men constituted the fort's garrison.

12. Merriam, Civil War Diary, Apr. 12, 1865.

13. Brig. Gen. William A. Pile to Sen. Henry Wilson, Feb. 9, 1867, contained in "Outline Statement of Services of Brig. Gen. Henry C. Merriam," Merriam Papers, Fort Laramie Archives; US House of Representatives, *Brig. Gen. H. C. Merriam.*

14. Maj. Gen. John P. Hawkins to Army Staff, Washington, DC, "Testifying to the character of Merriam for appointment in the Regular Army," Apr. 19, 1866, contained in "Outline Statement of Services"; Merriam, "Capture of Mobile," 21.

CHAPTER 2

1. Putnam, *Story of Houlton,* 126.

2. E. Smith, *Mayflower Hill,* 17–18.

3. Henry C. Merriam, "Maine in the War," n.d., Merriam Papers, Fort Laramie Archives. Elijah P. Lovejoy (1802–37) was an editor for the *St. Louis Observer* (1832–36) when he was forced to move to Alton, Illinois. He printed the *Alton Observer* and was attacked four times for his antislavery activity and eventually killed while defending his press.

4. *Maine Writers Research Club,* 284.

5. Ibid.; interview with Catherine (Kay) Bell, historian, Aroostook Historical and Art Museum, Houlton, Maine, Oct. 27, 2007; "Individual Service Report of Col. H. C. Merriam, 7th Infantry, for the fiscal year ended June 30, 1896," Merriam Papers, Fort Laramie Archives.

6. Bell interview; interview with Linda Faucher, librarian, Cary Library, Houlton, Maine, Oct. 27, 2007.

7. Knowlton, *Old Schoolmaster,* 139–41. Unfortunately, all individual and class records of Houlton Academy have been destroyed.

8. *Colby College Catalog of 1860,* 14, Colby College Special Collections, Waterville, Maine.

9. Ibid., 14–20; *Maine Writers Research Club,* 284; Putnam, *Story of Houlton,* 101.

10. Col. Henry C. Merriam, undated speech (given by at an alumni banquet at Colby College), Merriam Papers, Colby College Special Collections. On the outskirts of Houlton, near the Canadian border, there was a garrison established to protect Maine during the Aroostook War with the British. Merriam would have been aware of this presence, but there is no indication of any notable military influence on him.

11. Ibid.

12. Marriner, *History of Colby College,* 536. Also see Pullen, *Twentieth Maine,* 13.

13. Pullen, *Twentieth Maine,* 2.

14. Ibid., 3–4.

15. Ibid., 5, 12–13.

16. Henry C. Merriam, Civil War Diary, Nov. 7, 8, 1865, in private collection.

17. Pullen, *Twentieth Maine,* 18–19.

18. Ibid., 22.

19. Foote, *Civil War,* 1:683; Pullen, *Twentieth Maine,* 24–25.

20. Weigley, *Great Civil War,* 145.

21. Robertson, *General A. P. Hill,* 148–50.

22. Ibid., 150.

23. Pullen, *Twentieth Maine,* 27–30; Robertson, *General A. P. Hill,* 150.

24. Pullen, *Twentieth Maine,* 31.

25. Ibid., 35–36.

26. Ibid., 37–40.

27. Ibid., 42–43.

28. Ibid., 46–47.

29. Catton, *Picture History of the Civil War,* 266.

30. Pullen, *Twentieth Maine,* 52.

31. Ibid., 54–60.

32. Vandiver, *Their Tattered Flags,* 168; Catton, *Picture History of the Civil War,* 281.

33. Adelbert Ames to the President, Mar. 11, 1897, Merriam Papers, Fort Laramie Archives; Joshua L. Chamberlain to the President, Dec. 11, 1891, ibid.; Daniel Butterfield to Lieutenant General Schofield, Mar. 13, 1895, ibid.

CHAPTER 3

1. Military Order of the Loyal Legion of the United States, Commandery of the State of Maine, *In Memoriam: Henry Clay Merriam* (copy in Merriam Papers, Fort Laramie Archives); *Maine Writers Research Club,* 285. Also see US House of Representatives, *Brig. Gen. H. C. Merriam.*

2. E. Smith, *Mayflower Hill,* 19.

3. Official Statement of Service of Henry Clay Merriam, n.d., Merriam Papers, Fort Laramie Archives.

4. Foote, *Civil War,* 2:392–93; Camille Corte, "History of 73rd U.S.C.T.," Historic Blakeley State Park, http://www.blakeleypark.com/73rdusct.htm. Russell Weigley says that Butler had quietly commissioned African American company officers for the 1st, 2nd, and 3rd Louisiana Native Guards. *Great Civil War,* 187.

5. Weigley, *Great Civil War,* 401; Condensed Record of Col. H. C. Merriam, 7th Infantry, n.d., Merriam Papers, Fort Laramie Archives; *The Coloradan* 2, no. 4 (June 1, 1893): 13.

6. Wright, *Timeline of the Civil War,* 93.

7. Weigley, *Great Civil War,* 185; Claxton and Puls, *Uncommon Valor,* 26–27.

8. Weigley, *Great Civil War,* 28, 188.

9. Dobak and Phillips, *Black Regulars,* 50.

10. Catton, *Picture History of the Civil War,* 423.

11. Official Statement of Service of Henry Clay Merriam, Merriam Papers, Fort Laramie Archives.

12. Foote, *Civil War,* 3:89.

13. Ibid., 496, 508.

14. Ibid., 738.

15. Henry C. Merriam, Civil War Diary, Jan. 4, 15, 18, 27, 1865, in private collection.

16. Ibid., Jan. 15, 20, 24, 1865.

17. Ibid., Jan. 8, 9, 11, 1865.

18. Ibid., Jan. 12, 30, Feb. 20, 1865.

19. Ibid., Jan. 2, 10, 13, 1865.

20. Ibid., Jan. 15, 22, 23, 1865.

21. Mrs. H. was the wife of a Captain Hurts, and Arab was Merriam's trusted horse.

22. Merriam, Civil War Diary, Feb. 15, 17, 18, 1865.

23. Ibid., Feb. 18, 1865.

24. Ibid., Feb. 21, 22, 1865.

25. Ibid., Feb. 25, 26, 27, 1865.

26. Ibid., Feb. 28, 1865.

27. Ibid., Mar. 1, 2, 3, 1865.

28. Ibid., Mar. 4, 1865.

29. Ibid., Mar. 20, 21, 1865.

30. Ibid., Mar. 21–26, 1865.

31. Ibid., Mar. 26, 1865.

32. Ibid., Mar. 27–31, 1865.

33. Ibid., Apr. 2, 1865.

34. Ibid., Apr. 3, 4, 1865.

35. Ibid., Apr. 5, 1865.

36. Ibid., Apr. 6–8, 1865.

37. Ibid., Apr. 9, 1865.

38. Ibid., Apr. 1–17, 1865.

39. Ibid., Apr. 10, 1865.

40. McPherson, *Battle Cry of Freedom,* 564; Weigley, *Great Civil War,* 190–91.

CHAPTER 4

1. H. C. Merriam, Civil War Diary, Apr. 16, 1865, in private collection.

2. Gallman, *Civil War Chronicle,* 521.

3. Merriam, Civil War Diary, Apr. 18, 1865.

4. Ibid., Apr. 20, 21, 1865.

5. Ibid., Apr. 24–25, 1865.

6. Ibid., Apr. 26, 1865.

7. Ibid., Apr. 28, 1865.

8. Ibid., May 3–5, 1865.

9. Ibid., May 5, 1865.

10. Ibid., May 8, 19, 1865.

11. Ibid., May 11, 1865.

12. Ibid., May 25–26, 1865.

13. Gallman, *Civil War Chronicle,* 530; Merriam, Civil War Diary, June 11, 1865.

14. Merriam, Civil War Diary, June 14, 1865.

15. Ibid., June 18, 19, 20, 21, 1865.

16. Ibid., June 23, 1865.

17. Ibid., June 26, 27, 28, 29, 30, July 1, 1865.

18. Ibid., July 2, 3, 4, 1865.

19. Ibid., July 5, 1865.

20. Ibid., July 19, 1865.

21. Ibid., July 12, 23, 1865.

22. Ibid., July 8, 24, 1865.

23. Ibid., July 13, 1865.

24. Ibid., Aug. 7, 23, Sept. 1, 3, 1865.

25. Ibid., Sept. 15, 16, 17, 1865.

26. Col. W. A. Gordon to Lt. Col. H. C. Merriam, July 23, 1865, Special Collections, Colby College Library; Lt. Col. H. C. Merriam to Commander, Northern District of Mississippi, July 23, 1865, ibid.

27. Merriam, Civil War Diary, Sept. 18, 19, 1865.

28. Ibid., Sept 27, 1865.

29. Ibid., Sept. 29, Oct. 2–3, 1865.

30. Ward, *The Slaves' War,* 116.

31. Ibid.

32. Weigley, *History of the United States Army,* 251.

33. Merriam, Civil War Diary, Nov. 13–14, 1865.

34. Ibid.

CHAPTER 5

1. Military Order of the Loyal Legion of the United States, Commandery of the State of Maine, *In Memoriam: Henry Clay Merriam* (copy in Merriam Papers, Fort Laramie Archives).

2. Henry C. Merriam to Editors of *The Boston Daily Advertiser,* Sept. 4, 1865, Merriam Papers, Special Collections, McFarlin Library, University of Tulsa.

3. Headquarters, Jefferson Barracks, General Orders 12, Feb. 28, 1867, Merriam Papers, Fort Laramie Archives.

4. Headquarters, Department of the Missouri, Special Orders 36, Oct. 6, 1866, ibid.

5. Dobak and Phillips, *Black Regulars,* 20–24.

6. Headquarters, Regiment Recruiting Service, Jefferson Barracks, Special Orders 42, Apr. 29, 1867, Merriam Papers, Fort Laramie Archives.

7. Headquarters, District of the Upper Arkansas, Field Orders 41, June 14, 1867, ibid.; Frazier, *Forts of the West,* 53–54; Hart, *Old Forts of the Southwest,* 159–61; Headquarters, 38th Infantry, Special Orders 66, June 27, 1867, Merriam Papers, Fort Laramie Archives.

8. Headquarters, District of New Mexico, Special Orders 63, Aug. 12, 1867, Merriam Papers, Fort Laramie Archives.

9. Utley, *Indian Frontier,* 112–16. Also see Nye, *Carbine and Lance.*

10. Dobak and Phillips, *Black Regulars,* 140.

11. Maj. H. C. Merriam, "Enroute near Arkansas River," to Assistant Adjutant General, Department of the Missouri, July 12, 1867, Merriam Papers, Special Collections, McFarlin Library, University of Tulsa.

12. Ibid.

13. Ibid.

14. Ibid.

15. "Excursionists" to Maj. H. C. Merriam, July 19, 1867, Special Collections, Colby College Library.

16. Lahti, "Colonized Labor," 283–302.

17. Ibid.

18. Brig. Gen. H. C. Merriam to Dr. [E. C.] Marriner, May 10, 1902, Special Collections, Colby College Library.

19. Utley, *Indian Frontier,* 135, 196; Utley, "Victorio's War," 21–29.

20. Condensed Record of Col. H. C. Merriam, 7th Infantry, n.d., Merriam Papers, Fort Laramie Archives; "Outline Statement of Service of Brig. Gen. Henry C. Merriam," ibid., 6.

21. Headquarters, Fifth Military District, Special Orders 178, July 30, 1869, ibid.; Headquarters, District of New Mexico, Special Orders 52, Sept. 2, 1869, ibid.; Headquarters, District of New Mexico, Special Orders 3, Jan. 13, 1869, ibid.

22. Dobak and Phillips, *Black Regulars,* 14–15, 73.

23. Headquarters, District of New Mexico, Special Orders 100, Sept. 2, 1869, Merriam Papers, Fort Laramie Archives; Frazier, *Forts of the West,* 143–44.

24. Dobak and Phillips, *Black Regulars,* 16–20, 92.

25. Ibid., 20; Robinson, *Bad Hand,* 52, 70.

26. Carter, *On the Border with Mackenzie,* 17.

27. Chaplain John N. Schultz to *Waterville Mail,* May 20, 1870, Special Collections, Colby College Library.

28. Ibid.

29. Ibid.

30. Merriam's descriptive account of the flood was published in the *Army and Navy Journal* 7 (May 28, 1870), 643.

CHAPTER 6

1. Robinson, *Bad Hand,* 49–54.

2. Headquarters, Department of Texas, Special Orders 76, Apr. 18, 1871, Merriam Papers, Fort Laramie Archives; Robinson, *Bad Hand,* 162.

3. Frazier, *Forts of the West,* 154–55.

4. Headquarters, Department of Texas, Special Orders 47, Mar. 9, 1872, Merriam Papers, Fort Laramie Archives.

5. Headquarters, Department of Texas, Special Orders 200, Nov. 7, 1872, ibid.; Headquarters, Department of Texas, Special Orders 2, Jan. 3, 1873, ibid.

6. Headquarters, Ringgold Barracks, Special Orders 31, Mar. 8, 1873, ibid.

7. Maj. H. C. Merriam to Assistant Adjutant General, Department of Texas, Apr. 22, 1872, Merriam Papers, Special Collections, McFarlin Library, University of Tulsa.

8. Headquarters, Department of Texas, Special Orders 93, May 22, 1873, Merriam Papers, Fort Laramie Archives.

9. Telegram, Headquarters, Department of Texas, to Col. Abner Doubleday, June 12, 1873, ibid.; Headquarters, Department of Texas, Special Orders 108, June 12, 1873, ibid.; Headquarters, Department of Texas, handwritten order, Oct. 9, 1873, ibid.

10. Merriam, *Captain John Macpherson,* 141–61.

11. Ibid., 161.

12. Ibid., 161–62.

13. Ibid., 162–63. Henry's brother Rufus joined the couple at New York and traveled with them to Fort Brown.

14. Ibid., 163.

15. Ibid., 164.

16. Headquarters, District of the Rio Grande, Special Orders 2, Feb. 22, 1876, Merriam Papers, Fort Laramie Archives.

17. Headquarters, Department of Texas, Annual Report to Assistant Adjutant General, Military Division of the Missouri, Sept. 26, 1876, ibid.

18. Ibid.

19. Dobak and Phillips, *Black Regulars,* 70–75.

20. Frazier, *Forts of the West,* 154; Dobak and Phillips, *Black Regulars,* 102.

21. Headquarters, Department of Texas, General Orders 5, Apr. 7, 1876, Merriam Papers, Fort Laramie Archives.

22. Merriam, *Captain John Macpherson,* 164–65.

23. Adams, *Conflict and Commerce,* 99.

24. Merriam, *Captain John Macpherson*, 165–66.

25. Cutting from *Mexican Herald,* Nov. 21, 1905, Merriam Papers, Fort Laramie Archives.

26. Merriam, *Captain John Macpherson,* 167.

27. Telegram, Maj. H. C. Merriam to Headquarters, Department of Texas, and District Headquarters, Apr. 9, 1876, Merriam Papers, Fort Laramie Archives.

28. Telegram, Headquarters, Department of Texas, to Maj. H. C. Merriam, Apr. 10, 1876, ibid.

29. Telegrams, Maj. H. C. Merriam to Headquarters, Department of Texas, and District Headquarters, Apr. 10, 1876, ibid.

30. Telegrams, Maj. H. C. Merriam to Headquarters, Department of Texas, and District Headquarters, Apr. 11, 1876, ibid.

31. Telegram, Maj. H. C. Merriam to District Headquarters, Apr. 11, 1876, ibid.; Telegram, Maj. H. C. Merriam to Headquarters, Department of Texas, Apr. 12, 1876, ibid.

32. Telegram (quoting a "Dispatch now received as follows"), Maj. H. C. Merriam to District Headquarters, Apr. 14, 1876, ibid.

33. Telegram, Maj. H. C. Merriam to District Headquarters, Apr. 16, 1876, ibid.; Telegram, Headquarters, Department of Texas, to Maj. H. C. Merriam, Apr. 19, 1876, ibid.

34. Telegram, Maj. H. C. Merriam to Headquarters, Department of Texas, Apr. 20, 1876, ibid.

35. Headquarters of the Army, Special Orders 137, July 8, 1876, ibid.

36. Telegram contained in Headquarters, Department of Texas, Annual Report, Sept. 26, 1876.

37. These letters and messages are contained in a report with attachments in the Merriam Papers, Fort Laramie Archives.

38. Telegram, Lt. Col. H. C. Merriam to District Headquarters, Sept. 7, 1876, Merriam Papers, Fort Laramie Archives; Telegram, District Headquarters to Lt. Col. H. C. Merriam, Sept. 7, 1876, ibid.

39. Robinson, *Bad Hand,* 1.

40. Headquarters, Department of Texas, Annual Report, Sept. 26, 1876.

41. Telegram, Lt. Col. H. C. Merriam to Headquarters, Department of Texas, and District Headquarters, Sept. 8, 1876, Merriam Papers, Fort Laramie Archives.

42. B. Garcia to Lt. Col. H. C. Merriam, Sept. 7, 1876, ibid.

43. Telegram, District Headquarters to Lt. Col. H. C. Merriam, Sept. 8, 1876, ibid.; Gen. E. O. C. Ord to J. J. Haynes (through Colonel Merriam), Sept. 8, 1876, ibid.

44. Telegram, Lt. Col. H. C. Merriam to Headquarters, Department of Texas, Sept. 12, 1876, ibid.

45. Telegram, Lt. Col. H. C. Merriam to Headquarters, Department of Texas, Sept. 20, 1876, ibid.; Telegram, Headquarters, Department of Texas, to Lt. Col. H. C. Merriam, Sept. 21, 1876, ibid.

46. Ord Annual Report, Sept. 26, 1876, ibid.

47. This sword can be found in the Fort Laramie Archives.

48. Comments contained in "Outline Statement of Services of Brig. Gen. Henry C. Merriam," Merriam Papers, Fort Laramie Archives.

49. Ibid.

50. Merriam, *Captain John Macpherson*, 167.

51. Ibid., 168.

CHAPTER 7

1. Merriam, *Captain John Macpherson*, 168.

2. Ibid., 169.

3. Ibid.

4. Ibid., 169–70.

5. Ibid.

6. Ibid., 170–71.

7. Documents concerning these courts-martial charges and specifications can be found in the Merriam Papers, Fort Laramie Archives. Merriam's appointment as "Special Inspector" is in Headquarters, Fort Brown, Special Orders 8, Jan. 11, 1876.

8. See Lt. Col. H. C. Merriam to Gen. John S. Mason, marked "confidential," Dec. 7, 1876, Merriam Papers, Fort Laramie Archives.

9. Headquarters of the Army to Commanding General, Military Division of the Missouri, Oct. 24, 1876, third endorsement to Lt. Col. H. C. Merriam, Nov. 15, 1876, ibid.

10. Merriam, *Captain John Macpherson*, 171.

11. Special orders for such assignments can be found in the Merriam Papers, Fort Laramie Archives.

12. Telegram, Headquarters, Division of the Atlantic, to Lt. Col. H. C. Merriam, July 6, 1877, Merriam Papers, Fort Laramie Archives; Telegram, Lt. Col. H. C. Merriam to Col. Frank Wheaton, July 7, 1877, ibid.; Telegram, Col. Frank Wheaton to Lt. Col. H. C. Merriam, July 8, 1877, ibid.

13. Merriam, *Captain John Macpherson*, 170–71.

14. Ibid., 171.

15. Ibid., 172.

16. Ibid.

17. See Utley, *Indian Frontier*, 181–86.

18. Brandon, *American Heritage Book of Indians*, 312.

19. Frazier, *Forts of the West*, 45. Also see Nelson, *Fighting for Paradise*, 172, 278. "Lapwai" is a Nez Perce word meaning "place of butterflies."

20. Nelson, *Fighting for Paradise*, 200.

21. Ibid.

22. Condensed Record of Col. H. C. Merriam, 7th Infantry, n.d., Merriam Papers, Fort Laramie Archives.

23. Headquarters, District of the Clearwater, Special Orders 7, Feb. 9, 1878, ibid.; Commander, Department of the Columbia, to Col. Frank Wheaton, Mar. 27, 1878, ibid.

24. Maj. Gen. O. O. Howard to Adjutant General, US Army, Dec. 17, 1891, contained in "Outline Statement of Services of Brig. Gen. H. C. Merriam," Merriam Papers, Fort Laramie Archives.

25. Chief of Ordnance, War Department, to Lt. Col. H. C. Merriam, Apr. 25, 1877, ibid.; Army Equipment Board to Lt. Col. H. C. Merriam, Feb. 5, 1879, ibid.

26. Lt. Col. H. C. Merriam to Adjutant General, US Army, May 9, 1879, ibid.

27. Adjutant General's Office, US Army, to Lt. Col. H. C. Merriam, June 14, 1879, ibid.

28. Merriam, *Captain John Macpherson,* 172–73.

29. Ibid., 173.

30. Ibid.

31. Ibid.

32. Ibid., 174.

33. Ibid., 175.

34. Ibid.

35. Lt. Col. H. C. Merriam to Adjutant General, Military Division of the Pacific, Aug. 4, 1879, Merriam Papers, Fort Laramie Archives.

36. Lt. Col. H. C. Merriam to Adjutant General, Department of the Columbia, Oct. 10, 1881, ibid. This document provides a summary of some of Merriam's actions.

37. Telegram, Commander, Department of the Columbia, to Commanding Officer, Fort Walla Walla, Aug. 27, 1879, ibid. This telegram directed, "Forward following by Indian Courier."

38. "Early Impressions: Euro-American Explorations and Surveys," Oct. 12, 2004, pp. 1–2, North Cascades National Park, http://www.nps.gov/noca/hrs2-3e.htm.

39. Lt. Col. H. C. Merriam to Assistant Adjutant General, Department of the Columbia, Sept. 10, 1879, Merriam Papers, Fort Laramie Archives.

40. Note, Lt. Col. H. C. Merriam to Adjutant General, Department of the Columbia, Sept. 3, 1879, ibid.

41. "Early Impressions: Euro-American Explorations and Surveys."

42. Merriam to Assistant Adjutant General, Dept. of the Columbia, Sept. 10, 1879. Merriam Papers, Fort Laramie Archives.

43. Ibid.

44. Ibid.

45. Schubert, *Vanguard of Expansion,* 145; Merriam to Assistant Adjutant General, Sept. 10, 1879; "Early Impressions: Euro-American Explorations and Surveys."

46. Headquarters, Department of the Columbia, Special Orders 94, July 24, 1879, Merriam Papers, Fort Laramie Archives. These same orders indicated that the 2nd Infantry's regimental headquarters would be at Fort Coeur d'Alene, with Companies A, B, F, and G posted there.

47. Undated newspaper clipping, *Spokane Times,* ibid.

48. Merriam, *Captain John Macpherson,* 176–78.

49. Ibid.

50. "Early Impressions: Euro-American Explorations and Surveys."

51. Commander, Department of the Columbia, to Lt. Col. H. C. Merriam, Sept. 22, 1880, Merriam Papers, Fort Laramie Archives; Headquarters, Department of the Columbia, to Lt. Col. H. C. Merriam, Dec. 20, 1881, ibid.

52. Merriam to Adjutant General, Oct. 10, 1881.

53. Ibid.

54. Lt. Col. H. C. Merriam to Assistant Adjutant General, Department of the Columbia, Aug. 1, 1880, Merriam Papers, Fort Laramie Archives.

55. Kit Oldham, "U.S. Army Establishes Fort Spokane at the Junction of the Spokane and Columbia Rivers in 1882," Mar. 4, 2003, Essay 5358, HistoryLink.org, http://www.historylink.org/index.cfm?DisplayPage=output.cfm&file_id=5358.

56. Headquarters, Department of the Columbia, Special Field Orders 10, Oct. 23, 1880, Merriam Papers, Fort Laramie Archives.

57. "Memorandum of Recommendations," n.d., ibid.

58. Miles, *Personal Recollections,* 404–405. For a discussion of Chief Moses and his efforts to protect Sinkiuse lands, see Ruby and Brown, *Indians of the Pacific Northwest,* 243–62.

59. Brig. Gen. O. O. Howard to Lt. Col. H. C. Merriam, Sept. 11, 1879, Merriam Papers, Fort Laramie Archives.

60. Headquarters, Department of the Columbia, to Lt. Col. H. C. Merriam, July 10, 1880, ibid.

61. Lt. Col. H. C. Merriam to unidentified newspaper editor, Fort Spokane, May 14, 1883, ibid.

62. Frazier, *Forts of the West,* 172–74; Merriam, *Captain John Macpherson,* 178.

63. Ficken, *Washington Territory,* 75, 151; Henry Villard to Col. H. C. Merriam, n.d., contained in "Outline Statement of Services."

64. Newspaper clipping, *Spokane Times,* Aug. 28, 1880, Merriam Papers, Fort Laramie Archives; Fort Colville, Special Order 115, Sept. 20, 1882, ibid.; Headquarters, Department of the Columbia, Special Orders 131, Sept. 13, 1882, ibid.

65. Oldham, "U.S. Army Establishes Fort Spokane."

66. Headquarters, Department of the Columbia, to Lt. Col. H. C. Merriam, Apr. 18, 1883, Merriam Papers, Fort Laramie Archives.

67. This letter to an unidentified newspaper can be found in Merriam, *Captain John Macpherson,* 182.

68. Ibid.

69. Miles, *Personal Recollections,* 404–405.

70. Col. H. C. Merriam to Professor Hall, Colby College, Mar. 28, 1886, Special Collections, Colby College Library; Merriam, *Captain John Macpherson,* 181.

71. Headquarters, Department of the Columbia, to Merriam, Apr. 18, 1883.

72. Merriam, *Captain John Macpherson,* 181–82.

73. Ficken, *Washington Territory,* 179; undated newspaper clipping, *Spokane Chronicle,* Merriam Papers, Fort Laramie Archives.

CHAPTER 8

1. Hafen and Young, *Fort Laramie and the Pageant of the West,* 25, 70, 153. Also see Frazier, *Forts of the West,* 181–82.

2. Report, Aug. 1885, Medical History of Posts, Fort Laramie, sec. 3, Jan. 1885–Mar. 1890, Fort Laramie Library; McManus, *7th Infantry,* 11.

3. Merriam, *Captain John Macpherson,* 182–83.

4. Ibid., 183.

5. Ibid.

6. Ibid., 184.

7. Ibid., 184–85.

8. Ibid.

9. Bvt. Col. Guy V. Henry to Col. H. C. Merriam, Aug. 13, 1887, Merriam Papers, Fort Laramie Archives; Condensed Record of Col. H. C. Merriam, 7th Infantry, n.d., ibid.; Sharpshooter's Certificates No. 6, Aug. 25, 1884, and No. 256, Sept. 12, 1888, ibid.; R. Anderson to Col. H. C. Merriam, Oct. 20, 1887, ibid.

10. Hafen and Young, *Fort Laramie and the Pageant of the West,* 389.

11. Report, Oct. 9, 1885, Medical History of the Posts, Fort Laramie; Report, Jan. 1886, ibid.

12. Hafen and Young, *Fort Laramie and the Pageant of the West,* 390.

13. Ibid., 393.

14. Ibid., 388.

15. "Circumstances of the Introduction of My Infantry Pack into the Austrian Army," Dec. 26, 1893, Merriam Papers, Fort Laramie Archives.

16. Col. Henry C. Merriam, "The Foot Soldier's Kit and How to Carry It," 1888, Merriam Knapsack Collection, Stephen H. Hart Library, Colorado Historical Society, Denver, 23.

17. McChristian, *U.S. Army in the West,* 78–79.

18. Lt. Col. H. C. Merriam to Gen. William T. Sherman, May 1, 1878, Merriam Papers, Fort Laramie Archives.

19. F. W. Elbrey to Lt. Col. H. C. Merriam, Mar. 1, 1877, Merriam Knapsack Collection.

20. Col. H. C. Merriam to Adjutant General, US Army, Feb. 3, 1886, Merriam Papers, Fort Laramie Archives.

21. Adjutant General's Office, US Army, to Col. H. C. Merriam, Feb. 11, 1886, ibid.; Adjutant General's Office, US Army, to Col. H. C. Merriam, Sept. 9, 1886, ibid.

22. McChristian, *U.S. Army in the West,* 79–80.

23. US Chargé d'Affaires, Madrid, to Col. H. C. Merriam, Sept. 5, 1887, Merriam Papers, Fort Laramie Archives; Director of Infantry, Ministry of War, to Col. H. C. Merriam, May 7, 1887, ibid.

24. Merriam prepared a long memorandum of his visit to Vienna and his problems with Dr. Thomas. See Merriam, Memorandum, Fort Logan, CO, Dec. 26, 1893, ibid.

25. Merriam, *Captain John Macpherson,* 185.

26. Ibid., 185–86.

27. Report, Oct. 1887, Medical History of Posts, Fort Laramie, sec. 3, Jan. 1885–Mar. 1890, Fort Laramie Library, Fort Laramie, 90–92.

28. Report, Nov. 1888, ibid.; Headquarters, Department of the Platte, to Col. H. C. Merriam, Sept. 25, 1888, Merriam Papers, Fort Laramie Archives.

29. Col. H. C. Merriam to Assistant Adjutant General, Department of the Platte, Dec. 23, 1888, Merriam Papers, Fort Laramie Archives.

30. Ibid.

31. Col. H. C. Merriam to Assistant Adjutant General, Department of the Platte, Mar. 14, 1888, ibid.

32. Col. H. C. Merriam to Assistant Adjutant General, Department of the Platte, "Report of Camp of Instruction near Old Fort Casper, Wyo.," Oct. 17, 1888, ibid.

33. Ibid.

34. Ibid.

35. Ibid.

36. Brig. Gen. George W. McIver, "Service at Old Fort Laramie, Wyoming, June 1887, till April, 1890," Feb. 1943, Fort Laramie Library.

37. Ibid.

38. Annual Report, Col. H. C. Merriam to Assistant Adjutant General, Department of the Platte, Aug. 6, 1889, Merriam Papers, Fort Laramie Archives.

39. Ibid.

40. Ibid.

41. Telegram, Col. H. C. Merriam to Assistant Adjutant General, Department of the Platte, Oct. 14, 1889, ibid. Bordeaux was the nearest railhead to Fort Laramie, approximately twenty-eight miles away.

42. McIver, "Service at Old Fort Laramie."

43. Ibid.; Merriam, *Captain John Macpherson*, 186.

CHAPTER 9

1. Col. H. C. Merriam to Assistant Adjutant General, Department of the Platte, "Annual Report," Aug. 6, 1889, Merriam Papers, Fort Laramie Archives; M. C. Blaine to Col. H. C. Merriam, May 15, 1889, ibid.

2. Col. H. C. Merriam to Assistant Adjutant General, Department of the Platte, Oct. 14, 1889, ibid. Capt. L. E. Campbell arrived in November 1887 to become quartermaster and to supervise construction at Fort Logan.

3. Capt. Levi F. Burnett to Assistant Adjutant General, Department of the Platte, Dec. 11, 1889, ibid.

4. Capt. Levi F. Burnett to Mr. W. L. Ryder, Feb. 24, 1890, ibid.

5. Burnett to Assistant Adjutant General, Dec. 11, 1889; Brig. Gen. George W. McIver, "Service at Old Fort Laramie, Wyoming, June, 1887, till April, 1890," Feb. 1943, Fort Laramie Library.

6. Pfanner, "Genesis of Fort Logan," 43–50; Pfanner, "Highlights in the History of Fort Logan," 82. Pfanner says the date troops moved to the fort site was October 26, but the monthly report for October 1887 says, "October 31st permanent camp was made on the U.S. Military Reservation about nine miles S.W. of Denver, Colorado."

7. Merriam, *Captain John Macpherson*, 186–87.

8. Ibid., 187.

9. Utley, *Indian Frontier*, 244–45.

10. Maj. Gen. Nelson A. Miles to Col. H. C. Merriam, Dec. 11, 1890, Merriam Papers, Fort Laramie Archives.

11. Pfanner, "Highlights in the History of Fort Logan," 89; Utley, *Last Days of the Sioux*, 132.

12. Pfanner, "Highlights in the History of Fort Logan," 89. Regarding the death of Sitting Bull, see Utley, *Lance and the Shield*.

13. Telegram, Brig. Gen. Thomas Ruger to Col. H. C. Merriam, Dec. 16, 1890, Special Collections, Colby College Library.

14. Telegram, Brig. Gen. T. H. Ruger to Col. H. C. Merriam, Dec. 18, 1890, ibid.

15. Report, Capt. J. H. Hurst to Assistant Adjutant General, Department of Dakota, Jan. 9, 1891, ibid.

16. Ibid.; Col. H. C. Merriam to Capt. J. H. Hurst, Dec. 22, 1890, ibid.

17. Telegram, Headquarters, Department of Dakota, to Col. H. C. Merriam, Dec. 21, 1890, Merriam Papers, Fort Laramie Archives.

18. Report, Capt. J. H. Hurst to Headquarters, Department of Dakota, Jan. 9, 1891.

19. Brig. Gen. Thomas Ruger to Col. H. C. Merriam, Feb. 26, 1891, Special Collections, Colby College Library; Col. H. C. Merriam to Brig. Gen. Thomas Ruger, Mar. 1, 1891, ibid.

20. Report, Lt. F. C. Marshall to Col. H. C. Merriam, Jan. 13, 1891, contained in Report, Col. H. C. Merriam to Assistant Adjutant General, Department of Dakota, Jan. 14, 1891, ibid. This incident is described in considerable detail in Utley, *Last Days of the Sioux*.

21. Gen. I. S. Bangs to Col. H. C. Merriam, Jan. 1, 1891, Merriam Papers, Fort Laramie Archives; Gen. I. S. Bangs to Col. H. C. Merriam, Feb. 17, 1891, ibid.

22. Merriam, *Captain John Macpherson*, 188.

23. Gen. I. S. Bangs to Col. H. C. Merriam, Feb. 7, 1891, Merriam Papers, Fort Laramie Archives. Many decades later, such sentiments might have been heard with respect to the Korean, Vietnam, or Iraq Wars.

24. Merriam, *Captain John Macpherson*, 188.

25. McCoy, "From Infantry to Air Corps," 8; Utley, *Last Days of the Sioux*, 260.

26. Grand Army Executive and Memorial Association, Denver, to Col. H. C. Merriam, Apr. 9, 1891, Merriam Papers, Fort Laramie Archives.

27. Merriam, *Captain John Macpherson*, 187.

28. Ibid.

29. Ibid., 188.

30. "Extract of Report of Inspection of Fort Logan, Colo.," contained in Report, War Department Inspector General's Office to Col. H. C. Merriam, Dec. 11, 1891, Special Collections, Colby College Library.

31. Numerous letters and petitions (copies sent to inform Merriam) regarding Merriam's promotion efforts can be found in Special Collections, Colby College Library.

32. Col. H. C. Merriam to Sen. F. M. Cockrell, Aug. 20, 1891, Special Collections, Colby College Library.

33. Ficken, *Washington State*, 4, 254; Amelia Bagnall to Col. H. C. Merriam, Aug. 8, 1889, Merriam Papers, Fort Laramie Archives; Dr. Cyrus K. Merriam to Col. H. C. Merriam, Aug. 18, 1893, ibid.; Dr. Cyrus K. Merriam to Col. H. C. Merriam, Aug. 29, 1893, ibid.

34. Arps, *Denver in Slices*, 33.

35. Merriam, *Captain John Macpherson*, 189.

36. Ibid.; Maj. W. H. Powell to Col. H. C. Merriam, Apr. 4, 1891, Merriam Papers, Fort Laramie Archives; Col. H. C. Merriam, to Adjutant General, US Army, Sept. 1, 1894, ibid.; Col. H. C. Merriam to Maj. Gen. T. H. Ruger, Oct. 2, 1895, ibid.

37. Ordnance Office, War Department, to Col. H. C. Merriam, July 29, 1892, Merriam Papers, Fort Laramie Archives; Col. H. C. Merriam to Adjutant General, US Army, Feb. 4, 1896, ibid.

38. National Guard of Pennsylvania, Special Orders 1, "Proceedings of a Group of Officers," Jan. 16, 1886, Stephen H. Hart Library, Colorado Historical Society, Colorado History Museum, Denver; Office of Adjutant General, State of New Jersey, General Order 10, May 10, 1892, Merriam Papers, Fort Laramie Archives; Company E, 22nd Regiment, National Guard State of New York, Oct. 2, 1893, second endorsement to Headquarters, 12th Infantry, to Adjutant General State of New York, Sept. 19, 1893, ibid.

39. Unidentified newspaper clippings, Merriam Papers, Fort Laramie Archives. Merriam's letter to Lt. Col. G. V. Henry, 3rd Cavalry, is dated April 10, 1896. Henry's

reply is dated April 13, 1896. The originals of both are found in Merriam Papers, Fort Laramie Archives.

40. Maj. Gen. O. O. Howard to Col. H. C. Merriam, July 18, 1893, Merriam Papers, Fort Laramie Archives.

41. Receipt, T. B. Peddie & Co., Newark, NJ, Aug. 30, 1893, ibid.; T. B. Peddie & Co. to Col. H. C. Merriam, Jan. 22, 1895, ibid.

42. Extract of Report, Capt. William Quenton to Adjutant, 1st Battalion, 7th Infantry, n.d., ibid.

43. *Denver Republican,* Mar. 16, 1894, 1–2.

44. Smiley, *History of Denver,* 921–25. Also see Arps, *Denver in Slices,* 34; and Pfanner, "Highlights in the History of Fort Logan," 89.

45. McCoy, "From Infantry to Air Corps," 9.

46. Ibid., 9–10.

47. Merriam, *Captain John Macpherson,* 189–90.

48. Report, Col. H. C. Merriam to Assistant Adjutant General, Department of the Colorado, Sept. 23, 1894, Merriam Papers, Fort Laramie Archives.

49. Ibid.

50. Headquarters, 7th Infantry, Order 33, June 4, 1895, ibid.

51. Ibid.

52. Lt. Col. J. P. Sanger (for Lt. Gen. J. M. Schofield) to Col. H. C. Merriam, June 13, 1895, ibid.

53. *Littleton (CO) Independent,* June 28, July 5, 1895.

54. Assistant Adjutant General, Department of the Colorado, to Col. H. C. Merriam, Feb. 24, 1896, Merriam Papers, Fort Laramie Archives.

55. *Denver Rocky Mountain News,* May 1, 1897, 4.

56. "Outline Statement of Services of Brig. Gen. H. C. Merriam," Merriam Papers, Fort Laramie Archives.

57. *Denver Rocky Mountain News,* May 1, 1897, 4.

58. Clipping from the *Army-Navy Register,* July 10, 1896, Special Collections, Colby College Library.

CHAPTER 10

1. Merriam, *Captain John Macpherson,* 190.

2. Ibid., 191. The sword was inscribed: "Brig. Gen. H. C. Merriam, U.S.A. From the Officers of the 7th U.S.A. Infantry, July, 1897."

3. Correspondence regarding Carry Merriam's engagement can be found in the Merriam Papers, Fort Laramie Archives.

4. Comments of Charles Merriam upon arriving at Vancouver Barracks can be found in ibid.

5. Frazier, *Forts of the West,* 176–77.

6. Merriam, *Captain John Macpherson,* 191; Borneman, *Alaska Saga of a Bold Land,* 133.

7. Borneman, *Alaska Saga of a Bold Land,* 133. Also see Miles, *Personal Recollections,* 420.

8. Borneman, *Alaska Saga of a Bold Land,* 136–43.

9. Ficken, *Washington State,* 219, 222, 223. Walter Borneman takes note of these factors in causing people to head to the Yukon region. See *Alaska Saga of a Bold Land.*

10. Ficken, *Washington State,* 223–24.

11. Portland (OR) Chamber of Commerce, Report, Oct. 28, 1897, Merriam Papers, Special Collections, Colby College Library.

12. Telegram, Adj. Gen. Samuel Breck to Brig. Gen. H. C. Merriam, Dec. 16, 1897, ibid.

13. Telegram, Asst. Adj. Gen. J. C. Gilmore to Brig. Gen. H. C. Merriam, Dec. 16, 1897, ibid.

14. Brig. Gen. H. C. Merriam, response to a toast at the Annual Banquet of the Commercial Club of Portland, Oct. 9, 1897, ibid.

15. Report, J. F. Pratt to Dr. Henry S. Pritchett, n.d., (made available to Merriam), ibid.

16. US Consulate, Victoria, BC, to Brig. Gen. H. C. Merriam, Dec. 24, 1897, ibid.

17. Brig. Gen. H. C. Merriam to Secretary of War R. A. Alger, Jan. 20, 1898, Merriam Papers, Special Collections, Colby College Library.

18. Ibid.

19. Borneman, *Alaska Saga of a Bold Land,* 131; Merriam, *Captain John Macpherson,* 191.

20. Clipping from *Morning Oregonian,* Jan. 20, 1898, 6, Merriam Papers, Special Collections, Colby College Library.

21. "Synopsis of Interview between Department Commander and Messrs Gardner and Dalton at Vancouver Barracks," Dec. 26, 1897, ibid.

22. Clipping, *Morning Oregonian,* Jan. 20, 1898, 6.

23. Brig. Gen. H. C. Merriam to Gen. R. Alger, Sec. of War, Jan. 20, 1898, Merriam Papers, Fort Laramie Archive; unidentified newspaper clipping, n.d., Merriam Papers, Special Collections, Colby College Library.

24. Brig. Gen. H. C. Merriam to Colonel Anderson, Mar. 23, 1898, ibid.; Brig. Gen. H. C. Merriam to Maj. Gen. Nelson A. Miles, Mar. 6, 1898, ibid.

25. Telegram, Adj. Gen. W. C. Corbin (by command of General Miles) to Brig. Gen. H. C. Merriam, date obscured, ibid.

26. Maj. Gen. Nelson A. Miles to Brig. Gen. H. C. Merriam, Feb. 4, 1898, ibid.; Brig. Gen. H. C. Merriam to Adjutant General, US Army, Mar. 29, 1899, Merriam Papers, Fort Laramie Archives.

27. Brig. Gen. H. C. Merriam to Commander, Alaskan Exploratory Expedition No. 2, June 10, 1898, Merriam Papers, Special Collections, Colby College Library; Brig. Gen. H. C. Merriam to Capt. E. F. Glenn, June 30, 1898, ibid.; Brig. Gen. H. C. Merriam to Capt. W. R. Abercrombie, June 10, 1898, ibid.

28. Merriam to Anderson, Mar. 23, 1898.

29. Report, Lt. W. P. Richardson to Brig. Gen. H. C. Merriam, July 7, 1898, Merriam Papers, Special Collections, Colby College Library; Alaska Commercial Company to Brig. Gen. H. C. Merriam, n.d., ibid.; Brig. Gen. H. C. Merriam to Lt. W. P. Richardson, Aug. 2, 1898, ibid.

30. Brig. Gen. H. C. Merriam to Maj. Gen. Nelson A. Miles, Apr. 12, 1898, ibid.; Headquarters, US Army, General Order 19, Apr. 15, 1898, Merriam Papers, Fort Laramie Archives.

CHAPTER 11

1. Gould, *Spanish-American War,* 69–70.

2. *New York Times,* May 5, 1898.

3. Comments by Charles Merriam, Merriam Papers, Fort Laramie Archives; Merriam, *Captain John Macpherson*, 192.

4. Telegram, Headquarters, Department of California, to Brig. Gen. H. C. Merriam, May 19, 1898, Merriam Papers, Fort Laramie Archives.

5. Headquarters, Department of California, General Orders 5, Apr. 20, 1898, RG 393, National Archives; Maj. Gen. H. C. Merriam to Maj. Gen. Wesley Merritt, Jan. 11, 1899, contained in "Outline Statement of Services of Brig. Gen. Henry C. Merriam," Merriam Papers, Fort Laramie Archives. General Shafter had only taken command of the Department of California on May 14, 1897, so his tenure had been less than a year.

6. Headquarters, Department of California, General Order 8, May 6, 1898, RG 393, National Archives.

7. Department of the Columbia, Annual Report, July 1, 1897 to June 30, 1898, App. A, ibid.; National Park Service, "Spanish American War—'A Splendid Little War,'" Presidio of San Francisco, http://www.nps.gov/prsf/historyculture/spanish-american war-a-splendid-little-war.htm.

8. *Colorado Transcript*, May 11, 1898, 3.

9. Sailings were identified by a large chart, which is now located in Merriam Papers, Fort Laramie Archives.

10. Gould, *Spanish-American War*, 63–64, 69.

11. Merriam to Merritt, Jan. 11, 1899.

12. Maj. Gen. Wesley Merritt to Maj. Gen. H. C. Merriam, Jan. 17, 1899, contained in "Outline Statement of Services."

13. Headquarters, Department of California, General Orders 16, Sept. 22, 1898, RG 393, Records of US Army Continental Commands, National Archives; Merriam, *Captain John Macpherson*, 192.

14. Report, Brig. Gen. Charles King to Adjutant General, Department of California, Oct. 10, 1898, Merriam Papers, Fort Laramie Archives; Merriam, *Captain John Macpherson*, 192.

15. Merriam, *Captain John Macpherson*, 192.

16. Headquarters, Department of California, General Orders 2, Jan. 19, 1899. The general orders read, in part, "the undersigned [Major General Shafter] resumes command of the Department of California." For Merriam's relinquishing command of the Department of California, see Headquarters, Department of California, General Orders 1, Jan. 19, 1899, RG 393, National Archives.

CHAPTER 12

1. *Denver Evening Post*, Jan. 31, 1899, 7.

2. Ibid., Jan. 30, 1899, 3.

3. *Rocky Mountain News*, Jan. 31, 1899, 1.

4. Ibid.

5. Ibid.

6. Headquarters of the Army, Special Orders 74, Paragraph 46, Mar. 31, 1899, Merriam Papers, Fort Laramie Archives. Also see Headquarters, Department of the Missouri, Annual Report, Aug. 15, 1899, ibid.

7. Merriam, *Captain John Macpherson*, 192.

8. Telegram, Adjutant General, US Army, to Brig. Gen. H. C. Merriam, Apr. 30, 1899, Merriam Papers, Fort Laramie Archives.

9. J. Anthony Lucas believes that the selection of Merriam was simply geographic. *Big Trouble,* 116.

10. Berman, *Radicalism in the Mountain West,* xii.

11. *Idaho State Tribune,* May 3, 1899, 1. A copy of the article can be found in Headquarters, Department of the Colorado, July 31, 1899, App. A, "Report of the Idaho Riots," Denver Public Library [hereafter referred to as "Report of the Idaho Riots"].

12. Ibid.

13. *Wardner News,* May 6, 1899, copy contained in "Report on the Idaho Riots," App. B.

14. These messages are included in "Report on the Idaho Riots."

15. Lucas, *Big Trouble,* 117; "Report of the Idaho Riots."

16. "Report of the Idaho Riots."

17. Lucas, *Big Trouble,* 139; Message, Capt. J. B. Batchelor Jr. to Brig. Gen. H. C. Merriam, May 3, 1899, Merriam Papers, Fort Laramie Archives.

18. *Washington (DC) Sunday Star,* May 5, 1907; Aiken, *Idaho's Bunker Hill,* 30; Berman, *Radicalism in the Mountain West,* 120. The newspaper comments are from a summary account of events leading up to ex-Governor Steunenberg's assassination and the indictment of WMF union leaders in 1907.

19. Message, Maj. Charles Morton to Brig. Gen. H. C. Merriam, May 4, 1899, RG 393, National Archives; Message, Capt. J. M. Thompson to Brig. Gen. H. C. Merriam, May 4, 1899, ibid.

20. "Report on the Idaho Riots."

21. Message, Brig. Gen. H. C. Merriam to Lt. H. G. Lyon, May 7, 1899, RG 393, National Archives; Lucas, *Big Trouble,* 144. Lucas asserts, "Altogether, Lyon's raid seemed 'a gross violation of the law' as later charged by congressional Democrats."

22. Gov. Robert B. Smith to Brig. Gen. H. C. Merriam, May 12, 1899, contained in "Report on the Idaho Riots"; Brig. Gen. H. C. Merriam to Gov. Robert Smith, May 15, 1899, contained in ibid.; Gov. Robert B. Smith to Brig. Gen. H. C. Merriam, May 17, 1899, contained in ibid.

23. "Report on the Idaho Riots."

24. Brig. Gen. H. C. Merriam to Governor Steunenberg, May 11, 1899, contained in ibid., 14.

25. "Report on Idaho Riots."

26. Unidentified newspaper clipping contained in a scrapbook of such items in RG 393, National Archives.

27. *Wallace Idaho State Tribune,* May 31, 1899, RG 393, National Archives; *Spokane Spokesman Review,* May 14, 1899, ibid.; *American Federationist* 6, no. 5 (July 1899): 108.

28. Telegram, Adjutant General, US Army, to Brig. Gen. H. C. Merriam, May 29, 1899, RG 393, National Archives; Telegram, Brig. Gen. H. C. Merriam to Adjutant General, US Army, May 30, 1899, ibid.

29. Telegram, Secretary of War R. A. Alger to Brig. Gen. H. C. Merriam, May 31, 1899, ibid.; "Report on the Idaho Riots."

30. "Report on the Idaho Riots." The text of Merriam's request included the following: "As I do not find the instruction referred to as my 'original instructions' and have no recollection of having received any instructions to the particular purpose named, I beg to be supplied with the paper to which reference is made, in order that I

may have a clear understanding on the subject." Brig. Gen. H. C. Merriam to Adjutant General, US Army, June 6, 1899, RG 393, National Archives.

31. Telegram, Brig. Gen. H. C. Merriam to Adjutant General, US Army, May 12, 1899, RG 393, National Archives; Telegram, Adjutant General, US Army, to Brig. Gen. H. C. Merriam, May 12, 1899, ibid.; Telegram, Brig. Gen. H. C. Merriam to Adjutant General, US Army, May 16, 1899, ibid.

32. Telegram, Brig. Gen. H. C. Merriam to Adjutant General, US Army, May 17, 1899, ibid.

33. Ibid.

34. Telegram, Brig. Gen. H. C. Merriam to Adjutant General, US Army, May 25, 1899, ibid.

35. Brig. Gen. H. C. Merriam to Maj. Allen Smith, May 24, 1899, copy contained in "Report on the Idaho Riots."

36. Telegram, Assistant Adjutant General, US Army, to Brig. Gen. H. C. Merriam, June 5, 1899, RG 393, National Archives; Telegram, Brig. Gen. H. C. Merriam to Adjutant General, US Army, June 5, 1899, ibid.

37. Brig. Gen. H. C. Merriam to Adjutant General, US Army, Aug. 24, 1899, ibid.

38. Lucas, *Big Trouble,* 150.

39. Brig. Gen. H. C. Merriam to Adjutant General, US Army, Sept. 7, 1899, RG 393, National Archives; Capt. William S. Graves to Brig. Gen. H. C. Merriam, Sept. 12, 1899, ibid.

40. Material on this subject contained in RG 393, National Archives.

41. Brig. Gen. H. C. Merriam to Adjutant General, US Army, Oct. 11, 1899, RG 393, National Archives.

42. Telegram, Adjutant General, US Army, to Brig. Gen. H. C. Merriam, Oct. 12, 1899, ibid.; Laurie, "Army and the Labor Radicals," 27.

43. Telegram, Brig. Gen. H. C. Merriam to Maj. Allen Smith, Dec. 7, 1899, RG 393, National Archives.

44. US House of Representatives, *Coeur d'Alene Labor Troubles,* 84, 125. The committee began taking testimony on February 20, with the hearings continuing until May 8, 1900.

45. Ibid., 129.

46. See Laurie, "Army and the Labor Radicals," 12–29.

47. Unidentified Denver newspaper clipping, n.d., Merriam Papers, Fort Laramie Archives.

CHAPTER 13

1. Report, Brig. Gen. H. C. Merriam to Adjutant General, US Army, Aug. 12, 1899, Merriam Papers, Special Collections, Colby College Library.

2. *Denver Times,* Sept. 22, 1899, 1.

3. For background on the Meeker murder, see Ubbelohde, Benson, and Smith, *Colorado History.*

4. Report, Maj. James F. Randlett to Commissioner of Indian Affairs, Sept. 12, 1896, Merriam Papers, Special Collections, Colby College Library; Report, Brig. Gen. H. C. Merriam to Adjutant General, US Army, Nov. 28, 1899, ibid.; Maj. M. B. Hughes to Adjutant General, Department of the Colorado, Jan. 15, 1901, 1st Endorsement, Brig. Gen. H. C. Merriam to Adjutant General, US Army, Jan. 21, 1901, ibid.

5. Maj. M. B. Hughes to Adjutant General, Department of the Colorado, Jan. 15, 1901, ibid. This information contained in the 1st endorsement.

6. Board of Ordnance and Fortifications to Brig. Gen. H. C. Merriam, Apr. 9, 1900, Merriam Papers, Fort Laramie Archives.

7. Chief of Artillery, War Department, to Maj. Gen. (ret.) H. C. Merriam, Mar. 30, 1906, ibid.

8. Chief of Ordnance, War Department to Maj. Gen. (ret.) H. C. Merriam, June 2, 1906, ibid.

9. War Department to Brig. Gen. H. C. Merriam, July 24, 1900, ibid.; Brig. Gen. H. C. Merriam to Adjutant General, US Army, Sept. 10, 1900, ibid.

10. Merriam, *Captain John Macpherson,* 194–95; Headquarters, US Army, General Order 131, Oct. 29, 1900, Merriam Papers, Fort Laramie Archives.

11. Headquarters, US Army, General Order 140, June 17, 1901, Merriam Papers, Fort Laramie Archives.

12. Merriam compiled and published these events in his "Outline Statement of Services of Brig. Gen. Henry C. Merriam." One section, "Why Was He Not Promoted before Retirement?," specifically addresses the promotion issue.

13. Rep. C. E. Littlefield to Pres. Theodore Roosevelt, Nov. 5, 1901, Merriam Papers, Fort Laramie Archives.

14. US House of Representatives, *Brig. Gen. H. C. Merriam.* H. Rep. 3154.

CHAPTER 14

1. "On the Difficulty of Being a Contemporary Hero," *Time,* June 24, 1966, 32–33.

BIBLIOGRAPHY

ARCHIVES

Primary-source material for this biography essentially comes from five main archives. Foremost are primary documents, letters, telegrams, military orders, and reports found at Fort Laramie National Historic Site, Wyoming (herein listed as Fort Laramie Archives). A second major source of primary documents is a similar collection of letters, messages, orders, newspaper clippings, and reports located in Special Collections, Miller Library, Colby College, Waterville, Maine. A third collection of documents, including a ledger book, resides in Special Collections, McFarlin Library, University of Tulsa. Some Merriam materials, including photographs and his important but sparse Civil War diary, are held by W. Bart Berger, a Merriam descendant in Denver, Colorado. A fifth deposit of papers, almost exclusively related to the Merriam Pack and his three patents, is in the Stephen H. Hart Library, Colorado Historical Society, Colorado History Museum, Denver. These five principal collections provided most of the basic research material for this volume. Many of the key documents had never been noted nor published previously.

There are Merriam materials scattered in several places in the National Archives. The items in the files of Record Group 393, Records of US Army Continental Commands, proved most useful for this biography.

GOVERNMENT DOCUMENTS

US House of Representatives. *Brig. Gen. H. C. Merriam.* 57th Cong., 2nd sess., January 15, 1903. H. Rep. 3154, to accompany HR 14375, February 5, 1903.
———. *Coeur d'Alene Labor Troubles.* 56th Cong., 1st sess., June 5, 1900. H. Rep. 1999.
US Senate. *Coeur d'Alene Mining Troubles.* 56th Cong., 1st sess., 1899. S. Doc. 24.
———. *Report on Miner's Riots in Idaho.* 56th Cong., 1st sess., 1899. S. Docs. 86, 142.
War Department. *Medals of Honor Circular.* Washington, DC: GPO, 1897.

BOOKS AND ARTICLES

Adams, John A., Jr. *Conflict and Commerce on the Rio Grande: Laredo, 1755–1955.* College Station: Texas A&M University Press, 2008.
Aderkas, Elizabeth von. *American Indians of the Pacific Northwest.* University Park, UK: Osprey, 2005.
Aiken, Katherine G. *Idaho's Bunker Hill: The Rise and Fall of a Great Mining Company, 1855–1981.* Norman: University of Oklahoma Press, 2005.
———. "It May Be Too Soon to Crow: Bunker Hill and Sullivan Company Efforts to Defeat the Miners' Union, 1890–1900." *Western Historical Quarterly* 24, no. 3 (August 1993).

Andrist, Ralph K. *The Long Death: The Last Days of the Plains Indians.* New York: Macmillan, 1964.

Arps, Louisa Ward. *Denver in Slices.* Athens, OH: Swallow, 1983.

Arrington, Leonard J. *History of Idaho.* Moscow: University of Idaho Press, 1994.

Ash, Stephen V. *Firebrand of Liberty: The Story of Two Black Regiments that Changed the Course of the Civil War.* New York: W. W. Norton, 2008.

Athearn, Robert G. *William Tecumseh Sherman and the Settlement of the West.* Norman: University of Oklahoma Press, 1995.

Bangs, I. S. *The Ullmann Brigade.* War Papers. N.p.: Military Order of the Loyal Legion of the US, Commandery of the State of Maine, 1902.

Berman, David R. *Radicalism in the Mountain West, 1890–1920: Socialists, Populists, Miners, and Wobblies.* Boulder: University Press of Colorado, 2007.

Berton, Pierre. *Klondike: The Last Great Gold Rush, 1896–1899.* Toronto: McClelland and Stewart, 1972.

Borneman, Walter R. *Alaska Saga of a Bold Land.* New York: HarperCollins, 2003.

Bowers, William T., William M. Hammond, and George L. MacGarrigle. *Black Soldier, White Army: The 24th Infantry Regiment in Korea.* Washington, DC: US Army Center of Military History, 1996.

Brandon, William. *The American Heritage Book of Indians.* New York: American Heritage, 1961.

Brewer, Paul. *The Civil War State by State.* San Diego: Thunder Bay, 2004.

Byler, Charles A. *Civil-Military Relations on the Frontier and Beyond, 1865–1917.* Westport, CT: Praeger, 2006.

Carlson, Paul H. *Pecos Bill: A Military Biography of William R. Shafter.* College Station: Texas A&M University Press, 1989.

Carroll, John M., ed. *The Black Military Experience in the American West.* New York: Liveright, 1971.

Carter, Capt. R. G. *On the Border with Mackenzie: Or Winning West Texas from the Comanches.* New York: Antiquarian, 1961.

Catlett, Sharon R. *Farmlands, Forts, and Country Life: The Story of Southwest Denver.* Boulder, CO: Big Earth, 2007.

Catton, Bruce. *The American Heritage Picture History of the Civil War.* New York: American Heritage, 1982.

Chamberlain, John. "My Story of Fredericksburg." *Cosmopolitan Magazine.* January 1913.

Chamberlain, Katherine P. *Victorio: Apache Warrior and Chief.* Norman: University of Oklahoma Press, 2007.

Claxton, Melvin, and Mark Puls. *Uncommon Valor: A Story of Race, Patriotism, and Glory in the Final Battles of the Civil War.* Hoboken, NJ: John Wiley and Sons, 2006.

Coakley, Robert W. *The Role of the Federal Military Forces in Domestic Disorders, 1789–1878.* Washington, DC: US Army Center of Military History, 1989.

Cohen, Stan. *Gold Rush Gateway: Skagway and Dyea.* Missoula, MT: Pictorial Histories, 1986.

Connelly, Donald B. *John M. Schofield and the Politics of Generalship.* Chapel Hill: University of North Carolina Press, 2006.

Converse, George L. *A Military History of the Columbia Valley.* Walla Walla, WA: Pioneer, 1988.

Cooper, Bryan. *Alaska: The Last Frontier.* New York: William Morrow, 1973.

Cooper, Jerry M. *The Army and Civil Disorders: Federal Intervention in Labor Disputes, 1877–1900.* Westport, CT: Greenwood, 1980.

Cornish, Dudley Taylor. *The Sable Arm: Black Troops in the Union Army, 1861–1865.* Lawrence: University Press of Kansas, 1967.

Cozzens, Peter. *Eyewitness to the Indian Wars, 1865–1890: Wars for the Pacific Northwest.* Mechanicsburg, PA: Stackpole, 2002.

Cresap, Bernard. *Appomattox Commander: The Story of General E. O. C. Ord.* San Diego: A. S. Barnes, 1981.

Derickson, Alan. *Workers' Health, Workers' Democracy: The Western Miners' Struggle, 1891–1925.* Ithaca, NY: Cornell University Press, 1988.

Dobak, William A., and Theodore D. Phillips. *The Black Regulars, 1866–1898.* Norman: University of Oklahoma Press, 2001.

Dolph, Jerry. *Fire in the Hole: The Untold Story of Hardrock Miners.* Pullman: Washington State University Press, 1994.

Dorsett, Lyle W., and Michael McCarthy. *The Queen City: A History of Denver.* Boulder, CO: Pruett, 1986.

Dunn, J. P., Jr. *Massacre of the Mountains: A History of the Indian Wars of the Far West.* Mechanicsburg, PA: Stackpole, 2002.

Downey, Fairfax. *The Buffalo Soldiers in the Indian Wars.* New York: McGraw Hill, 1969.

Etulain, Richard W. *Beyond the Missouri: The Story of the American West.* Albuquerque: University of New Mexico Press, 2006.

Etulain, Richard W., and Glenda Riley, eds. *Chiefs & Generals: Nine Men Who Shaped the American West.* Golden, CO: Fulcrum, 2004.

Fahey, John. "Coeur d'Alene Confederacy." *Idaho Yesterdays,* Spring 1968.

———. "Ed Boyce and the Western Federation of Miners." *Idaho Yesterdays,* Fall 1981.

Ficken, Robert E. *Washington State: The Inaugural Decade, 1889–1899.* Pullman: Washington State University Press, 2007.

———. *Washington Territory.* Pullman: Washington State University Press, 2002.

Fletcher, Marvin. *The Black Soldiers and the Officer in the United States Army, 1891–1917.* Columbia: University of Missouri Press, 1974.

Fowler, Arlen L. *The Black Infantry in the West, 1869–1891.* Norman: University of Oklahoma Press, 1996.

Foote, Mary Hallock. *Coeur d'Alene.* Boston: Houghton Mifflin, 1898.

Foote, Shelby. *The Civil War: A Narrative.* 3 vols. New York: Random House, 1958.

Frazier, Robert W. *Forts of the West.* Norman: University of Oklahoma Press, 1965.

Gaboury, William J. *Dissension in the Rockies: A History of Idaho Populism.* New York: Garland, 1988.

———. "From Statehouse to Bull Pen: Idaho Populism and the Coeur d'Alene Troubles of the 1890s." *Pacific Northwest Quarterly* (January 1967).

Gallman, J. Matthew, ed. *The Civil War Chronicle.* New York: Gramercy, 2003.

Glatthar, Joseph T. *Forged in Battle: The Civil War Alliance of Black Soldiers and White Officers.* New York: Free Press, 1990.

Gould, Louis L. *The Spanish-American War and President McKinley.* Lawrence: University Press of Kansas, 1982.

Hafen, LeRoy R., and Francis Marion Young. *Fort Laramie and the Pageant of the West, 1834–1890.* Lincoln: University of Nebraska Press, 1938.

Harriman, Job. *Class War in Idaho: The Horrors of the Bullpen, 1900*. Reprint, Seattle: Shorey Book Store, 1965.

Hart, Herbert M. *Old Forts of the Southwest*. Seattle: Superior, 1940.

Hays, Samuel H. *Report to the Governor on the Insurrection in Shoshone County, Idaho*. Boise: Idaho State Historical Society, 1900.

Haywood, William D. *Bill Haywood's Book: The Autobiography of William D. Haywood*. New York: International, 1929.

Higginson, Thomas Wentworth. *Army Life in a Black Regiment*. New York: W. W. Norton, 1984.

Hoagland, Alison K. *Army Architecture in the West: Forts Laramie, Bridger, and D. A. Russell, 1849–1912*. Norman: University of Oklahoma Press, 2004.

Hoig, Stan. *Tribal Wars of the Southern Plains*. Norman: University of Oklahoma Press, 1993.

Holzman, Robert S. *Stormy Ben Butler*. New York: Macmillan, 1954.

Hunt, William R. *North of Fifty-Three Degrees: The Wild Days of the Alaskan-Yukon Mining Frontier, 1870–1914*. New York: Macmillan, 1974.

Hutton, May Arkwright. *The Coeur d'Alenes; or, A Tale of the Modern Inquisition in Idaho, 1900*. Reprint, Fairfield, WA: Ye Galleon, 1974.

Hutton, Paul Andrew, and Durwood Ball, eds. *Soldiers West: Biographies from the Military Frontier*. Norman: University of Oklahoma Press, 2009.

Jenson, Vernon H. *Heritage of Conflict: Labor Relations in the Non-Ferrous Metals Industry up to 1930*. Ithaca, NY: Cornell University Press, 1950.

Johnson, Jeffrey A. *"They Are All Red Out Here": Socialist Politics in the Pacific Northwest, 1875–1925*. Norman: University of Oklahoma Press, 2008.

Johnson, Virginia Weisel. *The Unregimented General: A Biography of Nelson A. Miles*. Boston: Houghton Mifflin, 1962.

Kip, Lawrence. *Indian Wars in the Pacific Northwest*. Lincoln: University of Nebraska Press, 1999.

Knowlton, William Smith. *The Old Schoolmaster*. Augusta, ME: Burleigh and Floyd, Printers, 1905.

Lahti, Janice. "Colonized Labor: Apaches and Pawnees as Army Workers." *Western Historical Quarterly* 39, no. 3 (Autumn 2008).

Laurie, Clayton D. *The U.S. Army and the Labor Radicals of Coeur d'Alenes: Federal Military Intervention in the Mine War of 1892–1899*. Washington, DC: US Army Center of Military History, 1990.

———. "The United States Army and the Labor Radicals of the Coeur d'Alenes: Federal Intervention in the Mining Wars of 1892–1899." *Idaho Yesterdays* (Summer 1993).

Leckie, William. *The Buffalo Soldiers: A Narrative of the Negro Cavalry in the West*. Norman: University of Oklahoma Press, 1967.

Leech, Margaret. *In the Days of McKinley*. New York: Harper and Brothers, 1959.

Leiker, James N. *Racial Borders: Black Soldiers along the Rio Grande*. College Station: Texas A&M University Press, 2002.

Linderman, Gerald F. *Embattled Courage: The Experience of Combat in the American Civil War*. New York: Free Press, 1987.

Lingenfelter, Richard E. *The Hardrock Miners: A History of the Mining Labor Movement in the American West, 1863–1893*. Berkeley: University of California Press, 1974.

Livingston-Little, D. E. "An Economic History of North Idaho: Discovery and Development of the Coeur d'Alene Mines." *Journal of the West* (July 1964).

Lubetkin, M. John. *Jay Cook's Gamble: The Northern Pacific Railroad, the Sioux, and the Panic of 1873.* Norman: University of Oklahoma Press, 2006.

Lucas, J. Anthony. *Big Trouble.* New York: Touchstone, 1997.

Madsen, Brigham D. *The Bannock of Idaho.* Moscow: University of Idaho Press, 1996.

Maine Writers Research Club, Just Maine Folks. Lewiston, ME: Journal Printshop, 1924.

Marriner, Ernest Cummins. *The History of Colby College.* Waterville, ME: Colby College Press, 1963.

Mattes, Merrill J. *Indians, Infants, and Infantry.* Lincoln: University of Nebraska Press, 1988.

Mayer, Frederick W. "Two Cavalrymen's Diaries of the Bannock War, 1878." *Oregon Historical Quarterly* (December 1967).

McChristian, Douglas C. *Fort Laramie: Military Bastion of the High Plains.* Norman, OK: Arthur H. Clark, 2008.

————. *The U.S. Army in the West, 1870–1880: Uniforms, Weapons, and Equipment.* Norman: University of Oklahoma Press, 1995.

McCoy, Earl. "From Infantry to Air Corps: History of Fort Logan." *Denver Westerners Roundup* (November–December 1986).

McDermott, John D. *A Guide to the Indian Wars of the West.* Lincoln: University of Nebraska Press, 1998.

McManus, John C. *The 7th Infantry Regiment: Combat in an Age of Terror, the Korean War through the Present.* New York: A. Tom Doherty Assoc., 2008.

McPherson, James M. *Battle Cry of Freedom.* Oxford: Oxford University Press, 1988.

————. *The Negro's Civil War.* New York: Vintage Books, 1967.

Merriam, Cyrus L., comp. *Captain John Macpherson of Philadelphia.* Brattleboro, VT: Griswold, 1966.

Michino, Gregory F. *Encyclopedia of Indian Wars: Western Battles and Skirmishes, 1850–1890.* Missoula, MT: Mountain, 2003.

Miles, Nelson A. *Personal Recollections and Observations of General Nelson A. Miles.* Chicago: Werner, 1896.

Military Order of the Loyal Legion of the United States, Commandery of the State of Maine. *In Memoriam: Henry Clay Merriam.* Circular 12, Series of 1912, no. 314. Portland, ME: December 4, 1912.

Minter, Roy. *The White Pass: Gateway to the Klondike.* Fairbanks: University of Alaska Press, 1987.

Murfin, James V. *The Gleam of Bayonets: The Battle of Antietam and the Maryland Campaign of 1862.* South Brunswick, NJ: A. S. Barnes, 1965.

Murray, Robert A., comp. *Fort Laramie: Visions of a Grand Old Post.* Fort Collins, CO: Old Army, 1974.

Nadeau, Rimi. *Fort Laramie and the Sioux.* Lincoln: University of Nebraska Press, 1982.

Nalty, Bernard C. *Strength for the Fight: A History of Black Americans in the Military.* New York: Free Press, 1986.

Naske, Claus-M., and Herman E. Slotnick. *Alaska: A History of the Forty-Ninth State.* Norman: University of Oklahoma Press, 1987.

Nelson, Kurt R. *Fighting for Paradise: A Military History of the Pacific Northwest.* Yardley, PA: Westholme, 2007.

Nevin, David, and Time-Life Editors. *The Old West: The Soldiers.* New York: Time-Life Books, 1978.

Nye, W. S. *Carbine and Lance: The Story of Old Fort Sill.* Norman: University of Oklahoma Press, 1969.

"On the Difficulty of Being a Contemporary Hero." *Time,* June 24, 1961.

Oliva, Leo E. *Fort Hays: Keeping Peace on the Plains.* Topeka: Kansas State Historical Society, 1980.

Pfanner, Robert. "The Genesis of Fort Logan." *Colorado Magazine* 19, no. 2 (March 1942).

———. "Highlights in the History of Fort Logan." *Colorado Magazine* 19, no. 3 (May 1942).

Pohanka, Brian C., ed. *Nelson A. Miles: Documentary Biography of His Military Career, 1861–1903.* Glendale, CA: Arthur H. Clark, 1985.

Pullen, John J. *The Twentieth Maine: A Volunteer Regiment of the Civil War.* Philadelphia: J. B. Lippincott, 1957.

Putnam, Cora Carpenter. *Story of Houlton.* Portland, ME: House of Falmouth, 1958.

Quarles, Benjamin. *The Negro in the Civil War.* Boston: Little, Brown, 1953.

Rickey, Don J. *Forty Miles a Day on Beans and Hay: The Enlisted Soldier Fighting the Indian Wars.* Norman: University of Oklahoma Press, 1956.

Rister, Carl Coke. *The Southwestern Frontier, 1865–1881.* Cleveland: Arthur H. Clark, 1928.

Robertson, James I., Jr. *General A. P. Hill: The Story of a Confederate Warrior.* New York: Random House, 1987.

Robinson, Charles M., III. *Bad Hand: A Biography of General Ranald S. Mackenzie.* Austin, TX: State House, 1993.

———. *Frontier Forts of Texas.* Houston: Gulf, 1986.

Ruby, Robert H., and John A. Brown. *A Guide to the Indian Tribes of the Pacific Northwest.* Norman: University of Oklahoma Press, 1986.

———. *Indians of the Pacific Northwest: A History.* Norman: University of Oklahoma Press, 1981.

Schubert, Frank N. *Vanguard of Expansion: Army Engineers in the Trans-Mississippi West, 1819–1879.* Washington, DC: Historical Division, Office of the Chief of Engineers, n.d.

———, ed. *Voices of the Buffalo Soldier.* Albuquerque: University of New Mexico Press, 2003.

Schwantes, Carlos. *In Mountain Shadows: A History of Idaho.* Lincoln: University of Nebraska Press, 1991.

———. *The Pacific Northwest.* Lincoln: University of Nebraska Press, 1989.

Schwatka, Frederick. *A Summer in Alaska in the 1880s.* Secaucus, NJ: Castle, 1988.

Sears, Stephen W. *Landscape Turned Red: The Battle of Antietam.* New York: Ticknor and Fields, 1989.

Sherwood, Morgan B. *Exploration of Alaska, 1865–1900.* Fairbanks: University of Alaska Press, 1992.

Shine, Gregory Paynter. "Respite from War: Buffalo Soldiers at Vancouver Barracks, 1899–1900." *Oregon Historical Quarterly* (Summer 2006).

Singletary, Otis A. *Negro Militia and Reconstruction.* Austin: University of Texas Press, 1957.

Smiley, Jerome C. *History of Denver.* Denver: Denver Times, 1901.

Smith, Duane A. *Rocky Mountain Mining Camps: The Urban Frontier.* Bloomington: Indiana University Press, 1967.

Smith, Earl H. *Mayflower Hill: A History of Colby College.* Hanover, NH: University Press of New England, 2006.

Smith, John David. *Black Soldiers in Blue: African-American Troops in the Civil War Era.* Chapel Hill: University of North Carolina Press, 2002.

Smith, Robert W. *The Coeur d'Alene Mining War of 1892.* Corvallis: Oregon State College, 1961.

Stackpole, Stephen W. *Drama on the Rappahannock: The Fredericksburg Campaign.* Harrisburg, PA: Military Service Publishing, 1957.

Stallard, Patricia Y. *Glittering Misery: Dependents of the Indian-Fighting Army.* Norman: University of Oklahoma Press, 1992.

Taft, Philip. *Organized Labor in American History.* New York: Harper and Row, 1964.

Trask, David H. *The War with Spain in 1898.* New York: Macmillan, 1981.

Twichell, Heath. *Allen: The Biography of an Army Officer, 1859–1930.* New Brunswick, NJ: Rutgers University Press, 1974.

Ubbelohde, Carl, Maxine Benson, and Duane A. Smith. *A Colorado History.* 9th ed. Boulder, CO: Pruett, 2006.

Utley, Robert M. *Frontier Regulars: The United States Army and the Indian, 1865–1891.* Lincoln: University of Nebraska Press, 1973.

———. *Frontiersmen in Blue.* Lincoln: University of Nebraska Press, 1967.

———. *The Indian Frontier of the American West, 1846–1890.* Albuquerque: University of New Mexico Press, 1984.

———. *The Lance and the Shield: The Life and Times of Sitting Bull.* New York: Ballantine, 1993.

———. *The Last Days of the Sioux Nation.* New Haven, CT: Yale University Press, 1963.

———. "Victorio's War." *Quarterly Journal of Military History* (Autumn 2008).

Vandiver, Frank E. *Their Tattered Flags: The Epic of the Confederacy.* New York: Harper and Row, 1970.

Villard, Oswald Garrison. "The Negro in the Regular Army." *Atlantic Monthly* (June 1903).

Ward, Andrew. *The Slaves' War: The Civil War in the Words of Former Slaves.* Boston: Houghton Mifflin, 2008.

Webb, Melody. *Yukon: The Last Frontier.* Lincoln: University of Nebraska Press, 1993.

Weigley, Russell F. *A Great Civil War: A Military and Political History, 1861–1865.* Bloomington: Indiana University Press, 2000.

———. *History of the United States Army.* New York: Macmillan, 1967.

Wharton, David B. *The Alaska Gold Rush.* Bloomington: Indiana University Press, 1972.

Whiting, J. S. *Forts of the State of Washington.* Seattle: Kelly Printing, 1951.

Wiley, Bell Irvin. *Southern Negroes, 1861–1865.* New Haven, CT: Yale University Press, 1938.

Wilson, Frederick T. *Federal Aid in Domestic Disturbances, 1787–1903.* Washington, DC: Government Printing Office, 1903.

Wilson, Keith P. *Campfires of Freedom: The Camp Life of Black Soldiers during the Civil War.* Kent, OH: Kent State University Press, 2002.

Woodworth-New, Laura. *Mapping Identity: The Creation of the Coeur d'Alene Indian Reservation.* Boulder: University Press of Colorado, 2004.

Wooster, Robert. *Nelson A. Miles and the Twilight of the Frontier Army.* Lincoln: University of Nebraska Press, 1993.

Wright, John D. *The Timeline of the Civil War.* San Diego: Thunder Bay, 2007.

Wyman, Mark. *Hard Rock Epic: Western Miners and the Industrial Revolution, 1860–1910.* Berkeley: University of California Press, 1979.

NEWSPAPERS AND PERIODICALS

American Federationist 6, no. 5 (July 1899).

Army and Navy Journal. Vol. 7, May 28, 1870.

Army and Navy Register. July 10, 1896.

Denver Evening Post, 1899.

Denver Republican, 1894.

Denver Times, 1899.

Golden Colorado Transcript, 1898.

Idaho State Tribune, 1899.

Littleton (CO) Independent, 1895.

Morning Oregonian (Portland), 1898.

New York Times, 1898.

Rocky Mountain News (Denver), 1897, 1899.

Spokesman Review (Spokane), 1899.

Washington (DC) Sunday Star, 1907.

Wardner (ID) News, 1899.

INDEX

and Merriam's Medal of Honor,
1–6
Merriam's return to fort, 69–70,
71
and Mudgett, 29
Fort Bliss, 57–59, 60
Fort Boise, 181
Fort Bowie, 149
Fort Brown, 67–68, 71, 79, 88
Fort Coeur d'Alene, 94–96, 98, 100, 108,
118
Fort Colville, 98, 102–4, 106–7
Fort Concho, 63, 65, 66
Fort Duchesne, 194–95
Fort Duncan, 66, 67
Fort Grant, 193
Fort Harker, 52
Fort Hill, 93
40th Infantry Regiment, 58
Fort John, 111
Fort Lapwai, 90, 92–93, 99, 108
Fort Laramie
    closure of, 127, 129, 131
    establishment of, 111
    illnesses at, 121–23
    and the Merriam family, 113–14,
    116, 121, 196
    Merriam's assumption of
    command, 110, 111–12
    Merriam's quarters, 113
    poor condition of, 114–16, 122–23
    and railroads, 112, 115, 123, 124–
    25, 126
    social life of, 113–14
    training and drilling at, 114, 126–
    27
Fort Leavenworth, 117, 119
Fort Logan
    and closure of Fort Laramie, 127
    commanding officer's quarters,
    133
    and construction issues, 134
    and Denver City Hall War, 148–49
    establishment of, 132
    and labor strikes, 149
    and the Merriam family, 128,
    133–34, 142

Merriam's assumption of
    command, 130–32
observation balloon, 149–50, 154
parades at, 134, 143, 152
7th Infantry at, 127–28, 130–32,
    142–43
Fort McIntosh, 66–67, 72–77, 82–83, 86,
202
Fort McKavett, 60, 65–66
Fort Meade, 186
Fort Morgan, 25, 29, 40, 45
Fort Nelson, 157
Fortnightly Club, 145
Fort Niobrara, 123
Fort Reliance, 157
Fort Riley, 149, 188, 190
Fort Robinson, 115–16, 123, 125, 186,
190
Fort Russell, 131
Fort Sherman, 94, 156, 177. See also Fort
Coeur d'Alene
Fort Spokane, 107, 109, 156, 181
Fort St. Michael, 165
Fort Sully, 135, 137, 139, 142
Fort Union, New Mexico, 52
Fort Vancouver, 156, 181
Fort Walla Walla, 169, 181
Fort William, 111
Fort Wrangel, 161
41st Infantry Regiment, 58, 59
Forty Mile Creek, 164
42nd Infantry Regiment, 48
47th US Colored Troops, 38–39
Foster's Creek, 100–101, 108
14th Infantry Regiment, 162, 169
4th Cavalry Regiment, 61, 65, 79, 169
Franklin, William B., 17
Fredericksburg, Battle of, 16–18, 19
frugality of Merriam, 28

Gallagher, Philip, 138
game preserves, 193
Garcia, B., 80, 84
General Order (12), 51
General Quitman (steamboat), 41
Geronimo, 56, 57
Gerrish, Theodore, 13

Merriam, Una (wife), 69, 70, 128, 172, 198
    and Atlanta life, 87
    death, 199
    and Denver, 175–76
    and Fort Coeur d'Alene, 95–96
    and Fort Colville, 103–4, 106
    and Fort Laramie, 113–14, 116, 121, 129
    and Fort Logan, 133–34, 142–43, 145
    and Fort McIntosh, 74, 83
    and Fort Spokane, 109
    illness, 121
    introduction and marriage to Merriam, 68–70
    and McPherson Barracks, 86
    and Merriam's career, 85
    on moonshiners, 89
    pregnancy, 90
    and the Presidio, 168
    religious devotion, 10
    and San Antonio, 83
    and social life, 134
    and son's injury, 150
    travels to New York, 112, 133–34
    travels west, 95
    and Vancouver Barracks, 155
    and Wheaton's retirement, 153
    on Yukon relief expedition, 162
Merriam Pack. See knapsack (Merriam Pack)
Merrimack (steamboat), 13, 48
Merritt, Wesley, 167, 169, 170, 173
Mescalero Indians, 56
messianic religions, 135
Mexican revolutionaries, 66–68, 76–82
Mexico, 72–73
Miles, Nelson
    and Alaska explorations, 163–64
    and establishment of forts, 102
    and Idaho mining conflict, 177, 181
    and Indian conflicts, ix, 91, 108–9, 135, 140–41
    and Merriam's career, 142, 144
    and the Spanish-American War, 165
    and Yukon relief mission, 156–58
Military District of Hawaii, 171
Military Division of West Mississippi, 24
military education of Merriam, 10–11, 15–16
military protocol, 15–16
Mimbres Indians, 56, 57
miners and mining
    and Idaho mining conflict, 178–92, 202–3
    and Indian conflicts, 52, 91, 109–10, 132, 202
    Klondike gold rush, 156–65, 157, 202
Miniconjou Indians, 136
Missouri, 51
Mobile, Alabama, 24–25, 29, 31–33, 37, 39–40, 69–71
mobilization for war, 168, 173
Mogollon Mountains, 57
moonshiners, 89
Moore, Thomas, 21
Morell, George W., 13
Morgan (steamboat), 48
Morganza, Louisiana, 25–28
Mormons, 111
Morning Oregonian, 162–63
Morris, Louis T., 169
Morton, Howard, 3
Moses, Chief (Sinkiuse leader), 97–98, 104–9, 200, 203
Mudgett, Lewis P., 1–2, 4, 29, 33
Mullan, Idaho, 181–82, 186
mumps, 122

N. P. Banks (ship), 29
National Guard units
    and the Denver City Hall War, 149
    and the Idaho mining conflict, 179, 190
    and the Merriam Pack, 146–47
    Merriam's command of, 150
    and reception for Merriam, 153
    and the Spanish-American War, 168, 171, 173